PRAISE FOR *WILD BILL*

"To a wider audience that has grown up with a romanticized and possibly sanitized version of this slice of America's story, Clavin's book will offer a well-researched, **ENTERTAINING,** and more realistic version of America's past." —*Missourian*

"**A VIGOROUS YARN** . . . Clavin writes fluently and often entertainingly of a man shrouded in legend while being all too human." —*Kirkus Reviews*

"**WELL WRITTEN,** full of vivid characters, and detailed. Fans of the Old West and the HBO show *Deadwood* will appreciate the wild ride." —*Booklist*

"**ROLLICKING** . . . an entertaining tale of the man and the legend." —*Publishers Weekly*

"Mr. Clavin's **FAST-PACED** biography does a good job of laying out the facts, but ultimately lets the reader decide. . . . We shouldn't like [Wild Bill], much less respect him, but somehow, despite it all, in some deep part of us we do." —*The East Hampton Star*

"Tom Clavin . . . gives a nod to every gunslinger and scout of Hickok's time, and if that's not **CATNIP TO WESTERN FANS,** nothing is. This book sweeps cross-country, around Indian villages and through decades as it busts myths and sets records straight, pulling readers into cow towns and across prairies and putting mistruths to rest. That allows this to be more than strictly a history book: Clavin can also make this tale seem as comfortable as a Saturday afternoon sofa-and-blanket session with an old black-and-white western." —*Times Record*

WILD BILL

ST. MARTIN'S GRIFFIN
NEW YORK

WILD BILL

The True Story of the American Frontier's First Gunfighter

TOM CLAVIN

Published in the United States by St. Martin's Griffin,
an imprint of St. Martin's Publishing Group

www.stmartins.com

Frontispiece courtesy of the Kansas State Historical Society

The Library of Congress has cataloged the hardcover edition as follows:

Names: Clavin, Thomas, author.
Title: Wild Bill : the true story of the American frontier's first gunfighter / Tom Clavin.
Description: First edition. | New York : St. Martin's Press, 2019. | Includes bibliographical
  references and index.
Identifiers: LCCN 2018041162 | ISBN 9781250173799 (hardcover) | ISBN 9781250237729
  (signed edition) | ISBN 9781250174017 (ebook)
Subjects: LCSH: Hickok, Wild Bill, 1837–1876. | Peace officers—West (U.S.)—Biography. |
  Frontier and pioneer life—West (U.S.) | West (U.S.)—Biography. | West (U.S.)—History—
  1860–1890.
Classification: LCC F594.H62 C55 2019 | DDC 978/.02092 [B]—dc23
LC record available at https://lccn.loc.gov/2018041162

ISBN 978-1-250-17816-9 (trade paperback)

Our books may be purchased in bulk for promotional, educational, or business use. Please
contact your local bookseller or the Macmillan Corporate and Premium Sales Department at
1-800-221-7945, extension 5442, or by email at MacmillanSpecialMarkets@macmillan.com.

First St. Martin's Griffin Edition: January 2020

10 9 8 7 6 5 4 3

To Brendan Clavin

Contents

Author's Note		xi
Prologue		1

ACT I

1.	A New England Clan	7
2.	Bloody Kansas	17
3.	Death at Rock Creek Station	31
4.	Behind Enemy Lines	48
5.	The Gunfighter	66

ACT II

6.	Along the Chisholm Trail	83
7.	Frontier Fame	93
8.	Life of a Frontier Marshal	108
9.	Buffalo Bill and Wild Bill	114
10.	"They Killed Me"	128

11. The Man-Killer   140

12. The Two-Fisted Marshal   152

13. The Streets of Abilene   166

14. A Three-Ring Romance   179

ACT III

15. The Running of the Bulls   195

16. The Reluctant Thespian   210

17. The Cheyenne Loafer   226

18. A Woman Called Calamity   240

19. A Married Man   247

20. Deadwood Days   255

21. The Premonition   267

22. Dead Man's Hand   278

Epilogue   288

Acknowledgments   295

Selected Bibliography   297

Index   303

Author's Note

After finishing *Dodge City*, about the lawmen and cowboys and outlaws who made it the wildest of Wild West cow towns in the 1870s, and especially after it became a national bestseller, a natural question was "What's next?" Well, "next" turned out not to be going forward in time but to step back a few years. Before the heyday of Wyatt Earp, Bat Masterson, Doc Holliday, and other iconic figures who continue to populate our books and screens, there was arguably the most iconic of all: James Butler Hickok.

Some people may think we know his story, the gallant plainsman and gunslinger who helped dozens of villains to meet their maker and who romanced perhaps the most notorious female figure of the Wild West, Calamity Jane. Those are indeed elements of the "Wild Bill" story, but, thankfully, the true and still to some degree untold—accurately—tale of the man known as Wild Bill is pretty surprising. Once again, as with *Dodge City*, it was a delight to discover that the truth—as far as we can know it—is at least as exciting and fascinating, if not more so, than the legends that have been attributed to Wild Bill Hickok.

The legends can't be ignored, however. For the most part, they are why we know (or think we know) Wild Bill today. He was indeed the first gunfighter on the expanding American frontier, and he was the first post–Civil War celebrity of the West. There had been legendary figures before Hickok, especially Daniel Boone and Davy Crockett and Kit Carson. But Wild Bill became bigger than all of them in the mind of a gullible and impressionable public, especially those on the east side of the Missouri River. He was an American legend by the time he was thirty years old, and by the end of the nineteenth century, only his good friend Buffalo Bill Cody, who transformed from army scout and hunter to shameless showman, and outlived Hickok by four decades, came close to Wild Bill's legendary status in the public imagination.

That Hickok was famous while still young was something of a curse. To me, one of the most important aspects of the life of James Butler Hickok is his story would have fit snugly in a portfolio of Shakespeare's tragedies. (Remarkably, and suitably, there was a connection between the Hickok family and the Bard of Avon.) From humble origins, Hickok ascended to a great height, and then, from a combination of his own flaws and the cruelties of fate, he fell. There was one final opportunity for redemption and lasting love, and then suddenly his life was snatched away. Still, the fame he left behind has continued for 150 years with Wild Bill Hickok being depicted in countless books and movies and television shows.

Today, Wyatt Earp, perhaps, equals Hickok as an icon of the American West. But Wild Bill's adventures and exploits, his triumphs and tragedies, came first. And during the finest years of his all-too-brief life, which ended at thirty-nine, there wasn't a man alive who could beat him. Looking at the landscape, I really had no choice but to answer the question "What's next?" with Wild Bill Hickok.

A quick note about sources and the "true story": A good amount of material has been published about Hickok, beginning with the so-called dime-store novels that began appearing while he was still alive. Even more serious attempts, such as *The Plainsman, Wild Bill Hickok* by Frank J. Wilstach and *Wild Bill and His Era* by William Connelley, liberally included fictions as well as a generous sprinkling of embellishments and exaggerations. The Englishman Joseph G. Rosa found a career in writing about Hickok, and one has to admire his relentless, decades-long efforts to track down every tidbit of information, though the result of his 1964 biography was a somewhat mind-numbing saga of facts and disclaimers and rebuttals ricocheting off each other.

As with *Dodge City*, I sifted through every source I could get my hands on, and at the end of each day, a little more gold had been collected in the pan. These nuggets added up to a book that once more demonstrates that the truth can be at least as dramatic and potent as the fabrications. What is no exaggeration is that the man we know as Wild Bill Hickok was one of the most intriguing figures in American history.

WILD BILL

PROLOGUE

The gunfight between Davis Tutt and Wild Bill Hickok on July 21, 1865, was to be recorded as the first quick-draw duel on the American frontier. While this has not been disputed, there was another very significant aspect to the duel: Hickok emerged as the most famous gunfighter—often, the term "shootist" was used—on the frontier. When the duel was detailed in an article published eighteen months later in *Harper's New Monthly Magazine*, Hickok, not yet thirty years old, was catapulted from local folk hero to national legend . . . and thereby, he became a marked man. During the ensuing decade, many men with six-shooters on their hips would measure themselves against the Hickok legend, and a few would ponder the value to their own reputations by gunning him down.

The duel took place in Springfield, Missouri. From the perspective of today, this town would not be considered part of the American West, but in the 1860s, Missouri and Kansas and Nebraska comprised much of the mid-American frontier. In July 1865, Springfield was one of the jumping-off points for people heading west, to Kansas next door or beyond to what had been known before the Civil War as the Great American Desert.

The participants in the "High Noon"–like shoot-out had once been friends. Davis Tutt had been born in Yellville, Arkansas, in 1836, and thus was or close to twenty-nine years old on that fateful July day. The Tutts were well known in Arkansas politics until the Tutt-Everett War. Also known as the Marion County War, it began when two prominent families took opposite sides in the presidential election of 1844 involving Henry Clay and the winner, James Polk. There were escalating confrontations—a scenario to be repeated decades later by the Hatfield and McCoy families—until 1850, when Hansford "Hamp" Tutt, Davis's father, was ambushed and shot. On his deathbed, he requested that there be no revenge and no more fighting over politics, and the war ended.

The younger Tutt enlisted in the Twenty-Seventh Arkansas Infantry Regiment in 1862 and fought on the Confederate side during the Civil War, seeing action in Mississippi and elsewhere. At the war's conclusion in April 1865, Tutt was sent home, but by then, Arkansas had lost its allure. Like thousands of other postwar young men, he turned his attention west. First, though, he ambled north, into Missouri, stopping for a spell in Springfield. Soon afterward, Hickok hit town, another postwar drifter killing time at the city's gaming tables.

The major difference between Hickok and Tutt was they had served on opposite sides during the Civil War. By that July, though, what mattered more was a mutual love of gambling. For a time, they were fast friends, enjoying the same card games. But a couple of issues involving women began to spill over onto the gaming tables, and worse, Hickok went on a cold streak and accepted loans from Tutt rather than be broke and idle. In the third week of a typically steamy July, he was already in a foul mood and needed no further provocation . . . but then there was a card game at the Lyon House Hotel.

As will be detailed later in these pages, the outcome of that card game was that Hickok and Tutt completed the journey from friends to enemies . . . and Tutt had taken Hickok's gold watch. It was only because Tutt was surrounded by friends at the hotel that Wild Bill did not confront him with guns drawn.

But it was a different story the next day. On the morning of July 21, there was Davis Tutt, strolling through the town square, sunlight glinting off the gold watch. By this point in his life, Hickok was no stranger to gunplay and people dying from it, yet when word reached him about Tutt's performance, he did not go for his gun. He did approach Tutt, but to negotiate getting the watch back. He was rebuffed.

The day wasn't over, though. Late that afternoon, Tutt was back in the Springfield town square, brandishing the pocket watch. Witnesses noted that a few minutes before six o'clock, Hickok was observed entering the town square from the south. In his right hand was one of his Colt Navy pistols. By the time he had drawn to within a hundred feet of Tutt, the latter was alone in one corner of the square, as townsfolk had rushed for cover in surrounding buildings. Dozens of pairs of eyes watched the scene unfold.

"Dave, here I am," Hickok said. In one last attempt to avoid a fight, he holstered the pistol and advised, "Don't you come across here with that watch."

Did Tutt underestimate Hickok, or, with all those witnesses, he could not possibly hand over the watch? He may have been debating his options as his right hand came to rest on his holstered gun. He turned sideways, and Hickok did the same. This was a maneuver associated with a traditional duel, but this wouldn't be the old-fashioned, Alexander Hamilton versus Aaron Burr kind of challenge, where the two men pace off and turn to each other, and each formally takes a shot, perhaps deliberately missing his opponent because just showing up and going through the motions was enough to have honor satisfied. This would be a quick-draw, shoot-first-and-ask-questions-later event.

A few seconds passed, then Tutt's hand jerked and his pistol came with it. In a smoothly coordinated series of motions, Hickok lifted his Colt, balanced the barrel on his bent left arm, and pulled the trigger the same instant Tutt tugged his. In an abrupt and hushed silence, the gun smoke was swept away by the evening breeze. Then Tutt cried out, "Boys, I'm killed!" He began to move, staggering, toward the courthouse. He got as far as the porch, then weaved back into the sunbaked, dusty street. He fell and may have been dead before he hit the ground. The bullet had entered Tutt's torso between the fifth and seventh ribs and struck his heart. Hickok watched the man die as he holstered his pistol.

The story spread across the frontier like a prairie fire that there was a man named Wild Bill Hickok in Missouri who might well be the fastest gunslinger on the American frontier. For once, a story with such a swift circulation was true.

ACT I

One of the earliest portraits of young James Butler Hickok.

I am a pilgrim and a stranger and I am going to wander til I am twenty-one and then I will tarry a little while.

—JAMES HICKOK IN A LETTER TO HIS BROTHER HORACE, NOVEMBER 24, 1856

Chapter One

———◆◆◆———

A NEW ENGLAND CLAN

Wild Bill Hickok, who would forever be a firm fixture in the annals of the American West as a plainsman, gunfighter, and lawman, was born into a family that identified themselves as New Englanders.

Some accounts of Hickok's life contend his family, at least on his father's side, originated in Ireland. William Connelley, who bent over backward to romanticize Hickok, stated unequivocally in his 1933 biography that "it is established that the Hickok family is one of the oldest and most honorable in America. It was of pure Saxon blood, and Wild Bill bore the traits and characteristics of the Ancient Saxons." Apparently, he saw Hickok as a knight in shining armor, with a six-shooter replacing an Arthurian sword.

A tad closer to modern times, the genealogy becomes clearer. There was a Hiccox family in Warwickshire, England, in the 1600s. Records reveal that the family farmed 107 acres owned by William Shakespeare in Stratford-upon-Avon. The family remained in the area as farmers and in other humble occupations for decades. The first member to distinguish himself was John Hiccocks, son of William Hiccocs, who became a lawyer in 1690 and a judge in 1709. By the time of his death in 1726, the family had acquired a coat of arms, which offered a respectability above and beyond tilling land.

Sometime during this period, a family member became one of the early settlers of America. In May 1635, a William Hitchcock or Hickocks strode up the gangway of the *Plaine Joan*, and shortly afterward the ship left London and sailed west across the Atlantic Ocean. He brought farming skills with him, and he employed them after settling in Farmington, Connecticut. He married a woman named Elizabeth, and they had two sons, Samuel and Joseph. Only ten years after arriving in America, William died. Both sons did not survive the seventeenth century; however, according to Joseph Rosa, the most dogged of Hickok researchers, the brothers' descendants in Connecticut "were prolific and lusty, and soon spread all over New England."

The most direct connection to the man who would become Wild Bill Hickok was a great-grandfather, Aaron Hickok, who in 1742 was born in Woodbury, also in Connecticut. His family moved to Massachusetts—first to Lanesborough and then Pittsfield in the Berkshires. When the Revolutionary War began, Aaron and a brother named Ichabod enlisted in the Massachusetts militia, becoming Minutemen in a regiment led by a Colonel Patterson. They and their fellow Minutemen harassed British troops on April 19, 1775, during the Lexington and Concord engagements. It is believed that the brothers became members of the Continental army two years later.

If members of the Hickok family were indeed prolific and lusty, they had nothing on Aaron. In between his nonmilitary labors as a farmer and owner of a sawmill, he sired nineteen children with two wives. His third son was Oliver, who also went off to war when the

United States and Great Britain went at it again. Unlike Aaron, Oliver did not emerge unscathed. He was wounded severely in the Second Battle of Sacket's Harbor in upstate New York in July 1813 and died from those wounds three months later. In a way, his father was a casualty, too, because a grieving Aaron died soon after.

When Oliver died, he left behind a twelve-year-old son, William Alonzo Hickok, who was born and raised in Vermont near Lake Champlain and the border with Canada. His path was much more scholarly than military. Intending to become a Presbyterian minister, he attended Middlebury College in Vermont. While at a seminary in New York, William met Pamelia Butler, who was called Polly. Her father had been one of the Green Mountain Boys of Vermont, who had served under Ethan Allen in the Revolutionary War. Her nephew, Ben Butler, decades later, would find both fame and notoriety as a Union general in the Civil War (he was dubbed "Beast" Butler while in command of New Orleans), lead the effort to impeach President Andrew Johnson while in the House of Representatives, and be elected governor of Massachusetts.

William and Polly married in June 1829. He survived typhoid fever but in such a weakened state that continuing to study for the ministry proved too taxing. His mother gave them some seed money, and the couple moved to Broome County, New York, to open a small store. William was well enough to sire Oliver, born in 1830, and then Lorenzo in 1831. Sadly for the family, Lorenzo died soon after birth. What is curious is that the following year, William Hickok moved his family to Illinois. This would be far removed from the couple's extended family in New England and upstate New York, and the well-educated William was far from being a robust, rough-hewn pioneer. Yet off he went, to be a shopkeeper. By doing so, he put Polly and their children in harm's way.

They first settled in Union Center, Illinois, then moved on to Bailey Point (later renamed Tonica). There, in October 1834, Polly gave birth to their third child, a son, who was also named Lorenzo. Two years later, the family was on the move again, this time to Homer. None of these towns, though, were yet considered free of danger.

If one were asked to name an American Indian leader who accomplished the rare feat of pulling different tribes together to fight a common foe, names most likely to come to mind would be Sitting Bull, Red Cloud, or perhaps Quanah Parker. However, before all of them came Black Hawk, a leader of the Sauk. In 1832, he persuaded the Meskwaki and Kickapoo to join his tribe, and he led them across the Mississippi River from Iowa Indian Territory into Illinois. His intent was to return to tribal lands on that side of the river, which had been given away in the Treaty of St. Louis in 1804. This treaty was, of course, recognized only by the U.S. government, as the Sauk, like most other American tribes, had no idea that they had ceded anything until the army forced them off their land.

The combined Indian tribes who entered Illinois numbered around five hundred warriors and were known as the British Band, as it was first believed the incursion had been encouraged by British agitators, only seventeen years after the end of the War of 1812 and the end of Great Britain's presence in the eastern half of the United States. After a peace delegation was fired upon by Illinois militia, Black Hawk attacked, earning a victory at the Battle of Stillman's Run. Pursued by army regulars, he and his warriors found refuge in southern Wisconsin. The actions inspired other tribes to attack settlements in western Illinois, and thus the series of conflicts became Black Hawk's War. The most famous participants—though only in retrospect—were

Winfield Scott, Jefferson Davis, and two future U.S. presidents, Zachary Taylor and Captain Abraham Lincoln.

Colonel Henry Dodge (who would later, coincidentally, command the fort outside Dodge City) led a force that caught up to Black Hawk and the British Band and defeated them at the Battle of Wisconsin Heights. Another loss at the Battle of Bad Axe meant the end of Black Hawk's War. The Sauk leader escaped capture for a short time, then surrendered and spent a year in prison. After his release, Black Hawk returned to Iowa, authored the first autobiography of an American Indian, published in 1833, and died five years later at the age of seventy.

The amount of time between the Black Hawk War's end and the Hickoks arriving in Illinois was at most a year, so it cannot be said that this was a safe place to raise a family or a place for a man with fragile health. But the family managed to put down roots in Homer—which would be renamed Troy Grove in the 1860s—in LaSalle County, along with others heading west looking for good farmland. There was plenty of that near the Vermilion River as well as forest full of sturdy timber to erect houses and fences. William Hickok must have been feeling energized by the burgeoning community because he built a home, though he eschewed farming for opening a general store.

William's fourth son, Horace, was born in Homer in 1832, and his fifth, James Butler Hickok, entered the world on May 27, when the country was in the grip of the Panic of 1837. This was no quick-hitting economic anxiety attack. There had been an expansion in the American economy the previous two years; then the prices of land, cotton, and—in the South—slaves, rose dramatically, until there was a collapse. The resulting recession would last for seven years, with banks closing, businesses failing, and, in some parts of the United States, unemployment rates as high as 25 percent. Not long after the youngest Hickok was welcomed, William had to shut the doors of his store.

He could no longer afford to avoid the labors of farming. The family moved again, though this time only a way north of Homer, where even a nearly broke businessman could buy land. William's other labors produced two daughters, Celinda and Lydia, in September 1839 and October 1842. Apparently, during the first few years of farming near Homer, William's health was stable. It was of great help that he had four sons who, according to their ages and abilities, could share in the work.

William also had a sideline occupation: abolitionist. The Hickoks had brought their antislavery fervor from New England to Illinois. William went further than simply making speeches on Sunday—he offered his farm as a sanctuary stop on the Underground Railroad. This was potentially dangerous. While today Illinois is known as the Land of Lincoln and the state most associated with the president who issued the Emancipation Proclamation, people on both sides of the issue lived there in the 1840s, and no doubt, some were neighbors of the Hickoks. (Even those who did not support slavery as an institution could hold the belief that you don't interfere with another man's property, whether it be land, possessions, or people.) To the east of Illinois was Indiana, which would later host a rebirth of the Ku Klux Klan, and bordering Illinois to the southeast and southwest were Kentucky and Missouri. Very discreetly, William worked with local Quaker families who were part of the Underground Railroad that extended deep into the South.

As a child, James Hickok would at times enter the family barn to find frightened escaped slaves hiding there, or they would be in a second cellar under the house lined with hay that William had created for this purpose. The men and women, and sometimes children, were waiting to be taken to the next stop along the line to eventual freedom farther north. On occasion, William Hickok took them on that journey, hiding them in his wagon with one or more of his sons with him to present an image above suspicion.

Sometimes this didn't work as planned. An unpublished manuscript written by Howard Hickok, a grandson of William and a nephew of James, reported being told that one night the Hickok wagon was fired upon by bounty hunters. William pushed James and his brother from the front seat into the bed of the wagon, where they lay atop the hidden slaves. The darkness of the night and William's knowledge of the terrain allowed him to elude the pursuers and deliver his cargo.

"Running the Underground was a serious and dangerous undertaking," wrote Howard Hickok. "Besides the Provost Marshals, who were legally bound to reclaim the slaves, there were several men in the neighborhood who made the undertaking more difficult and dangerous. These were the kidnappers and bounty hunters. The kidnappers recaptured the slaves and resold them. The bounty hunters returned the slaves to their former owners." Howard estimated from what he had been told that his grandfather "helped hundreds of slaves to their northern goal." One of the fugitives, a woman named Hannah, was taken in by the Hickoks and remained for years with them as a domestic before marrying and moving away.

This secret operation came to an end on May 5, 1852, when William Hickok died. Given his decades of uncertain health and the routine harshness of farmwork, he was fortunate to have lived to age fifty-one. And he had lasted long enough that his youngest son was about to turn fifteen. Oliver, the oldest, had left Illinois the year before, lured west with thousands of other men in a rush for gold. That left Horace, Lorenzo, and James to carry on the outside work while Polly took care of the household and her two young daughters.

Ⓒ The chore of providing much of the family's food fell to James because he was the one most comfortable with guns and was already an excellent marksman. While William was still alive, his youngest son had saved some of the money earned doing chores for surrounding farmers and purchased his first gun, a rifle. Walking deep into the nearby woods, James practiced relentlessly, and with increasing frequency he found his way back to the farm with dead animals to be skinned and cooked. This became more of a necessity with William and Oliver gone and more work spread among fewer hands.

James may have been content with his rural surroundings for years to come, but life on the farm ended. Lorenzo and Horace made the decision to sell it and buy a house back in Homer, and the remaining Hickoks moved there. While this kind of life was less interesting to James, it did mean regular schooling. Previously, he had received only as much formal education as farm chores and being able to get to the nearest one-room schoolhouse allowed. It was not unusual in an Illinois farm community in the 1850s that boys were educated fitfully and for the most part remained illiterate into adulthood. (Girls may not have received any schooling at all.) But James had shown ability, and he enjoyed reading pamphlets that carried tales of adventure, featuring Daniel Boone and Kit Carson. And he could write. Given his original life plans and education, William (as well as Polly) may have actively encouraged his children to learn, and thus the Hickoks became regular letter writers, including James, who to the end of his life would write to his family and others back east from wherever he was on the frontier.

The time came when James heard the siren call of California, possibly in a letter from big brother Oliver. He became increasingly restless in Homer, and approaching his seventeenth birthday, James announced he wanted to head west, too. Horace and Lorenzo persuaded their headstrong brother to postpone his trip for a few months, until the family could become more settled and solvent in town. James took a job as a driver of horse and mule teams with the Illinois and Michigan Canal company, living for a time in Utica, Illinois.

Up to this time, when he was approaching his eighteenth birthday in 1855, the life of James Butler Hickok was free of legend. The combination of being an excellent woodsman and able to read and write well enough might be unusual at that time and place, but these were good qualities for a restless young man yearning for more adventure than the humble Homer could provide. How he came to leave his hometown has been portrayed in many accounts that have more to do with enriching the Wild Bill Hickok legend as folk hero than with the truth.

According to a typical account, James, when about sixteen, was swimming with friends in a stream, and a local bully began picking on one of his friends. The young Hickok, described as "always a defender of the weak," lifted the bully off the ground and tossed him in the water. Another account has it that around the time James had expressed a desire to venture west, he threw his boss into the Illinois and Michigan Canal after the older man had mistreated horses. This was viewed as an early indication of Hickok's "life long habit of interposing himself between the oppressed and the oppressor." Connelley has a man named Charles Hudson, both a boss and a bully, fall into the canal after being beaten severely by the younger James: "The boy, believing that his antagonist was dead, and fearful of the results in case that should be true, immediately ran away."

His departure was less dramatic and far more practical. Polly

Hickok and her children discussed relocating to Kansas. This might offer the compromise of satisfying James's desire to explore new lands to the west and finding good, less expensive land to farm. So, in June 1856, a month after James had turned nineteen, he and his older brother Lorenzo set off on foot, aiming to make St. Louis their first stop.

Chapter Two

BLOODY KANSAS

Soon after the brothers arrived in St. Louis, they parted ways. Thanks to the uncanny reliability of the U.S. mail system in the 1850s, letters from Homer, Illinois, had outpaced them and were waiting for pickup at the St. Louis post office. One reported that Polly Hickok was ill, causing Lorenzo to have second thoughts about continuing the trip. He did not share his younger brother's restless spirit, and he was somewhat overwhelmed being in a loud, dusty city teeming with trappers, hunters, prospectors, immigrants, and others passing through the gateway to the West. The news about his mother convinced Lorenzo that St. Louis was enough of an adventure for now. He gave James most of the money he had brought along, and he prepared to begin the journey back to LaSalle County.

James booked passage on a steamer traveling up the Missouri River. During the trip, he began to be called Bill Hickok. For whatever reason—possibly because he had been named for a brother who died—within the family, Lorenzo had often been addressed as "Bill." Several passengers on the steamer had heard James do the same to his brother when they parted on the dock, and now they called their new acquaintance Bill. Hickok apparently did not mind, and he adopted the name as his own, with only immediate family continuing to call him James or Jim. As the years went on, "Wild Bill" was considered to be William B. Hickok, even though he always signed official documents using his true initials and name, J. B. Hickok.

In the unpublished manuscript titled *The Hickok Legend*, his nephew Howard wrote that the young pioneer would soon also be referred to as "Shanghai Bill on account of his slim and supple form." His uncle is further described as "much over six feet in height, strong and self confident, still attuned to a code of quiet gentle speech and manner; trained to a skill seldom attained in the use of firearms; skilled in woodcraft; taught to champion the weak, but encouraged never to let himself be 'put upon.' He was taught to believe in the freedom and equality of men." Perhaps a few grains of salt are needed here for an account written decades later with "Legend" in the title, but the physical portrait is consistent with ones in subsequent years.

The steamboat bearing "Bill" Hickok and other travelers paddled north and west on the Missouri River toward Kansas. Newcomers could not have arrived in the state at a more dangerous time, and the risks faced on this particular frontier in the summer of 1856 had little to do with Indians. The term beginning to be used in newspapers back east, Bleeding Kansas, was not an understatement.

Two years earlier, President Franklin Pierce had signed the Kansas-Nebraska Act, which opened up 140,000 square miles of territory to westbound adventurers and settlers. Most of this swath of land—in the heart of America and ending at the Continental Divide—was occupied by various Indian tribes and animals, especially millions of buffalo. Congress had left open to the people who would reside in this territory whether Kansas or Nebraska would become states, and if so, as free or slave states.

Given the influence exerted by his father, Hickok was strongly antislavery. However, he would encounter people who felt differently. Some of the people flooding into Kansas to farm and ranch the grass-covered prairie were aware that the Missouri Compromise of 1820, which had admitted Maine as a free state and Missouri as a slave state, had essentially been repealed by the Kansas-Nebraska Act, allowing that the next state to enter the Union could be a slave state. But there were many men like Hickok coming from the east bringing abolitionist views with them. And the act Pierce signed in 1854 did allow Kansans to make their own decision. Hence, conflict was inevitable—especially when fanatics like John Brown became involved.

The federal government thought it had avoided armed conflicts by removing Indian tribes, relocating them to the south on land called Indian Territory or the Cherokee Strip, later northwest Oklahoma. It had not anticipated the number of people coming in from proslavery Missouri. Residents on both sides of the issue set up their own communities, with Leavenworth and Atchison inhabited mostly by Missourians and Lawrence, Manhattan, and Topeka founded by New Englanders who would be called Free-Staters. This scenario made for an increasingly ungovernable situation. No wonder that beginning in 1854, there would be six governors of Kansas in seven years, each one finding frustration at the ballot box and in trying to maintain any semblance of law and order.

The first vote on free or slave state took place that November. Armed groups crossed the border from Missouri to tell people how to vote and to illegally cast votes themselves, and the results had to be nullified. This happened again the following March in 1855. The federal government sent troops to prevent bloodshed, and feeling somewhat protected, supporters of a free state held a convention that June in Lawrence. The result was a more militant faction determined to have Kansas enter the Union as a free state, led by James Lane, who would soon have Bill Hickok as a follower.

Lane had had a colorful career even before he arrived in Kansas. Born in Indiana in 1814, he followed in his father's footsteps and became a lawyer. Then he developed interests in the military and politics, the first while serving in an Indiana regiment of volunteers in the war against Mexico. Soon after Lane returned, he became Indiana's first lieutenant governor. In 1853, he traded in the state capital for the nation's center of power when he was elected to Congress. The debate on the 1854 Kansas-Nebraska Act (which he voted for) inspired Lane to see the territory for himself, and the following year, he traveled to Lawrence.

It was Lane who led what became known as the Free State Army. Given his relatively scant military experience, he was not immediately hailed as a leader come to save the free-state cause. But his timing was good, because he was well positioned when the so-called Wakarusa War began that November. It was a skirmish, really, instigated by Frank Coleman, a proslavery settler, who shot Charles Dow, who favored abolition. The more immediate dispute was over a land claim at a place called Hickory Point, ten miles south of Lawrence, but in that tinderbox atmosphere, the men's opposing views took precedence.

The local sheriff, Sam Jones, actually arrested a friend of the victim, who was soon freed by a group of gun-toting Free-Staters. This aggravated Sheriff Jones, who suddenly found himself the head of fifteen hundred men who had crossed the border from Missouri, looking for trouble. On their way west, they had broken into an army arsenal in Liberty, Missouri, and stolen guns, ammunition, swords, and even a cannon.

The latest ineffectual governor in Topeka called for militia to repel the incursion. This was ignored everywhere except in Lawrence, where eight hundred men grabbed guns and turned out. (Among them were John Brown and his sons.) Suddenly, there was the Free State Army. James Lane became second in command to the elected leader. The opposing Missourians established a camp six miles away, at the Wakarusa bottoms, and effectively placed Lawrence under siege. During this mostly lackluster effort, only one man was shot and killed.*

After a few weeks of hurled threats, posturing, and the occasional potshot, the opposing sides, especially with winter taking hold, felt inclined to sign a peace treaty, and the Missouri contingent left Wakarusa and headed home.

Such proslavery militants from Missouri were often called Border Ruffians, and their free-state adversaries were Jayhawkers. With no one inclined or powerful enough to keep the two sides apart—and with the government in Washington itself paralyzed by the issue of slavery, epitomized by the caning of abolitionist Charles Sumner by Preston Brooks on the floor of Congress—violence broke out in Kansas again in May 1856, shortly before Hickok arrived, when Border Ruffians once more showed up at Lawrence, hoping to intimidate convention attendees the same way they had voters in the two previous referendums. They went beyond attempts to frighten citizens, though, destroying two antislavery newspaper offices and the house

---

*The unfortunate casualty, Thomas Barber, at least had his demise memorialized in "Burial of Barber," a poem composed by John Greenleaf Whittier.

of Dr. Charles Robinson, who had been a member of a free-state militia. (Fortunately for him, Dr. Robinson was under arrest and confined in Lecompton at the time of the violation of his home.)

The Border Ruffians apparently thought little of the abolitionists' mettle . . . but they hadn't counted on John Brown, whose seething antislavery anger had reached the boiling point. He and a group of armed men, including four of his sons, set out for Lawrence. For whatever reason, they did not get there, and turned around to head back home. One night during the return trip, they came to the home of James Doyle, a supporter of slavery. Brown and his followers led Doyle and two adult sons into the woods, where they were hacked to death with swords. The next stop on this vengeance mission was the home of Allen Wilkinson, who suffered the same fate. A fifth man, William Sherman, at a third house, on the other side of the Pottawatomie Creek, was also killed in a similar fashion. Satisfied with such a productive outing, Brown and his fellow killers resumed their journey home.

What was called the Pottawatomie Massacre outraged proslavery residents and advocates. The federal government, fearing Kansas was descending into murderous chaos, sent more troops. Governors came and went (for three days in September 1856, there were two men holding the office simultaneously) and so did militias and groups of armed vigilantes. As much of a mess as things were in Kansas, they would only get worse after the Civil War began in 1861 with the brutal raids by guerrilla factions.

In June 1856, Bill Hickok disembarked at Leavenworth in Kansas. Though he was no longer accompanied by Lorenzo, his goal continued to be to find a good place to build a homestead, and the entire family would then relocate from Illinois. But he needed to find a job so as not to dip into the homestead money Lorenzo had given to him. Hickok couldn't help but be distracted by the turmoil in Kansas. Pro-

and antislavery positions were being debated in churches, in saloons, and on street corners, and violence simmered barely below the surface. Sometimes it boiled over; as Hickok wrote his mother after three months in Kansas, "I have seen since I have been here sites [*sic*] that would make the wickedest hearts sick, believe me mother, for what I say is true."

Trying to stay out of the fray, Hickok worked whatever jobs he could find. Having a strong constitution and years of farmwork on his résumé helped, as did a willingness to take on whatever was offered. When he wrote his brother Horace in November, he had not made any progress toward finding a site for the Hickok homestead, but there had been no lack of experiences and observations: "You wanted to no what was going on in Cansas. I looked ahead of me to where the roads crossed and saw about 500 soldiers agoing on and I looked down the river and saw some nice steamers and they were all agoing on and that is the way with all the people in Cansas, they are all agoing on. I guess they are going to hell so you see I have told you what is going on in Cansas."

The wide-open albeit dangerous atmosphere of Leavenworth could be catnip for a handsome young man. The end of that letter to Horace implies that Bill was no stranger to alcohol or other vices, and Leavenworth may have offered plenty more opportunity: "Now I will tell you a few lyes. I have quit swearing now. I have quit drinking but tell Bill [Lorenzo] I have quit dancing etc. I have quit chewing tobacco and don't touch any lager beer and I don't speak to the girls at all. I am getting to be the perfect hermit."

As an aside, Hickok had mentioned to his brother, "Thare is 29 of our company in custody at Lacompton yet. I have been out to see them once. I had as good as a horse and as good a gun as thare was in our company."

There has long been a murkiness to Hickok's history concerning his activities with James Lane and the Free-Staters. This is understandable because many of these activities were clandestine, and there was no reason to take any special notice of the newcomer from Illinois. Also, Hickok is discreet in his letters so as not to worry his family, especially his mother. However, references like "our company" imply he took up arms with the Free-Staters. His mention of Lecompton most likely refers to the engagements that took place in August and September of that year, 1856.

First, Lane led an army to Lecompton to oppose a force led by David Atchison, which had again marched across the border from Missouri. What could have been a bloody battle and Hickok's first significant military action was prevented by Colonel Philip St. George Cooke, commanding a contingent of army troops from Fort Leavenworth. The second week in September, yet another governor, John Geary, ordered both sides to disband. He probably would have been laughed out of the state, but Colonel Cooke and his troops backed Geary up. After the two-day Battle of Hickory Point, where Lane was in command of the Jayhawkers, the army arrived and order was restored. Arrests of about a hundred of Lane's men followed, but the men were later released. By this time, Hickok was a scout for Lane yet managed not to get caught in any roundup.

This had to be a heady time for a strapping young man who was finding some of the adventure he had sought. What could make life better for Bill Hickok? Falling in love.

This experience actually began when he met John Owen, who would have an impact on Hickok's life beyond having a fetching daughter. Owen, born in Tennessee, was forty-three or forty-four when he met Hickok in Kansas. He had moved there from Missouri in 1836 to work for the American Fur Company. During his travels trading among the Indian tribes, he fell in love with a Shawnee woman, Patinuxa. They had one child, named Mary Jane. Owen was adopted into the tribe, then kicked out when his active support of the Free State movement called unwanted attention to the Shawnee. He became a farmer, and he and his family settled on a tract of land on Mill Creek. It was there that Owen encountered Bill Hickok. Despite the age difference, they took a liking to each other.

They also went to work for Lane. Up to this point, Hickok may have been no more than an occasional follower and scout who could come in handy because of his marksmanship and comfort handling weapons. Owen was more of a participant in the Free State movement and knew Lane. He vouched for Hickok to Lane, and the two men became Lane's bodyguards. It was reported that when Lane made a speech in Highland, Kansas, in 1857—by then, he had become a fiery speaker quick to insult Missourians—Owen and Hickok were his armed guards.

Such proximity to Owen and to his farmhouse allowed a relationship to blossom between Hickok and Mary Jane Owen. While as a teenager Hickok had had a few flirtations back in Illinois, this appears to have been his first real romance. In a letter to his family, signed James Hickok, he refers to Mary as "my gall," and in another, signed James Butler Hickok: "I went to see my gall yesterday and eat 25 ears of Corn to fill up with. You ought to be here and eat some of hur buiskits. She is the only one I ever Saw that could beat mother making buiskits." And in a letter dated August 23, 1858, he reports that Mary had cut off a lock of his hair and that he should send it to his mother and sisters.

While the work with Owen and romance with his daughter continued, Hickok met another man who would play an important role in his life. Actually, it was a boy he met—an eleven-year-old named

Cody, whom everyone called Billy. The person who would achieve fame as Buffalo Bill was part of a wagon train in October when he met a handsome stranger who saved him from a severe beating.

William Frederick Cody had been born in February 1846 in Scott County, Iowa, the youngest of four children and the second son. His father was a farmer until Cody was seven, when he moved the family to LeClaire on the Iowa side of the Mississippi River and he operated a stage line between Davenport and Chicago. After an aborted attempt to go west to seek gold, Isaac Cody moved the family again, this time to return to farming. The youngest Cody attended school when he had to but otherwise trapped quails and small game and explored his surroundings. "Many a jolly ride I had and many a boyish prank was perpetrated after getting well away from and out of sight of home with the horse," Cody recalled in *Buffalo Bill's Life Story,* published in 1879. This was the first of three autobiographies he wrote and the one considered the most reliable, though in the very first sentence he gives an incorrect date of birth. Over the years, in the other two stories of his life, Cody remembered less about what actually transpired and put more stock in what had been said and written about him.

When Cody's brother, Samuel, died in a horse-riding accident, the family's grief resulted in a desire to leave Iowa. They loaded up wagons of possessions and traveled to Missouri, and after catching their breath with Isaac's brother Elijah, they pushed on into Kansas, arriving in 1852. Isaac combined farming with trading goods with the Kickapoo. After the enactment of the Kansas-Nebraska Act, that summer "was an exciting period in the history of the new territory," according to Cody. "Thousands and thousands of people, seeking new homes, flocked thither, a large number of the emigrants coming over from adjoining states. The Missourians, some of them, would come laden with bottles of whiskey, and after drinking the liquor would drive the bottles into the ground to mark their land claims, not waiting to put up any buildings."

Without wanting to, Isaac Cody was caught up in the free state versus slavery violence. Unlike Hickok, he was not antislavery . . . but he was not for slavery, either. In the middle of the rabid Kansas controversy was the Free Soil movement, and Isaac Cody adhered to some of its beliefs. One of them proposed a territory free of black men altogether, meaning slavery, pro or con, wouldn't be an issue in Kansas. Isaac did have some interest in the politics of the new territory and was known as a good speaker. Having a brother living in Missouri, it was believed that Isaac was not a free-state supporter.

One day, there was a gathering of about a hundred Missouri men and allies, and Isaac was asked to address them. When he revealed his leanings that Kansas should not be a slave or a free state, but a sort of neutral one, one of the enraged proslavery listeners attacked him. Isaac was stabbed twice with a bowie knife. He was severely wounded, but survived. However, the Cody family in Kansas now had a reputation as being Free-Staters.

For the rest of Billy's childhood and adolescence, there were verbal and some physical assaults, and Isaac at times had to go into hiding when a group bent on lynching him approached the property. In his autobiography, Cody recalls several harrowing escapes, including one when the youngster had to outride a gang of armed men to warn his father that they were on their way to murder him. Isaac Cody defiantly worked with Lane and others to make Kansas a free state until, never having completely recovered from his wounds, he died when his son was only eleven.

At a very tender age, Billy Cody became the man of the family, and he took whatever work he could find, which was how he met Bill

Hickok. One job in the summer of 1857 was helping teamsters headed by Lewis Simpson, a friend of the Cody family, drive a wagon train across the prairie and High Plains to Utah. His mother was very much opposed because, as Cody understates, "owing to the Indians, a journey over the plains in those days was a perilous undertaking." She relented when Simpson promised to keep a close eye on the boy. However, the danger came not from Indians but from within the ranks of teamsters.

As the trek progressed, Cody met one of the drivers, who identified himself as James B. Hickok, "a tall, handsome, magnificently built and powerful young fellow, who could out-run, out-jump and out-fight any man in the train." One evening, Cody ran afoul of "a surly, overbearing" teamster twice his size, who knocked the boy down with one swat. Cody got up holding a pot of coffee, and he threw the scalding contents in the face of the man, who in turn "sprang at me with the ferocity of a tiger, and undoubtedly would have torn me to pieces."

What prevented this was the appearance of Hickok, who knocked the teamster down. He warned, "If you ever again lay a hand on that boy—little Billy there—I'll give you such a pounding that you won't get over it for a month of Sundays." Hickok may have saved Cody's life—an act that would be reciprocated a decade later.

Most likely, this journey west was the only one Hickok undertook in 1857 because of his occasional employment with the Free-Staters and a new job he soon secured. At that time, Hickok called the small community of Monticello in Johnson County home. Probably because of his association with Lane, in March 1858, though only twenty years old, Hickok was elected the town constable. Also elected, as supervisor, was John Owen. This would be Hickok's first posting as a lawman.

Constable was not, however, much of an occupation, and if there was any pay, it had to be a pittance. With the intentions of settling down, perhaps with Mary Owen, and returning to the original plan of founding a new Hickok homestead, he traveled less and farmed more. He had purchased some land, and he wrote to his family that he was hard at work on it, also informing his mother and siblings—this time, he wasn't kidding—that he had given up drinking and gambling. Kansas offered opportunity: "I would like to have for us fore brothers" acquire another section of land "and the great butiful prairie cant be beat in the country."

❧ Back in Homer, the news about James being a disciplined farmer was good, but not so much the probability that he would marry Mary. Polly in particular did not want a half-Indian daughter-in-law and heathen grandchildren. While it was common on the frontier for white men to have children and even marry women from the tribes, that did not fly in Illinois, and certainly not with the Hickoks, who were probably thinking about preserving that Saxon blood. And apparently, the family's caring for people with black skin did not extend to those with red skin. Lorenzo was dispatched to talk some sense into the youngest son.

He arrived in Monticello to find his brother Jim virtually homeless. A disadvantage to being a close associate of James Lane was also being a target for proslavery militants. One night, a group of them set fire to the modest cabin Hickok had built, and crops that were soon to be harvested were also put to the torch. Moving to Monticello had not been enough for Hickok to escape the partisan violence and destruction.

He should have realized that nowhere in eastern Kansas was safe. Only a few months earlier, the Marais des Cygnes Massacre had occurred. Proslavery Bushwhackers had killed five men in a rural area.

After the massacre, John Brown constructed a fortified cabin on the site. However, this act of defiance did not bring the dead men back or protect future victims.

The sudden, surprise attack on his future homestead left Hickok angry and distraught. Lorenzo's arrival and the affection of his older brother could not have come at a better time. The same can't be said for the relationship with Mary, however. Part of the comfort Lorenzo offered was persuading his brother to give up farming, at least for now, and look for a more promising occupation.

Blood was thicker than the feelings for his girlfriend. Hickok waved good-bye to what was left of his farm and to a life with Mary Owen (who later married a doctor), and he and Lorenzo set off for Leavenworth.

Chapter Three

⸻✦⸻

DEATH AT ROCK CREEK STATION

Quitting Monticello and Mary Owen began a pattern of Wild Bill Hickok leaving discarded women in his wake as he set off for the next adventure. For him and Lorenzo in the latter part of 1858, that meant heading to Leavenworth to seek employment. The brothers were offered jobs with the Overland Stage Company, which had begun as the Russell, Majors, and Waddell partnership. Bill would work as a teamster for the company off and on, while the steadier and less restless Lorenzo would be in the Overland Stage's employ through the Civil War years.

Around this time, Bill had a photograph taken in Lawrence. He wears a dark wide-brimmed hat and a white shirt under a plaid shirt under a dark vest. His eyes gaze steadily at the camera, and there is no expression on his face except maybe a bit of apprehensiveness being that he was a twenty-one-year-old having his image captured for the first time. He has a long, slender nose and seemingly smooth skin, slightly protruding lips and ears, a thin mustache, and a sparse goatee. A distinguishing feature, though not uncommon on the frontier in the late 1850s, is long brown hair whose tendrils touch his shoulders.

While being a teamster and fulfilling other duties on wagon trains traversing hundreds of miles west did offer adventure, it was very hard work. The wagons set off at sunup and jostled along on trails that twisted or went monotonously straight depending on the topography, and they were filled with rocks and half-formed ruts. Axles broke, horses and mules died, travelers were harassed by clouds of insects, many days the sun beat down incessantly, water could become scarce, there was the ever-present fear of attacks by hostile Indians (stories circulated of the gruesome fates of those taken alive), and a welcome rainstorm could suddenly turn into a gully washer.

Adding to the teamsters' woes were outbreaks of smallpox and cholera and diseases that remained a mystery but whose fatal outcome was the same. For many, there was homesickness for who and what were left behind or the grinding misgivings of what a mistake this was to be out in the middle of nowhere. Not for nothing was this midsection of the country often ominously referred to and labeled on crude maps as the Great American Desert.

A wagon train employee had to have a hardy constitution, and apparently Bill Hickok did because this was the life he led for the rest of 1858 and for at least a year after that. He was a quick learner and very good with horses and other animals. If he drank, he must have held his liquor well because there are no reports of angry disputes. It probably helped that the wiser wagon masters banned alcohol, and high-proof watering holes were few and far between on the prairie, though that would change with the westward expansion of white settlement.

It was not uncommon—with Dodge City being just one example—that the first structure of what would become a settlement was a saloon.

More than a few towns got their start as simply being an oasis for thirsty travelers. "Saloons," such as they were, might be within riding distance of U.S. Army forts or share a place on the prairie with way stations that held horses for stagecoaches. A makeshift saloon—some were made of wood, most from sod—was nothing more than a tent or dugout, and the interior contained little else than a wooden plank supported by two beer kegs. Whiskey and beer were poured from jugs and tapped barrels into glasses that, with luck, had been swiped with a rag since the last use. During the cold-weather months, they offered some shelter from the wind, though were always in danger of being blown down. Even a solid shelter was of dubious advantage, as the interiors kept contained an almost combustible mixture of odors of wet furs, unwashed bodies, cigar smoke, and the vapors coming out of a stove that burned wood, sod, or kerosene.

Sometime during his travels on the rudimentary, dust-choked trails, Bill Hickok encountered one of his boyhood heroes. He had read about the trailblazing career of Kit Carson. He had no way of knowing how much of what he read was actually true, and to a youngster with imagination, it didn't matter. An irony was that the tales of Carson's exploits had been embellished—and some were outright fabrications—and a few years later, Hickok would receive the same treatment from writers.

But what *was* true about the legendary frontiersman was impressive enough. Christopher Carson was born on Christmas Eve 1809 in Madison County, Kentucky. Soon after, the Carson family, which would eventually include fourteen children, relocated to Boone's Lick, Missouri. As would be experienced by Hickok and Cody, Carson had to grow up fast because of a father's premature death. At age nine, Chris Carson found whatever work he could. And like those other two teenagers, he was restless and had a curiosity about what lay to the west. When he was fifteen, Carson hopped on a wagon that was part of one of the early trains on the Santa Fe Trail.

By nineteen, he was a fur trapper, going back and forth to California, journeys that took him through the Rocky Mountains and over the Sierra Nevada mountains. Carson became familiar with Indian tribes, and his first two wives were an Arapaho and a Cheyenne, Singing Grass and Making-Out-Road. And among trappers and explorers (often, one and the same), he earned a reputation for courage and honesty. "Clean as a hound's tooth" was one of the appraisals of him.

A significant turn in his life came in 1842 when he met John C. Frémont on a Missouri riverboat. Frémont, who would be dubbed "Pathfinder," was about to launch his first mapping expedition to the Pacific Ocean, and he hired Carson as his guide. His collaboration with Frémont would make both figures of national renown as mountain men and explorers when their experiences were written up (mostly ghostwritten by Frémont's wife, Jessie) and published in books devoured by a public eager for tales of the mysterious and fabulous American West.

When he was not blazing and mapping trails, Carson called Taos in New Mexico Territory home. His third wife was Maria Josefa Jaramillo, from a prominent family in the town. From their marriage in 1843—he was thirty-three, she was fourteen—to his death twenty-five years later, Carson made enough visits home to sire eight children. Away from Taos, his adventures included aiding Frémont in the Bear Flag Revolt in California in 1846, helping General Stephen Kearny to wrest that territory from Mexico in the subsequent war, and blazing more trails, sometimes as a federal Indian agent. In 1856, Carson stayed still long enough to write a book that was to be titled simply *Memoirs*. On its way to a potential publisher in New York City, the manuscript was lost; it was discovered in a trunk in Paris in 1905 and finally printed.

It was while acting as an Indian agent and trail guide that he met Hickok, probably in 1859, at the end of the trail in Santa Fe. Carson, who knew it very well, gave the man almost thirty years his junior a tour of the town's saloons and advised him against consorting with any of the Mexican women there. William Connelley, though he mistakenly mentions that Carson and Hickok "became good friends," offers a description of what the two men encountered at the United States Hotel: "In the bar-room there was a cosmopolitan crowd: Santa Fe traders and their customers, engaged in animated bargaining; trappers and hunters from the south ranges of the Rockies beyond Taos, armed with Bowies and Hawkins rifles, and wearing fringed buckskin; teamsters, freighters, travelers, and native greasers. There was a din of conversation, a jargon of tongues, and snatches of songs. There was constant serving of liquor and the clink of glasses."

After a night on the town, which included a good dose of gambling, as a parting gift, Carson presented Hickok with a Colt Dragoon pistol, which he kept for the rest of his life.

Though both men fought on the Union side in the Civil War, Carson's battles were farther west, in New Mexico and Texas, including the Battle of Adobe Walls against the Comanche.

Hickok and Carson may not have met again after their Santa Fe bacchanal. In 1868, an exhausted Maria Josefa expired while giving birth to her and Carson's eighth child, a loss the fifty-eight-year-old frontiersman found too great to bear. Soon afterward, in May, Carson died suddenly of an aortic aneurysm.

Given that Bill Hickok was just one of hundreds of men crisscrossing the country on the rough trails, there was no reason he would have attracted any notice from the press. But there have been backward glances to this time in his life. In March 1931, *The Denver Post* published a reminiscence by Truman Blancett. More than seventy years earlier, he and his father and brothers maintained a station at Ash Point, Kansas, 125 miles west of Leavenworth. They kept mules there, and when a mail coach arrived, the driver exchanged the six or eight mules that pulled it. Every week for several months, Hickok, one of the drivers, was at the station while the rotation of mules was under way, and "we would exchange stories," Blancett recalled. The visitor would also demonstrate skills of the future gunfighter.

"Hickok handled a pistol with the speed of lightning. When he wished to emphasize something he had a way of throwing his right hand or left hand towards you with the trigger finger pointed straight at you. His hands moved with incredible swiftness and I believe he practiced this mannerism with such purpose that it became part of his nature, and probably resulted in making him the fastest two-gun man of his day." Blancett concluded his account: "Anyone who wanted to make the acquaintance of Hickok and would mind their own business and not get too inquisitive would find him a perfect gentleman in every way. In those days he was not known as 'Wild Bill.'"

The James Butler Hickok of 1859 was not known at all outside his family, coworkers, a handful of Jayhawkers, the Owens, and a few acquaintances like Billy Cody. He was simply a young, adventurous man like many others on the American frontier, some of whom had ambitions while others just lived from day to day, content enough with survival and the bare necessities and the occasional pleasures. Hickok seems to have been generally well liked, with no hint of the legendary and even tragic figure he would become in American history. He wrote home to his mother and siblings, was guarded but could make friends when he wanted to, possessed skills with guns, and had a sense of humor. Connelley writes about Hickok as a stagecoach driver, "When he drove into Santa Fe, he entered with a flourish, and raised as much dust as he could. He took a mischievous delight in sending the lazy inhabitants scurrying out of his way."

Late that year, Hickok was a guest at the Cody house, along with Lew Simpson and two other men. Cody's mother and sister were quite taken by the young frontiersman. Buffalo Bill, decades later, recalled that because he had "become greatly attached to [Hickok], I asked him to come and make a visit at our house" in Leavenworth. "My mother and sisters, who had heard so much about him from me, were delighted to see him and he spent several weeks at our place. They did everything possible to repay him for his kindness to me." Cody added that Hickok, having become something like the older brother he had lost years before, frequented the Cody residence when he was in the area: "He used to call our house his home, as he did not have one of his own."

A Hickok legend that may well be fact is that around this time, after the stay at the Cody residence, he had an encounter with a bear that went badly for him. (One is reminded of the scene early in the film *The Revenant* when Leonardo DiCaprio's character barely survives a mauling.) A few researchers have disputed that the encounter ever took place. However, there are accounts of Hickok in 1860 into 1861 that make mention of him recovering from serious injuries. Given the harsh nature of life driving wagons on butt-bruising trails, there were any number of ways to be injured. Yet there is a mention in the Kansas paper *The Fort Scott Monitor* of a man identified as "Wild Bill" who "has proved himself a tight customer in a bear fight." Connelley claims Hickok killed a "huge grizzly bear" with his bowie knife after a furious fight, and that when he was found, he was barely alive, and that, among other injuries, "his left arm was crushed and still in the bear's mouth."

As Hickok himself told it, he was driving a freight team that had originated in Independence and was bound for Santa Fe. During an isolated stretch in a range of short hills, he found a bear blocking the road. She was a cinnamon bear—a subspecies of the American black bear, with red-brown fur—with two cubs. Hickok got down off the wagon, and obviously not inclined to entice the bear out of the way and knowing how ruthlessly violent a bear protecting cubs could be, he ran up to her and shot her in the head.

Whatever ammunition he was using, it wasn't enough. The bullet ricocheted off the cinnamon bear's skull. Being shot made her very angry. She attacked, crushing Hickok against her. He fired his gun again, and this time the bullet struck one of the bear's paws. In response, she shoved Hickok's left arm in her mouth and began to bite. His right hand found his bowie knife. He yanked it out of his belt and slashed the bear's throat. After several vicious thrusts, the bear fell dead.

Somehow, Hickok, in what must have been an excruciatingly painful journey, steered the freight wagon to the next town. There he was treated for broken bones in his chest, shoulder, and arm.

Three or four months later, in early 1861, because of his injuries and the slow recovery, the Overland Stage Company transferred Hickok from being a driver and guard on wagon trains to lighter duties at the Rock Creek Station in the Nebraska Territory. (More about this shortly.) Even Joseph Rosa, surely a doubting Thomas about so many of the tales told about Hickok, wrote about his posting at Rock Creek: "The effects of his recent battle showed in the clumsy way he walked, and his left arm was still useless."

Another legend is that Hickok was a founder of the Pony Express. This one is not quite true. The Russell, Majors, and Waddell company, which included Hickok as an employee, did initiate the mail-carrying

WILD BILL · 39

service in April 1860. On the third, one rider left Sacramento heading east and one left St. Joseph, Missouri, heading west, with the intent of carrying mail on horseback across two thousand miles in eight days. Hickok, however, was not one of the riders, then or ever. He was soon to turn twenty-three—not old by any means, but most of the riders, like Billy Cody, were under twenty-one and shorter and thinner than Hickok, who had filled out from years of steady labor.

Jack Slade deserves a detour here. For a time, until he was swept into the dustbin of history, he was a much-talked-about man whose legend grew as writers from the East, such as Bret Harte and Mark Twain, began to roam the frontier and send back dispatches in between making notes in their journals. Depending on the account, Slade was the epitome of villainy or a rough but decent fellow in a brutal business.

Joseph Alfred Slade was another Illinois product, born in Carlyle in January 1831. He was only sixteen when he enlisted in the army and went off to fight in the war with Mexico, though he got no farther than Santa Fe, where his regiment did mostly guard duty. Sometime in the 1850s, Slade worked as a freighting teamster and wagon master along the Overland Trail. This passage west had been used by explorers and trappers beginning in the 1820s, but it was in the 1850s that it began to see a steady traffic of gold-seekers and then stagecoaches carrying mail and adventurous passengers. The Overland Trail originated in Atchison, Kansas, and went into Colorado, then swung up to southern Wyoming, where, at Fort Bridger (named for the explorer and scout Jim Bridger), it intersected with the Oregon Trail, which would take travelers to the West Coast. It would become extinct in 1869, when the First Transcontinental Railroad was completed. A year or two later, Slade was in Texas and then moved around working for a succession of stage companies. Along the way, he was one of the founders of the Pony Express.

In 1859, he went to work for the Overland Stage Company, which would result in him encountering both Bill Hickok and the teenaged William Cody. Before long, Slade was in charge of a six-hundred-mile-long corridor of the country, and the freight had to get through no matter what. He acquired a ruthless reputation, inspiring fear among thieves and other outlaws, some of whom didn't have to wait for a judge and jury to stretch a rope. One incident involved one of his own employees, Andrew Ferrin, whom Slade shot when the worker was hindering the progress of a wagon train.

Another story that circulated about Slade was that when he tracked down a man named Jules Beni, who had previously shot him and robbed one of the Overland wagon trains, Slade tied him to a stake. He then occupied much of the day by shooting him bit by bit, none of the wounds immediately fatal, then cutting off his ears, before finally finishing Beni off. (One ear was always kept in his pocket, to display as a conversation piece or a warning to outlaws.) The only actual truth to this story was that Slade did kill a hiding Jules Beni after tracking him down in Wyoming, but the embellished tale—and subsequent accounts, including one by Mark Twain in *Roughing It* that he had killed at least twenty-six men—was useful in sometimes deterring mischief against the Overland Stage.

There are no reports of Hickok and Slade at odds. In the one event where they were known to be together, it was a festive occasion. Plant's Station was one of the stage company's transfer sites, this one in northeast Wyoming. One day, there was a potential disaster when Indians attacked and took all the horses and mules at the station. The value of the animals aside, mail-carrying and other activity on the trails would be at a standstill until they were replaced. Maybe the stock could be recovered.

A posse was put together—probably only as many men as there were horses left—led by Hickok. The would-be rescuers followed the raiding party's tracks to the Powder River, then beyond Crazy Woman's Fork to Clear Creek, and there they found the Indian camp. More importantly, they also found the stolen stock and about a hundred ponies belonging to the Indians, who were most likely Oglala Sioux whose head man was Red Cloud, the most powerful leader of the High Plains tribes. Hickok and the others waited until dark, then attacked. Their shouting and shooting set the Indians to running one way, and the attackers rounded up the horses and ponies and got them going the other way. The Indians had too few ponies remaining to give chase . . . even if they were of a mind to, not knowing how many armed banshees had suddenly appeared in the night.

Hickok herded the posse and the horses and ponies to the Sweetwater Bridge Station, where the successful mission was celebrated. Slade was there leading the cheers of congratulation.

Billy Cody saw only one side of Slade: "Although rough at times and always a dangerous character—having killed many a man—he was always kind to me. During the two years that I worked for him as pony express-rider and stage-driver, he never spoke an angry word to me."

The young Cody's impression was more a minority one as the years passed. Finally, it turned out to be a hard end for a hard man. Slade may have done his job the only way it could be done to keep the Overland Stage Company functioning and profitable, but he had made a lot of enemies along the way, and not just among outlaws. A decreasing ability to hold his liquor and a succession of drunken brawls because of boorish behavior didn't endear him to others, either. In November 1862, Slade was sacked by the Overland Stage Company for rampant drunkenness; one damaging incident was firing bullets at the Fort Halleck canteen.

This did not turn out to be a wake-up call. In March 1864, he was in Virginia City, Montana, indulging in an alcohol-fueled, violent tantrum. In the absence of any effective law enforcement, Slade was taken into custody by an ad hoc group of peacemakers. The "charge" was only disturbing the peace, but Slade had disturbed it so thoroughly that a resentful local citizenry decided to hang him. Without delay, Slade was marched down the main street and soon was swinging from the beam of a corral gate. Fittingly, his body was preserved in alcohol until the snows had melted and it could be transported to Salt Lake City for burial.*

The seemingly harmless position of assistant stock tender that the Overland Stage Company gave Hickok led to him killing a man for the first time. According to more colorful accounts, he killed several in a burst of brutality while working at the Rock Creek Station. And more than one account has Hickok dueling with and dispatching up to ten men, including via hand-to-hand combat. As Joseph Rosa remarks in *They Called Him Wild Bill*, "No single gunfight, with the possible exception of the Earp-Clanton fight in October 1881, in Tombstone, Arizona, has caused so much controversy as the Hickok-

---

*Slade would appear in several screen projects, including being played by Mark Stevens in the 1953 feature film *Jack Slade*, with Barton MacLane as Jules Beni, and an episode two years later on the TV series *Stories of the Century*, with Gregg Palmer as Slade and Paul Newman as Beni.

McCanles affair at Rock Creek on the afternoon of Friday, July 12, 1861."

The station site had the advantage of being on both the Oregon Trail and the California Trail six miles from Fairbury, Nebraska. The company had rented the station from the owner, David McCanles, a North Carolina native. By April 1861, Overland Stage ascertained that business was brisk enough that it would be a good investment to purchase the Rock Creek property.

A man named S. C. Glenn had established the small compound as a cabin, barn, and makeshift supply store. In 1859, he was visited by the brothers David and James McCanles, who aimed to find gold in Colorado. David changed his mind, though, and bought the property from Glenn. He sent for his wife, Mary. Their fifth child, Charles, would be born that year.

David McCanles turned out to be a pretty good entrepreneur. He added items to his store's inventory and constructed a toll bridge across Rock Creek. For ten to fifty cents, depending on what the driver could pay, wagons traversed the rough wooden bridge in a couple of minutes rather than having to spend hours hoisting and lowering their wagon into the creek and hoisting it back up on the other side. McCanles put up a cabin and dug a well on the other side of the creek, which he called, sensibly, East Ranch, with the original compound becoming the West Ranch. It was the east-side site, in 1860, that became the Rock Creek Station when the Overland Stage Company leased it.

Continuing to wheel and deal, McCanles sold and resold and sold again the toll bridge. Each buyer had the misfortune of not meeting one of the myriad stipulations in the sales contract, with ownership reverting to McCanles. He also sold the West Ranch at a good profit and moved his family to a new structure three miles away. The future for this frontier businessman looked bright, especially when the Over-land Stage Company offered a new deal.

To buy the Rock Creek Station, the company promised to give McCanles one-third of the price down and the remaining payment or payments made within four months. Horace Wellman was appointed to supervise operations at the station, and Bill Hickok, who turned twenty-four that May, was hired as the assistant stock tender, mostly to take care of the horses.

Months went by, and there was no further payment. Wellman was apologetic, but he personally could not produce the money. The non-payment became a burr under the saddle for McCanles, who reached the point where he told Wellman he was going to shut the station down. The owner had already acquired the reputation of being a hot-head and a bully. One of his frequent targets was the young stock tender, whom McCanles referred to as "Duck Bill" because of his long nose and slightly protruding lips. Also causing friction was his support of the South's recent declaration of independence and its taking of Fort Sumter that April.

If that were not enough to make the two men antagonists, there was the matter of Sandra Schull. She was twenty-six in the spring of 1861. Like McCanles, she was a North Carolina native. There are inferences that she was romantically involved with Hickok, or McCanles, or both, which could have been reason enough for an angry confrontation.

However, for an ambitious businessman like David McCanles, most likely money was a bigger issue than a woman. Wellman kept saying he would wring the next payment out of the Overland Stage, but he could not deliver. The company, he insisted, was in bad shape financially and could not complete the purchase of the property. On the afternoon of July 12, McCanles went to the station to again confront Wellman. He was accompanied by William, his twelve-year-old son, and two friends, James Woods and James Gordon. McCanles carried a shotgun. He and his son walked toward the ranch house that served as the Wellman home while the other two men, armed with pistols, stayed in the front yard.

McCanles stood in the doorway and demanded that Wellman appear. When he did, McCanles went into a rant about Wellman and his employer. Intimidated by the bigger man and the shotgun, Wellman retreated inside. He was replaced by his wife, who, demonstrating plenty of gumption, gave McCanles a piece of her mind, enraging the station owner even more. When she returned inside, the next person to appear was Bill Hickok. McCanles was taken aback. He did not expect to be confronted by the young man, and he told Hickok to mind his own business. Hickok responded that he was making it his business.

"Send Wellman out here," McCanles demanded, "so I can settle with him, or I will come in and drag him out."

Hickok went back inside, and McCanles followed. Finding Wellman, he continued his verbal abuse of him. When he gestured with the shotgun, Hickok raised his right hand. There was a Navy Colt in it, and before McCanles could turn the shotgun toward him, Hickok fired. The bullet went through McCanles's heart. He fell to the floor and died within seconds, his son kneeling beside him.

Out in the yard, Woods and Gordon heard the shot, and with pistols drawn, they started for the house. As soon as Woods entered, Hickok shot him. Woods went back outside, staggering, and fell into a weed patch. Then Hickok shot Gordon. He, too, was not killed; wounded enough, he turned and ran for the cover of the brush by the creek. Mrs. Wellman emerged from the house, saw Woods on the ground, and screamed with fury as she finished him off with a garden hoe. Hickok and two other men who worked at the station followed Gordon's bloodstained tracks to the creek, where he, too, was finished off, reportedly with the shotgun McCanles had brought with him.

The bodies of David McCanles and James Woods were tossed into the same wooden box, which was buried on nearby Soldier Hill. James Gordon's body didn't go as far—it was wrapped in a blanket and buried where he died close to the creek. McCanles and Woods rested in peace for about twenty years, until the construction of the Burlington and Missouri River Railroad required that tracks go onto and over Soldier Hill. The displaced bodies were reinterred at the Fairbury Cemetery.

Three days after the shootings, Hickok was arrested for murder, along with Wellman and J. W. "Doc" Brink, a Rock Creek Station employee. The only witness for the prosecution to actually see what had transpired was William McCanles, but at the trial, the judge ruled he was too young to testify. With no other witnesses and with the jury believing the Rock Creek Station employees' defense that they were protecting themselves from a sudden attack—no doubt, McCanles's notorious reputation helped here—a verdict of not guilty was rendered.

While there was no official testimony from her at the trial, Sandra Schull's version of events may have influenced the men on the jury. She maintained that McCanles and the two men had gone to the Rock Creek Station looking for trouble, to further force the issue with Wellman, which is why all three were armed. (This does not explain, however, why McCanles would put his twelve-year-old son in danger.) Schull contended that Hickok had fired in self-defense, he had no choice, and it was three against one. If there had indeed been something between Hickok and Schull, it is understandable that she would help get him acquitted. Though she wound up as another girl he left behind, this remained the tale she was still telling when interviewed at age ninety-one. (She died at ninety-eight in June 1932.)

Even though he had been acquitted, Hickok thought it a good idea to get far away from Rock Creek Station. Many men his age were choosing sides and signing up to fight in the war that was now over three months old. Hickok became one of them. He returned to Leavenworth and enlisted in the Union army. As would be true for whatever Hickok did during his life, it would not take long for him to see action.

Chapter Four

BEHIND ENEMY LINES

In a family full of abolitionists, James Butler Hickok would be the only member of his immediate family to directly serve the Union cause. And, ironically, he spent a considerable amount of time during the Civil War wearing Confederate uniforms.

It was out of the question for Horace to enlist because he had to remain in Homer to maintain the family farm and thus be the only means of support for his mother. Oliver may have sat out the war entirely while living on the West Coast. Lorenzo continued working for companies with government contracts to haul freight, which made him immune to being conscripted. Bill was the only one of the brothers to step forward and enlist, which he did in Leavenworth in July 1861. Because of his extensive travels, he offered himself as a scout; being cannon fodder in the infantry was out of the question. He saw action rather quickly—a little too quick for his taste.

Hickok was indeed selected as a scout, his first assignment being to accompany the force of fifty-five hundred Union troops commanded by General Nathaniel Lyon. Their mission was to defeat a hastily reorganized Missouri state guard led by a General Sterling "Old Pap" Price, who would wind up having one of the longest tenures of any Confederate general in the war. A Virginian born in 1809, he studied law and made his way west, arriving in Missouri at age twenty-two. Price served as a state representative and then as a member of the House of Representatives, resigning to take command of a regiment of Missouri volunteers in the Mexican-American War. He served with distinction, leading men in battle, and returned to Missouri as a hero and brigadier general. From 1853 to 1857, he was governor of the state. Afterward, Price was a slave-owning businessman; then when the war began he was back in uniform as leader of the state guard.

The Battle of Wilson's Creek, in which he opposed Nathaniel Lyon, was his first major Civil War action, and its success made Price a Confederate hero, too. On August 10, 1861, what was essentially Missouri militia (which included the soon-to-be guerrilla leader William Quantrill) beat the Union forces, killing General Lyon in the process. Hickok was at times in the thick of the action and later confessed to his brothers that especially the crashing artillery scared him to pieces. As the leaderless Union troops retreated, Hickok and the other scouts made for the rear and out of harm's way.

Alas, for Old Pap, it was pretty much downhill from Wilson's Creek. His force, which was absorbed into the regular Confederate army, was defeated at Pea Ridge in March 1862 (more on this later). The so-called Price Raid of 1864 was an unsuccessful effort to divert William Tecumseh Sherman's march toward Atlanta. The end of the war was not the end of Price as a Confederate general. He took the command he had left into Mexico, waiting for a Southern revival. Eighteen months later, when it was quite evident there wouldn't be one, Price returned. He died shortly afterward in St. Louis.

As with other periods in Hickok's life, there are gaps during the Civil War years, and thus it is not known exactly what he did where and when. For some of that time, he traded in his scout outfit to be a teamster again, here and there working for the same firms that employed Lorenzo. Beginning in October 1861, he was based in Sedalia, Missouri, and employed as a wagon master. He stayed at this job for a year, receiving a couple of promotions and a raise to a hundred dollars a month, not bad at all for a twenty-five-year-old on the frontier. He was certainly reminded there was a war going on in the spring of 1862. He was leading a wagon train from Independence to Sedalia when Johnny Rebs attacked and captured it. Hickok got away, returned to Independence, and rounded up some men, and they rode after the pilfered train. They attacked the next morning, and quickly it and the supplies for Union troops were theirs again.

There are several versions of how Bill Hickok became Wild Bill Hickok, including that he was out on the town one night with the mild-mannered Lorenzo, who was nicknamed "Tame Bill," and by obvious contrast his younger, whiskey-loving brother was "Wild Bill." But the tale that has the most support took place in Independence when he was a civilian wagon master. As Hickok walked through town one day, he came upon a disturbance in a bar. He was told that the bartender had incautiously spoken in favor of the rebellion and several drunken Union-favoring patrons inside were beginning to show the bartender the error of his ways with a severe beating. Though far from sharing the man's views, Bill believed in fair fights, and peering inside, he saw this wasn't one.

Drawing his pistols, Hickok stepped inside and told the attackers to back off. They did, because now they had a new target. As they moved at Hickok, he fired twice over their heads. "I'll shoot the next man who comes at me," he told them. Grumbling, they went out the saloon door. That night, as Hickok sauntered past a meeting being held to organize a vigilance committee, several people noticed him. Apparently, his somewhat reckless defense of the outnumbered bartender had made the rounds. One woman shouted, "Good for you, Wild Bill!" A name fit for a frontier legend was born.

Other times, when he was lured away from wagons by better pay (or simply ordered to report), Hickok was a scout for various Union army detachments. This sometimes put him, as in the Battle of Wilson's Creek, in the line of fire. In March 1862, he served as a scout under General Samuel Curtis. By then, General Price and his troops were in the process of being pushed out of Missouri and would soon take refuge in Arkansas. There he was reinforced by a two-thousand-man force led by General Earl Van Dorn. The combined command outnumbered Curtis, offering the Confederates an opportunity to gain back ground in Missouri.

But before the Confederate army could get there, Hickok and other scouts spotted them on the move. Curtis set up a defensive position on the Arkansas side, northeast of Fayetteville. On the seventh, Price attacked, and the two-day Battle of Pea Ridge began. Again and again, Curtis's lines repelled the rebels. Hickok was seemingly everywhere, riding between bullets to gather information to report to Curtis as well as carrying dispatches from the general to the front lines. On that first day, he went through four horses, three giving in to exhaustion and the other being shot out from under him. The fierce fighting took more of a toll on the attackers than on the defenders. One of the more famous deaths in the Civil War was recorded that day: when Confederate general Ben McCulloch was shot by a soldier in the Thirty-Sixth Illinois Infantry, he exclaimed, "Oh, hell!" and died.*

On the second day, the Union army shifted to offense, and their firepower forced Price to retreat. Part of that firepower was supplied by Hickok with a group of sharpshooters on a ridge offering a clear view of the Confederate troops. Curtis pressed forward, and the rebels quit the field entirely. A consequence of the battle was that Missouri would never be seriously threatened again by a Confederate army.

Kansas, however, did not enjoy such relative peace from conflict. In fact, quite the opposite: it was mostly during the Civil War years that the state was at its bloodiest. While there were Union troops stationed there, not enough of them could be spared to guard towns against various vigilante groups. Having almost free rein were the proslavery Missouri Bushwhackers for whom the war simply provided further opportunities for depredations. The Jayhawkers were not the only antislavery force. Early in the war, a company of border scouts formed what became known as the Red Legs because they wore red- or tan-colored leather leggings. The somewhat secret society of about a hundred men—one of whom might have been Bill Hickok, though he had plenty else to do—was under the direction of Thomas Ewing, Jr. He had been the first chief justice of Kansas and would go on to serve as a senior Union officer and, after returning to his native Ohio, in the House of Representatives.

Hickok certainly would have qualified for membership in the Red Legs, which included loyalty to the Union cause, shooting skills, and courage under fire. The organization's headquarters was near Wyan-

---

*Those concerned about General McCulloch's soul no doubt hoped his exclamation was not a greeting.

dotte. One of the Red Legs' officers was George Hoyt, an attorney whose clients had included John Brown at his trial in Virginia.* Initially, this group of militant abolitionists was viewed as modern-day Minutemen, protecting eastern Kansas from brutal invaders. However, it was at times infiltrated by less idealistic men who used the red leg decoration as a license to steal from and kill farmers and other settlers on the Missouri side of the border.

Even when the Jayhawkers and Red Legs were at full strength, they could not completely protect Kansans from the worst of the Southern-sympathizing guerrilla groups. And the worst of the worst, who truly made Kansas bleed, was William Clarke Quantrill, a schoolteacher turned vigilante leader.

Born in Ohio in 1837, Quantrill left his teaching position to move to Utah, then returned east, to Lawrence, Kansas. He didn't remain long there because his proslavery views found more of a welcome in Missouri. Soon after the Civil War began, Quantrill joined General Sterling Price's troops and thus was part of the force opposing General Lyon and Hickok at Wilson's Creek. He chafed, though, under authority and believed that the Southern troops were not brutal enough.

In the western part of the state, there were many former Border Ruffians who hadn't had their fill of violence against abolitionists and Kansas residents in general. They were quick to fall in behind Quantrill—who had deserted Price's army—as he formed a group of guerrillas. He did not have any particular ties to the South and was not a slave owner and had no desire to be one. However, according to the Civil War historian James McPherson, Quantrill "chose the

---

*Brown was found guilty of murder, conspiracy, and treason stemming from the raid on Harpers Ferry. He was executed in December 1859.

Confederacy apparently because in Missouri this allowed him to attack all symbols of authority. He attracted to his gang some of the most psychopathic killers in American history."

They were active early in the war, raiding civilian settlements in addition to Union outposts. In 1862, Quantrill and his guerrillas officially became a unit in the Confederate army, and he was appointed a captain. They conducted raids on isolated Union camps and for a short time took and ransacked Independence. They later did the same to Shawnee, Kansas. En route, they captured a dozen unarmed drivers of Union supply wagons. All were murdered. Over time, the band known as Quantrill's Raiders would include the future outlaws Frank and Jesse James, the Younger brothers, and William "Bloody Bill" Anderson.

Quantrill's raid on Lawrence on August 21, 1863, became one of the most notorious events of the entire war. The direct motive for the attack has often been attributed to the collapse of a federal prison in Kansas City, which killed several Confederate sympathizers being held there, including wives of the raiders, and crippled Josephine Anderson, Bloody Bill's fifteen-year-old sister. A week later, Quantrill gathered about four hundred men and off they rode. Entering Lawrence, they immediately set to work destroying as much property as they could. The raiders set fire to as many as two hundred buildings, and when panicked people ran out of the burning structures, they were gunned down. The fires and the bullets killed close to 150 people.

Remarkably, one of those who survived was James Lane, who during the attack had jumped out his bedroom window in his nightshirt and ran through a cornfield. Soon after Quantrill's Raiders left, Lane rounded up as many men with guns as he could find, and they hurried off in pursuit, the screams of terrorized citizens in their ears and the smell of woodsmoke and burning flesh still in their nostrils. But

Quantrill had gotten too big a lead on them, and his band of mur-
derers escaped across the river and into Missouri.

James Lane was in Lawrence after a stay in the nation's capital. In
January 1861, Kansas had become a state, and its first two senators
were S. C. Pomeroy and Lane. They were in Washington, D.C., on
April 17, 1861, when Virginia seceded from the Union. More than a
few people feared a newly formed Confederate army would march on
the city and possibly kidnap or even kill the new antislavery president, Abraham Lincoln. Lane didn't stand around wringing his
hands. He put out a call to all Kansans in the city, and within twenty-
four hours, he presented to the War Department an "army" of fifty
armed men.

Just in time, it seemed, because reports arrived from Baltimore that
Southern sympathizers there had attacked the Sixth Massachusetts
Infantry as it passed through the city. All that mob had to do was
travel forty miles south to be storming the capital. Rumors were ram-
pant that Lincoln was to be assassinated and Congress held hostage.
With the War Department's approval, Lane led his men to the White
House to protect the president.

As they stood guard, Lane was easy to spot—he brandished a shiny
saber. When night fell, the unit, an abrupt precursor of the Secret
Service, entered the building and practiced military drills in the East
Room. When Lincoln went to see what the commotion was all
about, the Kansan standing guard at the door refused to let him in
because the president did not know the countersign. When the exercises ended, Lane and his men camped out in the East Room.

These ad hoc occupants of the White House intended to remain
indefinitely and not be secretive about it. Calling themselves the
Frontier Guard and with Lane and his saber leading them, on
April 22, now numbering over a hundred men, they paraded down

Pennsylvania Avenue, displaying their rifles, pistols, and knives. Bring on those Confederate hooligans! However, three days later, a sufficient number of Union troops was bivouacked in and around Washington that when the Frontier Guard entered the East Room that evening, Lincoln was waiting with hastily printed discharge certificates. The president greeted each man and presented him with a certificate, and afterward, the Kansas contingent disbanded.

By this time, Lane and his former bodyguard Bill Hickok had lost most of their connection to each other, though their paths would sometimes cross during the Civil War in eastern Kansas military operations. During the conflict, Lane acquired the nicknames "the Grim Chieftain" and the simpler "Bloody Jim." The war afforded him the opportunity to become a brigadier general in command of the Kansas Brigade, consisting of the Third through Seventh Kansas Volunteers. Acting further on his abolitionist outlook, Lane formed the First Kansas Colored Volunteers, the first regiment of black troops to taste battle on the Union side in the war. In the summer of 1861, he led the brigade in numerous actions against the army of General Price and other Confederate forces. And, demonstrating there was a very thin line between him and Quantrill, there was the Osceola Massacre.

That September, Lane was told that hidden in Osceola, Missouri, were Confederate supplies and cash. He led his men into the town and ransacked it, stealing possessions from victims no matter what their political persuasion. Nine residents were accused of refusing to reveal where the Confederate material was—if indeed it was there, it was never found—and were immediately tried, found guilty, and shot. The looters became drunk, with some having to be loaded into wagons as Lane's brigade departed. They left behind several fires they had set, which destroyed the town, killing more of its citizens. Lane's personal wagon trundled out of town bearing a piano and a rack of silk dresses. Though his actions were widely condemned, even by senior Union commanders, Lane continued to lead Kansas troops in the war.

Considering how many enemies he had made and how many men had vowed revenge for their cutthroat activities, it is startling that both James Lane and William Quantrill survived the Civil War. With the latter, it was just barely. Blithely ignoring what was happening back east, in May 1865, Quantrill led the most recent edition of a band of guerrillas into western Kentucky. Union troops had been tipped off that Quantrill was on his way, and an ambush was set up. During it, Quantrill was shot in the back, paralyzing him from the chest down. He died on June 6, not having reached age twenty-eight.

In 1865, Bloody Jim Lane was reelected to the U.S. Senate. However, the mental instability that had been somewhat obscured by a general's uniform during the war became more apparent in civilian life. Almost as soon as Lane took his seat in the Senate, there were investigations into his finances, which of course included what he had plundered for years. Lane grew increasingly paranoid and morose, perhaps missing the glory days of guerrilla warfare. On July 1, 1866, while back in Leavenworth, he leaped from a moving carriage. To give the seeming suicide attempt a better chance at success, while doing so, he shot himself in the head. Lane died from his wound ten days later.

The newly christened Wild Bill Hickok was not wild enough to keep running with Lane as the war continued, and he was kept busy as a wagon master and Union army scout. Then he added espionage to his activities. More than a few writers and historians have attributed this aspect of Hickok's Civil War service to being part of his legend more than being factual. However, according to Joseph Rosa and his investigation, "Wild Bill graduated from sharpshooting to scouting and spying. Soon after the Pea Ridge battle he is alleged to have wangled himself on to Curtis's headquarters staff . . . it is probable that he was attached to the Eighth Missouri State Militia as a scout or spy. The regiment was organized in 1861 and saw active service until 1865. One of its roles was to provide scouts and spies to infiltrate Confederate-held territory."

This does seem to be what Hickok did from late 1862 into 1864—spy for the Union army, with many of his missions placing him behind rebel lines. The first major mission brought him into contact with Susannah Moore, another of his romantic partners.

Hickok was a member of a party of men who had gathered information and ridden back roads looking for the Union line. They came upon a cabin in a clearing, and a black man working outside told them there were four guerrillas inside holding two women. Guns drawn, Hickok entered the cabin. The men inside must have been thoroughly surprised, hungover, or just unaccustomed to facing a man with pistols because Hickok was able to disarm all four. One of the two women was Moore, who "seemed much impressed by Hickok's appearance and by his early mastery of the four guerillas," according to one account.

Suddenly, a squad of Confederate cavalry arrived at the cabin, and a firefight began. After the Union scouts wounded three of the enemy, the remaining rebel riders took off. Hickok and another scout gave chase. His horse was shot dead, but Moore, who had been following them, stopped and gave Hickok her horse. Off he went again, but he and the other scouts were by then too far behind. They returned to the cabin, picking Moore up along the way. It was too dangerous to stay there, so with directions from Moore as to where the Union forces were, they rode away.

She and Hickok would see each other again. Indeed, William

Connelley reports that the scouts did not ride away; instead, they and Hickok remained with Moore and her companion overnight. The next morning, he and his men were attacked by a fresh contingent of Confederates. They held out in a small fort against an assault for two hours. During it, Moore stood by Hickok's side, and she "proved one of the most savage and reckless fighters on the Union side," reports Connelley.

The truth about some of the tales told about Hickok's spying exploits will never be fully known. It is clear from collections like J. W. Buel's *Heroes of the Plains* (which falsely claimed that Hickok kept a journal of his daily activities, even while a captive) that stories were fabricated, turning them into dime-store novel fodder that would be gobbled up by gullible readers back east. Still, between what can be documented and a few experiences as Hickok himself related them after the war (before he became careless with facts), it appears that he was frequently on espionage missions, and he was a productive spy.

One reason was Hickok was by this point in his life a battle-tested man with steel nerves. He rode into dangerous situations—not just riding far afield from his own troops and behind enemy lines but dressing as a Confederate officer to more directly glean information. Of course, this meant execution if caught. He did not panic under pressure, and he survived a couple of narrow escapes.

Hickok told an interviewer after the war that one of his adventures had him spend five months traveling with General Price's army of rebels. He knew of a Confederate soldier named Barnes who had been killed at Pea Ridge, and he presented himself to a regiment of rebel mounted rangers as the dead man's brother. They believed Hickok, and he enlisted. During the months riding with them, Hickok collected information "until I knew every regiment and its strength; how much cavalry there was and how many guns the artillery had."

One account has Hickok finagling his way to being a scout directly under the command of General Price, and thus there would be times when he would be near the Confederate commander and eavesdropping on his conversations with subordinates and messengers giving him reports, gaining valuable information at the very top level. Getting that intelligence to General Curtis would be more difficult: "You see 'twas time for me to go, but it wasn't easy to git out, for the river was close picketed on both sides," Hickok told the postwar interviewer.

There is more than one story about Hickok barely escaping from the Confederate side. A version has it that he concocted a ruse to fight a sergeant in his regiment who claimed that there wasn't a man whom he could not beat, and Hickok suggested they go down to the river and let the Yankees across the way watch the fisticuffs. Somehow, the Union troops would know the rebel scout was Hickok, and perhaps he planned to outlast the sergeant and get a head start across the river. The plan went awry, though, when a Union soldier cried out, "Bully for Wild Bill!" He was heard loud and clear.

"Then the sargent suspicioned me, for he turned on me and growled, 'By God, I believe yer a Yank!' And he at onst drew his revolver; but he was too late, for the minute he drew his pistol I put a ball through him."

Hickok and his horse dove into the river. Bullets flew over his head as the Union troops provided covering fire. He held on to his horse's tail as they fought their way through deep water. The Confederate troops who had followed to watch the fistfight opened up, too, and "bullets zitted and skipped on the water. I thought I was hit again and again." Hickok survived to be personally thanked by General Curtis.

Another narrow escape was observed by young Bill Cody. There are actually at least three stories of Hickok making a dash for Union lines with a companion who was killed, and in each story, the unfortunate man has a different name. In one case, when one of the escape stories was published after the war, the companion supposedly killed read about it in the newspaper.

For a time during his spying activities, Hickok reunited with Cody. The latter was seventeen when his mother died in November 1863. Up to that point in the war, Cody had worked as a freight hauler and ridden with the Red Legs as they attacked settlements in Missouri. The reasoning of his unit, commanded by a man named Chandler, was that this pursuit was justified; since "the government was waging war against the South, it was perfectly square and honest, and we had a good right to do it," Cody recalled. "So we didn't let our consciences trouble us very much." His military status changed after his mother's death. He "continued my dissipation about two months," and then "one day, after having been under the influence of bad whisky, I awoke to find myself a soldier in the Seventh Kansas." Apparently, in a blackout, he had enlisted in the regiment—also known as Jennison's Jayhawkers—and he went off to war.

The Seventh Kansas fought in Tennessee and Mississippi in 1864 and then was sent to Missouri as part of the final campaign against General Price's army. By then, Cody was a corporal or sergeant and serving as a scout. One day, he was riding well ahead when he arrived at a farmhouse and found a man there wearing gray clothes, sitting at a table eating bread and milk, who addressed him with "You little rascal."

Cody recalled in his first autobiography, "Judge my surprise when I recognized in the stranger my old friend and partner, Wild Bill, disguised as a Confederate officer." Hickok informed him that he was disguised as an officer from Texas attached to General Marmaduke's division of Price's army. He gave to Cody what information he had collected in recent weeks and letters to bring back to Union commanders. Cody hoped he would return with him, but Hickok said, "I am getting so much valuable information that I propose to stay a little while longer in this disguise." And off he rode—perhaps on Black Nell. A piece of the Hickok legend that has little or no factual evidence is that he rode this magnificent mare who helped him get out of one scrape after another.

Cody claims to have witnessed one of Hickok's dashing escapes. The Union and Confederate forces were drawn up in a skirmish line near Fort Scott, Kansas, when Cody observed two men take off on horses away from the rebel position. Improbably, "some five hundred shots were fired at the flying men" with only one man—another of Hickok's unfortunate sidekicks—being felled. With Union troops returning fire, he made it safely to report to General Alfred Pleasonton that Price's force was weaker than it appeared. Based on this intelligence, an attack was ordered, and it was successful in driving Price back.

Hickok and Cody scouted together for a time during the campaign, then went to Springfield, Missouri. "Wild Bill and myself spent two weeks there 'having a jolly good time,' as some people would express it."

During this bacchanal, Cody may have been told of Hickok's close shave with being executed. While with Marmaduke's forces, a corporal recognized him as Union loyalist Bill Hickok. There was an immediate court-martial, and the prisoner was sentenced to die at dawn. Hickok was kept in a small cabin, guarded by six men, overnight until his appointment with the firing squad.

With something like divine intervention—or Connelley's invention, though Hickok later contended this happened—"a terrific storm rose." The flashes of lightning allowed the prisoner to scan the interior, and he spotted an old knife used to unlock the door. Hickok used the knife to laboriously cut through the rope binding his wrists. After whetting the knife against his boot sole, Hickok approached the door and spoke to the guard, who we can believe was pretty soaked and miserable by now. Maybe the prospect of shelter prompted him to enter the cabin. His harsh reality was having his throat cut. Hickok's "action was as quick as the lightning which was still flashing."

He exchanged clothes with the guard and took his place outside. The other guards were attempting to stay dry in a shed thirty or forty feet away. Hickok remained at his post until he thought the rebels were asleep; then he slipped away into the dark. All night he walked in the direction of where he thought the Union army was, moving more cautiously during the day, and found it the next evening.

Before the conclusion of 1864, Hickok left off being a Union spy in favor of being a military policeman with some detours to being a scout again. He was paid sixty dollars a month. The reduction from an earlier salary reflects less on Hickok's abilities than on the financial depletion of the U.S. treasury after three years of incessant war. At that time, he reported to General John Sanborn, who the previous October had been appointed commander of the District of Southwestern Missouri. Sanborn had distinguished himself during Grant's Vicksburg campaign, and after the war, he would team up with Kit Carson to negotiate peace treaties with several Indian tribes.

Transporting prisoners and chasing deserters probably was not too riveting an occupation, so Hickok may have welcomed participating in several battles that year. General Pleasonton had become commander of the District of Central Missouri, and his mandate was to finish off General Price's army as a plausible threat once and for all.

Pleasonton had come up the ranks as a cavalry officer and had been part of several major battles, including Antietam, Chancellorsville, and Gettysburg. He led the Union force against J. E. B. Stuart's troopers in the Battle of Brandy Station, the largest cavalry battle of the war. In Missouri, he got right to work.

The beginning of the end for Price occurred on October 21, 1864, at the Battle of Little Blue River in Jackson County, Missouri. Though Price had suffered one defeat after another, the Confederate general Edmund Kirby Smith ordered him to seize St. Louis. This quickly proved impossible, as the city and the route to it were too well defended. Plan B was to burst out of Missouri and into Kansas, even as far as Indian Territory in Oklahoma, capturing or if necessary destroying Union supplies. This plan looked less far-fetched when Price, still in Missouri, scored a minor victory at the Battle of Glasgow. Encouraged, Price headed toward Fort Leavenworth, which had become the headquarters of the Federal Department of Kansas.

On paper, the Battle of Little Blue River was another minor victory for Price, who succeeded in pushing Union troops (many of them militia) back through the streets of Independence. But the Yankees made the rebs pay dearly for every inch, allowing more Union forces to consolidate under the command of General Curtis—and setting up the decisive Battle of Westport, which many historians have regarded as the "Gettysburg of the West."

On October 23, General Curtis and his Union troops faced off against General Price outside Kansas City for what would be their last decisive confrontation and the defeat of the final major Confederate offensive west of the Mississippi River. Curtis had learned of Price's move on what was then called the Town of Kansas from several spies, including Hickok. An attack was launched against Marmaduke's division at 8 A.M. By the early afternoon, other attacks had been made, and Price's army was being hit from three different directions. Price was forced to set fire to prairie grass to set up a smoke screen to cover the withdrawal of his forces.

The rebels would continue to retreat out of Kansas. Another blow, which occurred before Price crossed into Missouri, was the Battle of Mine Creek, when two of his cavalry divisions were routed by Union brigades commanded by Colonels John Finis Philips and Frederick Benteen.* The remnants of Price's army would find some refuge in Texas, but they would have no further impact on events in the South.

When the Civil War ended, the scout and spy known as Wild Bill Hickok had one more message to deliver. On April 9, General Robert E. Lee surrendered to General Ulysses S. Grant, and the news of the momentous event spread as fast as the communications networks of 1865 would allow. Eventually, even those on the frontier heard of it. An elated Hickok could not contain himself. William Darnell was a young man who was part of a wagon train approaching Fort Zarah in Barton County, Kansas, near Great Bend, in mid-April. Decades later, he would recall that a rider went dashing by, shouting, "Lee's surrendered!" It was Hickok, and he kept calling that out until he had passed the wagon train, then he continued on to the fort— and beyond that, to the event that would define his life.

*Custer aficionados will recognize Benteen as one of the officers who served with the Seventh Cavalry at the Battle of Little Bighorn in June 1876.

Chapter Five

THE GUNFIGHTER

Most of the time during the months after the war ended found Wild Bill Hickok in a bustling Independence, Missouri. There he was reunited with Lorenzo, who was still busy hauling freight. And there was plenty of it, with the fighting over and interest in the American frontier being rekindled, especially among the young and the restless. That July, the editor Horace Greeley advised in the *New-York Tribune*, "Go west, young man, and grow up with the country," borrowing the phrase that John Babsone Lane Soule had written in *The Terre Haute Express* in 1851: "Go west, young man, go west."

Hickok was thinking about it. In Independence, he had found an opportunity to work with his brother in a business that could only grow in the expected postwar expansion of the frontier. The Bill Hickok of a few years earlier would have been tempted, tugged by family loyalty and a more nose-to-the-grindstone work ethic. But he was a twenty-eight-year-old Civil War veteran now.

The country had changed, and he had changed with it. True, by

this time, the Hickoks were no longer looking for a frontier homestead and were content to live on in Homer, which was soon to be
renamed Troy Grove, Illinois. The original purpose of his first foray
west no longer mattered. But mostly, James Butler Hickok was a different man. A routine job, farming, or any kind of simple labor was
not for him. He had seen some of the American West, and he wanted
more of it. He knew how to take care of himself in many situations,
including very dangerous ones involving men out to kill him. He had
killed men, an untold number during the war, after the initiation of
the McCanles killings. He wanted to fully embrace life as the man
known in the summer of 1865 as Wild Bill.

By this time, too, he had acquired a distinctive look to go with
his more ambitious life and with new adventures yet to come. By his
appearance, at least, he separated himself from many other men in
their late twenties to be found on the frontier. He was "the most striking object in camp," an army officer, Colonel James Meline, would
soon be including in a letter about Hickok. "Six feet, lithe, active,
sinewy, daring rider, dead shot with pistol and rifle, long locks, fine
features and mustache, buckskin leggings, red shirt, broad-brim hat,
two pistols in belt, rifle in hand—he is a picture. He goes by the name
Wild Bill and tells wonderful stories of his horsemanship, fighting,
and hair-breadth escapes." Tongue-in-cheek, Meline concluded, "We
do not, however, feel under any obligation to believe them all."

Hickok did not care what people believed or didn't. He wasn't
looking back, only forward. He said good-bye to Lorenzo and traveled to Springfield. Its saloons and gambling houses were looking to
lure men like Hickok, and he obliged. Whatever reputation Springfield may have today as a peaceful place, it was anything but tranquil
in the summer of 1865. There was a volatile mix of settlers and adventurers heading west, gamblers and prostitutes, entrepreneurs looking

for business opportunities or on the run from creditors after their previous businesses failed, and soldiers who had been mustered out, some ex-Union and some ex-Confederate. It was an exciting town for a man with no encumbrances and responsibilities, looking for card games and cheap liquor and other forms of entertainment.

What he also found in Springfield was Davis Tutt. Somehow, Hickok and the man from Arkansas had become friends, or at least acquainted with each other in a friendly enough way, even though they had been on opposite sides in the just-concluded war. There were even rumors that Hickok had impregnated Tutt's sister, though it is unclear how they would have encountered each other while there was a war going on (though Hickok may have done more than spying while behind enemy lines). A mutual love of gambling was enough to overcome any blue-gray obstacles and to resume that friendship in Springfield. Tutt, having been there longer and being among Southern sympathizers in Missouri, was a well-known man in Springfield, so a friend of his was welcome at the gaming tables.

They were viewed as something like two peas in a pod. "He is a noted scout, desperado and gambler," reported Albert Barnitz, who led the Second Ohio Volunteer Cavalry stationed at Springfield, about Tutt. "Both have been in the habit of appearing on the streets with two revolvers strapped on their belts. Both have been intimate for years and have been gambling together."

However, it soon became clear the friends had another mutual love: Susannah Moore. She may have been waiting for the war to be over, and Hickok would, perhaps, settle down, even take up farming again. Whatever the thinking, Moore was waiting for him in Springfield when he arrived. This may not have been the welcome Hickok was wanting. He was a free man with a thirst and an itch for gambling, and settling down in any capacity was not in the cards. If Susannah would be patient, or they could cohabit until . . .

Apparently, she was not so inclined. Moore was not scorned, exactly, but she had different thoughts about their relationship, and when he didn't share them, she got angry. Turned out, angry enough to take up with Davis Tutt, who possibly saw this as revenge for any dalliance Hickok had had with his sister.

Hickok was content to let matters take their course and probably valued a drinking buddy and fellow gambler more than an exgirlfriend, but Tutt was looking for trouble. He not only refrained from being in the same card games as Hickok, but he gave money to other players, underwriting an effort to clean Hickok out and presumably send him on his way.

But what led directly to what turned out to be a historic gunfight was Tutt's attempt to humiliate Hickok. Tutt's plan for the exiling of his former friend had gone awry when Hickok beat the other players at cards. Worse, the money he raked in was as much Tutt's as theirs. Frustrated, he told Hickok that he owed forty dollars from a deal the two men had made on a horse. Right then and there, without argument, Hickok took that amount from his winnings and attempted to give the money to Tutt.

That was not enough to appease him. Tutt then insisted that Hickok owed him an additional thirty-five dollars. "I think you are wrong, Dave," Hickok said. "It's only twenty-five dollars. I have a memorandum in my pocket."

The attempt to tamp down the tension that permeated the warm and smoky room failed. Tutt insisted on the higher amount. The two men disputed the ten-dollar difference. Suddenly, Tutt stepped forward, reached out, and snatched Hickok's watch off the card table.

This was not just any timepiece but a Waltham gold pocket watch. Tutt announced that Hickok would get his watch back when he paid a thirty-five-dollar ransom for it. Hickok was tempted to go for his guns, but the other men in the room were friends of Tutt's, and they were armed. With a grin, and the watch, Tutt walked out.

Soon after, Hickok was told that Tutt intended to parade in public with the confiscated watch dangling from the pocket of his vest. Hickok seethed, and he repaired to his room to make sure his .36-caliber Colt 1851 Navy revolvers were well-oiled and loaded. Word spread fast in Springfield that there could be a confrontation the next day.

Still, Tutt was given one last chance. "He shouldn't come across that square unless dead men can walk," Hickok told Tutt's friends.

Now Tutt risked being shamed if he *didn't* wear the watch while in the town square. He did; yet, showing remarkable restraint considering how much Tutt had turned against him, Hickok offered one more way out. Confronting Tutt in the square, he said he would pay the twenty-five dollars he owed Tutt to settle the supposed debt and the return of the watch. Tutt now insisted on forty-five dollars. Eli Armstrong, who knew both men, intervened, urging Tutt to compromise at the thirty-five dollars he'd originally demanded. Tutt refused. Incredibly, both he and Hickok contended they did not want to fight, and they strolled to a nearby saloon to have a drink. From there, Tutt left, the matter unresolved.

As previously described, the matter was resolved by the bullet that killed Davis Tutt. Immediately after he hit the ground, Hickok wheeled about to confront a group of the dead man's friends who had positioned themselves behind him. They had guns, and they were angry. However, they had also just witnessed a perfect performance by a coolheaded shootist.

"Aren't you satisfied, gentlemen?" Hickok demanded. "Put up your shooting irons or there'll be more dead men here." No one challenged him.

Word would spread far and wide that Wild Bill Hickok was not a man to be trifled with when he held a gun. Worse was when he held two, because he could shoot just as accurately with either hand.

An arrest warrant for murder was issued, and three days after the town-square duel, "William Haycocke" was taken into custody. A magistrate reduced the charge to manslaughter and set bail at two thousand dollars, which Hickok posted. On August 3, the trial began, with Judge C. B. M'Afee presiding.

Considering that Springfield had been more Tutt's town than Hickok's, and the gunfighter's having served the Union cause, one might expect that during the trial the deck and especially the jury would be stacked against him. That his lawyer was Colonel John Phelps, an army officer and former Union military governor of Arkansas, probably didn't help in Missouri. A finding of guilty could have resulted in years in prison, with Wild Bill Hickok never heard from again. However, it seems from the coverage in *The Missouri Weekly Patriot*—the trial transcripts having been lost—that witnesses testified during the three-day trial that Hickok tried to avoid an armed conflict, and when it was inevitable, he had allowed Tutt to draw first. Letting an adversary do that meant a finding of self-defense was automatic.

Still, the not guilty verdict the jury delivered after ninety minutes of deliberation was not greeted warmly. According to Captain Barnitz, "'Wild Bill' has been released on bail. Public sympathy seems about equally divided between him and his victim." A few of Tutt's friends even made noises about putting a noose around Hickok's neck. Leaving Springfield seemed like a good idea.

Tutt was buried in the Springfield City Cemetery, where he remained for almost eighteen years. In 1883, Tutt's body was dug up and reburied by Lewis Tutt, once a slave who was the son of Tutt's father and a black woman he owned back in Arkansas.

Hickok certainly had to consider that every time he turned his back in Springfield, a bullet would find its way into it. Yet he remained in Springfield. He did not want to be chased out; he would leave when it suited him. And he had a good streak going at the gaming tables.

Soon after the trial, Hickok was approached by Colonel George Ward Nichols. Their subsequent conversations, gathered in an interview for an article published in *Harper's New Monthly Magazine,* would do much to create the Wild Bill Hickok legends that exist to this day. It even contained a few facts.

Nichols was a New Englander, having been born in Maine in 1831. As a young man, he worked his way down to Boston, where he wrote for newspapers. His first foray as a sort of foreign correspondent was when he journeyed west in the late 1850s to report on the bloody doings in Kansas. When Nichols returned east, it was to become an editor at *The New York Evening Post.* A year after the Civil War began, he was commissioned a captain in the Union army.

By the end of the Civil War, he was indeed a colonel, having served in campaigns headed by the generals John C. Frémont and William Tecumseh Sherman. He was also a somewhat celebrated author because his book published in 1865, *The Story of the Great March: From the Diary of a Staff Officer,* about Sherman's march to the sea, was a bestselling crowd-pleaser. That year, he became a correspondent for *Harper's New Monthly Magazine.* It is not clear how he happened to interview Hickok, though one explanation was that while roaming the frontier looking for a good story, he heard about the deadly gunfight in Springfield.

In any case, he interviewed Hickok at length and spent some time with a man he identified as "Captain Honesty." This was a pseudonym for the second man named Owen to have an impact on Hickok's life. Captain Richard Bentley Owen had been a regimental quartermaster in the Union forces that had battled General Sterling Price for years and had been a supervisor of Hickok when the latter was a military policeman. It was Captain Owen who, during the last year of the war, often dispatched Hickok on his policing missions, which included tracking down deserters and mule stealers. Apparently, they had remained friends and had reconnected in Springfield.

It would not be until early 1867 that the lengthy article written by Nichols would appear in *Harper's New Monthly Magazine,* when it would cause a national sensation. Hickok had no inkling of this when he and Nichols parted. Even if he indeed did trust the man, he had no idea what would be written—and how much of that would be within shooting distance of the truth. He would have gotten a pretty fair idea had Nichols shared the thoughts that later comprised just one paragraph of the magazine piece:

> *Whenever I had met an officer or soldier who had served in the Southwest I heard of Wild Bill and his exploits, until these stories became so frequent and of such extraordinary character as to quite outstrip personal knowledge of adventure by camp and field; and the hero of these strange tales took shape in my mind as did Jack the Giant Killer or Sinbad the Sailor in childhood's days. As then, I now had the most implicit faith in the existence of the individual; but how one man could accomplish such prodigies of strength and feats of daring was a continued wonder.*

According to Nichols, as he was leaving Springfield, he asked Hickok if it was all right to publicize a few of the scout's adventures.

(This, of course, begs the question of what Hickok thought he was being interviewed for.) "Certainly you may," he responded, adding a curious statement: "I am sort of public property." Hickok was reported to have tears in his eyes when he prevailed upon Nichols to reassure him that his "old and feeble" mother—sixty-one was practically elderly in 1865—in Illinois would not be embarrassed by anything she read. "I'd like her to know what'll make her proud," Hickok said. "I'd like her to hear that her runaway boy has fought through the war for the Union like a true man."

The details of the magazine article, some of which might have made even Polly Hickok gag, will be discussed in the next chapter, to coincide with its publication and impact.

Obviously, Hickok did not count political advisers among his few friends in Springfield, because that fall, he decided to run for office there. He set his sights on becoming the marshal. He did have law-enforcement experience, beginning as a constable in Monticello and carrying out Captain Owen's assignments in the war. That experience did not count as much as his lingering unpopularity, and he was defeated at the polls.

Hickok might have continued in Springfield out of sheer spite—or with Tutt in his grave, he might have reawakened the romance with Susannah Moore—but an appealing offer came his way. It was from Captain Owen, who as the winter of 1865–66 took hold was the assistant quartermaster at nearby Fort Riley. Hickok could wear a badge as a deputy U.S. marshal.

The turmoil at the fort went beyond it being a main hub for travelers going west. Army money was being embezzled, soldiers were deserting with alarming frequency, and worse, often they made their getaways on stolen horses and mules. Hickok made his way into north-central Kansas and was appointed to the position in February

1866. A plus was finding Lorenzo there, his brother having moved on from Independence and now undertaking what hauling trips the winter would allow, earning a decent seventy-five dollars a month as a wagon master. Officially, Wild Bill's duties were to "hunt up public property," man or beast, and for this, he would earn the same salary as his brother. He could not take advantage of the shelter the frontier fort provided the rest of that winter. (It was established in 1853, named after General Bennett Riley, who had led the first military escort along the Santa Fe Trail.) Owen had him back on his horse to make arrests.

One mission was to track down several men who had all deserted together, on four-legged government property that was probably viewed as more valuable than they were. Hickok tracked the deserters south through Council Grove to the upper waters of the Little Arkansas River. When he returned, three weeks after leaving Fort Riley, he had three of the deserters and nine of the stolen mules. The army was especially glad to have the mules back. What observers noticed was that the biggest of the three deserters was riding on a mule next to Hickok.

One man wondered if that was taking too much of a chance, that the deserter under arrest could have suddenly lunged for one of the marshal's six-shooters. The confident Hickok answered that he would have drawn his other gun and killed all three deserters before the first one had fired a shot. This same observer, George Hance, who would write an article titled "The Truth About Wild Bill" published thirty-five years later, claimed to have seen Hickok "draw a pistol and hit a spot, not larger than a silver dollar, at 20 to 30 steps, before an ordinary man could fire a shot into the air or into the ground."

It would seem that seventy-five dollars a month, Lorenzo to hang around with, rounding up stolen property, tracking down fleeing men, all that fresh air and exercise, and putting on demonstrations of fantastic marksmanship would constitute a fine life. But Hickok quickly grew bored. As it turned out, midspring was a good time for him to again turn his eyes westward. By then, the war had been over for a year, and some of the men who had returned to their homes in the Northeast and Midwest became restless or desired new opportunities for farming or owning a business. Some of the men who had returned home from the Confederate army felt similarly in addition to chafing under Yankee occupation and the implementation of Reconstruction. To the west was the so-called Great American Desert with its wonders to be explored and its millions of acres of free or at least very cheap land to be exploited.

But all that territory contained an obstacle: Indians. While some easterners advocated for the rights of America's indigenous people, to many people west of the Missouri River, being a Native American conferred no rights. And anyway, they were savages—not white, not educated, not Christian, not civilized, and not deserving of any charitable feelings. Let them be exiled or pushed to places where they weren't going to bother westbound explorers and those in their wake aboard wagons that would be dubbed "prairie schooners" as they yawed and creaked along trails created through the tall grass.

During the Civil War, some tribes had returned to the hunting grounds and other lands abandoned by earlier settlers and left virtually unprotected by army forts that had been surviving with bare-minimum contingents of Bluebellies or had shut down altogether. A few Indian leaders had allowed themselves to dream that the white men had hurt themselves so badly making war on each other that they would not return.

In 1866, those dreams were about to be dashed. The tribes of the prairie and Great Plains were to experience the nightmare of westward expansion—Manifest Destiny—with a new wave of white men coveting their land and buffalo and protected by a fresh influx of soldiers. Those army units needed scouts to guide them to where forts could be built, and between them would be long trains of supplies hauled by heavily laden wagons steered by men like Lorenzo.

In May, General William Tecumseh Sherman arrived at Fort Riley. He was taking a tour of the West as commander of the Military Division of the Mississippi. Sherman, who doubled as general of the army, was in charge of most of the territory between St. Louis and the Rocky Mountains. His immediate destination was Omaha, Nebraska, and from there he would travel to St. Paul, Minnesota. When he requested someone to be his scout and guide, Captain Owen readily suggested Hickok, who was hired for the first leg of the trip, which would take Sherman and his party to Fort Kearny in Nebraska.

Soon after they arrived, "there was little of anything exciting to report about it," writes Robert G. Athearn in his *William Tecumseh Sherman and the Settlement of the West*. "The dilapidated frame buildings, standing gauntly out on a vast, treeless plain, were desolate and lonely. Despite the barrenness of the country, there were a few farms dotting the landscape. The land to the east was more heavily settled and was generally safe from hostile Indians. Sherman wondered why there were any settlers around the place at all."

Perhaps this unpromising route was not worth further exploring, because Hickok parted ways with Sherman at Fort Kearny. He was soon hired to scout for another well-known—though less successful—Civil War general, John Pope. His greatest achievement was being appointed by President Lincoln to command the Army of Virginia in the summer of 1862. His greatest failure came soon after, when Generals Robert E. Lee, Stonewall Jackson, and James Longstreet gave him a good drubbing at the Second Battle of Bull Run. By that

September, Pope had been banished to Minnesota. In the summer of 1866, his exile was over, and he was leading an expedition to Santa Fe, a route well traveled by Hickok.

In September, Hickok returned from this sun-drenched excursion. Beginning the previous month at Fort Riley, the Seventh Cavalry Regiment was being organized. Soon, both it and the fort would have a new commander: Lieutenant Colonel George Armstrong Custer. He had with him his beautiful wife. At the fort, the Custers made the acquaintance of the buckskin-wearing scout called Wild Bill, who made an immediate impression on the twenty-four-year-old Libbie Custer. She would spend the rest of her life—a long one, not ending until four days before her ninety-first birthday in April 1933, stretching from the presidencies of John Tyler to Franklin Delano Roosevelt—refuting rumors that she and Hickok had engaged in an affair. Libbie was not especially aggressive in her denials, and her view of Hickok certainly allowed for some speculation.

"Physically, he was a delight to look upon," is how the description begins in *Following the Guidon*, her memoir published in 1890.

> *Tall, lithe, and free in every motion, he rode and walked as if every muscle was perfection, and the careless swing of his body as he moved seemed perfectly in keeping with the man, the country, the time in which he lived. I do not recall anything finer in the way of physical perfection than Wild Bill when he swung himself lightly from his saddle, and with graceful, swaying step, squarely set his shoulders and well-poised head, approached our tent for orders. He was rather fantastically clad, of course, but all seemed perfectly in keeping with the time and place. He did not make an armory of his waist, but carried two pistols. He wore top-boots, riding breeches, and dark blue flannel shirt, with scarlet set in the front. A loose neck-handkerchief*

left his fine firm throat free. I do not remember all his features, but the frank, manly expression of his fearless eyes and his courteous manner gave one a feeling of confidence in his word and his undaunted courage.

Wild Bill Hickok was about to become a new kind of plainsman on the American frontier—part explorer, part hunter, part romantic figure, and part gunslinger. One-third of the nation, its entire middle section, was relatively untouched, a temptation many men could not resist, and experienced guides into that territory were in much demand. For the rest of the year, Wild Bill spent a lot of time in the saddle, becoming a familiar and striking figure across the frontier.

While Hickok rode with the Custers, the article written by Colonel Nichols was being prepared for publication. A legend that would increasingly deviate from reality was about to be born.

ACT II

Wild Bill Hickok when he was a lawman
in Hays City in the 1860s.

Wild Bill was a Plainsman in every sense of the word,
yet unlike any other of his class.

—LIEUTENANT COLONEL GEORGE ARMSTRONG CUSTER, 1872

Chapter Six

ALONG THE CHISHOLM TRAIL

The world of Wild Bill Hickok was about to expand to include much of the American West, with his adopted state of Kansas as the main gateway to it. Looking at a map today, one might wonder about Kansas being considered part of the West at any time in American history. At most, the state was sort of the eastern edge of the vast American West and resided in the central time zone, not even the mountain zone. And being pretty much smack in the center of the continental United States and thus not at all remote, could Kansas ever have been included in what was once called the Great American Desert?

Yes. The plains west of Topeka when the Civil War ended had only a handful of inhabitants. In all of Kansas, the population in the mid-1860s was only around 250,000 people, and they were easily outnumbered by millions of American bison (or buffalo). There were also untold numbers of antelope, coyotes, wolves, snakes, and the inescapable prairie dogs. Most tribes had been decimated by diseases communicated by white men, or those who once occupied Kansas had been moved south into the Indian Territory that had been carved out of Oklahoma. Still, until the postwar migration really gathered steam, a westbound traveler was more likely to encounter an Indian than a white man. The weather could be harsh for the hardiest of hunters and settlers, with the sun baking the prairie in the summer and brutal winds and days-long blizzards collecting fatalities in the winter.

Like Hickok had before the war, the increasing numbers of travelers heading west were discovering not just the promise of Kansas but its beauty. As in other years, in 1866, from the middle of spring into late September, the state and its four-hundred-mile width offered a wide array of green prairie grass and colorful flowers. Most of the land the migrants plodded through was covered with waves of grass, in some areas six inches high or even taller. Among the flowers they observed were plum blossoms, elderberries, blue lupine, primroses, and wild strawberries. Above this verdant and radiant pageantry was a limitless blue sky. Though this was beautiful to look at, cloudless days meant no escape from the relentless sun. Narrowing and swelling with the seasons, rivers and streams coursed through the prairie, and near them could be found such trees as hickory, willow, elm, walnut, oak, cottonwood, and buttonwood.

Men looking for homesites could pick the most appealing combination of fresh water and sturdy timber. And there would be no lack of food as long as one had a rifle, as there were plenty of wild turkeys, prairie chickens, quail, and other readily available game. There were travelers who intended to push through to Nebraska or even Colorado, but the grasslands and fertile beauty of Kansas persuaded some of them to pick a spot and begin to put down roots.

The promise of Kansas was more immediately realized precisely because of its central location. The end of the war produced the peak years of the cattle trade, and most of the cattle would be coming up from Texas. Driving them due north meant cutting through a piece of Indian Territory / western Oklahoma and up into Kansas. At the same time, railroad companies were laying track from east to west, and the most desirable avenue was through the state. Kansas was not only in the middle of the country, its flat grassland occasionally interrupted by modest ranges of brown hills made for efficient track-laying. Eventually, the Kansas Pacific Railway and the Atchison, Topeka, and Santa Fe Railway would become the dominant companies, and their lines would allow for a virtually straight run to Colorado.

Though not a cattleman or a Kansan or Texan, Jesse Chisholm was the man the business leaders in the cow towns could thank once they began to benefit financially from the cattle trade. Legend may have him depicted as a big, strapping American frontiersman who blazed the trail brandishing smoking six-shooters. The real story of this true pioneer is not quite that dramatic but still colorful. Chisholm was born in 1805 or 1806 in Tennessee. His father had emigrated from Scotland, and his mother was Cherokee. In his early twenties, he was living near Fort Gibson, on land given to the Cherokee Nation in Oklahoma, and working as a hunter and trail guide. When he married in 1836, Chisholm relocated to Creek Nation territory, also in Oklahoma. There, he established a trading post, and certainly one reason why it was successful was he was fluent in fourteen different Indian dialects.

His linguistic talents not only appealed to Indians with goods to trade but made Chisholm much in demand as an interpreter between various tribes and U.S. government emissaries as treaties were being negotiated. He traveled regularly from his trading post in Hughes County, Oklahoma, to other sites in Indian Territory as well as Texas, Nebraska, and Kansas. During one of his journeys, Chisholm rescued several Mexican children who were prisoners of the Kiowa and

Comanche tribes and brought them back home, adopting them as his own. With an expanding family, he focused more on also expanding his business, establishing trading posts elsewhere in Oklahoma and in Kansas. He was living in Wichita during the Civil War. At first, he traded with the Confederate army. Then as the winds of war blew the other way, the Union army became his primary customer.

What would be called the Chisholm Trail began in 1865. He and a partner led a train of wagons weighed down with supplies out of Fort Leavenworth in Kansas and took them south to one of his trading posts, at Council Grove, near the future Oklahoma City. Chisholm hadn't used this route arbitrarily. Based on his experience as a wide-ranging scout and interpreter, he followed a path worn by the feet and hooves of Indian raiding and hunting parties. Other traders followed his lead, and it became a popular route, named for its first and most prominent traveler. The trail lengthened with the coming of the cattle drives, though Chisholm, past sixty years old after the war, never drove a single steer himself. Indeed, he did not last long enough to reap any possible reward for the Chisholm Trail, dying of food poisoning in March 1868. His grave can be found in Geary, Oklahoma.

At the time of Chisholm's death, the trail was still a work in progress. Ranchers began their cattle drives in San Antonio—or even as far south as the Rio Grande—and took them due north to Red River Station. From there, cowboys continued to drive the cattle north, through the Oklahoma Indian Territory (over what is U.S. Highway 81 today) and into Kansas near Caldwell. As the railroads laid track west, most of the herds pushed on up to Abilene. It is estimated that by the time the cattle drives from Texas were pretty much done in the late 1870s, close to five million head had churned up dust on the Chisholm Trail.

Even with the relative efficiency of the trail, it could take as long as two months to complete it from south Texas, and this was even in friendly weather conditions. The terrain cattle had to plod along was sometimes treacherous, and water barriers such as the Washita, Canadian, Red, Arkansas, and Smoky Hill Rivers were death-defying to cross. The occasional thunderstorm or just the crack of a Sharps hunting rifle could set the jittery longhorns stampeding. An annoying threat was rustlers and marauding Indians, who quietly picked off cattle by the twos and threes under the cover of darkness.

Being a cowboy was a lonely occupation. For most of the trek north, the drovers saw only the outskirts of small settlements and few people, and the menu did not stray far from beef and beans and coffee. Trail bosses prohibited alcohol. Women were available only in the cowboys' feverish imaginations. Men could start fights out of boredom as much as genuine irritation. After weeks upon weeks of smelling cattle and eating dust, the cowboys entered a town demanding that it accommodate their thirst and other needs.

The impact on the cow towns was prosperity and plenty of it, though the towns flamed out rather quickly. Across Kansas, the convergence of the railroad and the cattle drives created boomtowns. Saloons seemed to pop out of the ground like the heads of prairie dogs. Bartenders could not dispense liquor fast enough to the tired, dirt-streaked, and parched cowboys whose pockets were filled with their pay. Bordellos also prospered, as did other businesses like dry goods stores and dance and gambling halls and hotels. It was difficult for a reasonably competent man to not make money.

But for each town, the boom began to fade. The railroads moved relentlessly west, and with them went the trail bosses and their herds. Many citizens were glad to see them go because the rowdiness and violence had become too high a price to pay for prosperity. The cow towns had to find ways to survive without cows. Gamblers like Wild Bill Hickok moved on, too, following the action.

The first of the major postwar cow towns in Kansas was Abilene. The town that within a few years would play a major role in the life of Hickok had, like many of the frontier towns springing up, a modest origin but drew men with vision.

One morning in July 1856, Timothy Hersey guided a wagon out of the gates of Fort Riley and rode west. With the sun at his back and then climbing up his neck and warming his hat, he drove up the Smoky Hill River, camped along Chapman Creek, and set off again the next day. On the bottoms between present-day Detroit, Kansas, and the banks of Mud Creek, Hersey encountered a large herd of buffalo. He shot a few—it was hard to resist; the dumb beasts simply stood there and took it—and he camped there for the night. On this site, what is today the intersection of First and Vine Streets, Abilene was founded.

Hersey built a log cabin. He had left a wife and child behind in Illinois, and the following year, he returned there to fetch them. Back in Abilene, he made additions to his cabin, including a store and bedrooms and stables, necessitated both by business and by Mr. and Mrs. Hersey having eight more children. It was Elizabeth Hersey who gave the town its name. The devout Methodist was a fervent Bible reader, and soon after relocating from Illinois and taking stock of her surroundings, she was struck by a passage in the book of Luke that mentions Abilene as a province in Judea that is described as a "beautiful area of the plains."

The coming of the railroad was still years away, but Abilene became a stop on the Overland Stage route from Leavenworth to Denver. Inside his corral, Timothy Hersey kept horses and a few mules for the stagecoaches, and his wife took care of feeding the dust-caked travelers. Hersey would later claim that the phrase "a square meal" originated at his outpost. The food that he and his wife provided was, he contended, the last and best of its kind for hundreds of miles, and he advertised that at his outpost, travelers would have the "last square meal east of Denver." That meal typically consisted of bacon and eggs, some beef when available, hot biscuits, coffee, dried peaches and apples, and Elizabeth's pies. The entrepreneur also contracted with the Overland Stage to supply it with hay and feed for the company's animals, some of which were kept in his own corral.

Perhaps to his eventual regret, Hersey was a restless man, and he lived in restless times on the American frontier. He stayed with his family in Abilene until the town grew up around him. During the Civil War, he was a lieutenant in the Kansas militia. With a partner, C. H. Thompson, who had built Abilene's first hotel, on the east bank of Mud Creek, Hersey bought large tracts of land and sold parcels at a good profit as more visitors decided to become residents. Another sign of progress came in 1864, when W. S. Moon built the Frontier Store, which also served as the post office and where court sessions were held. The first saloon was simply called Old Man Jones and was, for whatever reason, constructed in the middle of a prairie dog town, which must have made for treacherous going for tipsy travelers.

"By 1867, more than a score of adults had established themselves in the usual one-room homes on the east side of the creek," wrote Stewart P. Verckler in his history of Abilene. "These homes consisted partly of logs plastered together with clay and mud; dirt was banked around the bottom to keep out the weather and the wind. The roofs were of poles, brush and grass held down by dirt. Hersey had built the only decent home."

Hersey could have had a long and prosperous life in Abilene, especially being on the ground floor when the lucrative cattle trade began. But one morning, he was once again setting off on a wagon heading west. He went on to found the town of Benoit by building a sawmill and then a gristmill at Willow Springs. As the town grew, Hersey became restless again. He moved on, constructing another sawmill and gristmill, these on the Solomon River. When his pockets were full enough, he packed supplies and tools into five wagons and left Kansas altogether, driving his teams to Wyoming. There, the Panic of 1873 caught up to Hersey, and his pockets were emptied. For some reason, he thought Los Angeles was the answer. If it was, he never found out. He got only as far as Denver, where he had health problems while trying to make money investing in mines. However, though his pioneering days were over, Hersey would wind up with a long life, not dying until 1905, in Castle Rock, Washington.

Whatever credit Hersey deserves, he alone did not turn Abilene into a boomtown. That happened because of another visionary entrepreneur, Joseph McCoy, and the railroads working their way west. It would make Abilene the first of the boisterous cow towns, to be followed in the late 1860s and early '70s by Ellsworth, Hays City, Newton, Wichita, and Dodge City. And as the people moved west with the railroad, they carried tales of the famous frontiersman Wild Bill Hickok—famous, thanks to the *Harper's New Monthly Magazine* article, which had finally appeared in February 1867.

Hickok could not have known in advance the contents of the article with any certainty, so he was surprised when he heard people talking about it and questions were put to him, and even newspapers of the day began commenting on it. When people encountered Hickok, they found the man to be as described by George Ward Nichols: He was over six feet tall and wore bright yellow moccasins. A deerskin shirt hung jauntily over his shoulders, revealing, as Nichols offered, echoing Libbie Custer's bodice-ripping estimation, "a chest whose breadth and depth were remarkable. His small round waist was girthed by a belt which held two of Colt's Navy revolvers. His legs sloped gradually from the compact thighs to the feet, which were small and turned inward as he walked."

The enraptured writer added, "There was a singular grace and dignity of carriage about that figure which would have attracted your attention, meet it where you would." On Hickok's head was a large sombrero, and out of it "a mass of fine brown hair falls below the neck to the shoulders."

And there were the guns. Hickok would have thrived with the double-action Colt .44s, but as they would not be introduced until 1877, he continued to make do with the .36 Navy Colt, and when it became available in 1873, he would switch to the single-action Army Colt .45. With both pistols, the catch was filed down for hair-trigger quickness. In his side pockets, he carried .41-caliber derringers, and in his belt was a bowie knife. Later, as a lawman, he also carried a shotgun or repeating rifle. A decade later, another lawman, Wyatt Earp, would extoll the effectiveness of shooting deliberately over shooting first and furiously. Though this had worked well enough in his gunfight with Davis Tutt in July 1865, by early 1867, Hickok's approach was if forced to draw, he would do it faster than his opponent and pump out several bullets while his victim was still thinking about squeezing the trigger.

During idle periods when he was not a scout for the army or a deputy U.S. marshal or gambling, Hickok enjoyed putting on shooting exhibitions. Especially impressive was his ambidextrous accuracy. Witnesses report seeing Hickok driving a cork through the neck of a whiskey bottle at twenty paces, splitting a bullet on the edge of a dime at the same distance, and putting as many as a dozen bullet holes in a tomato can that had been tossed in the air. No doubt Hickok enjoyed the expressions of astonishment on the faces of his ad hoc audiences, but such exercises also kept him in practice. And letting the public know he was always at the top of his game could dissuade ambitious gunmen from trying to take Hickok on. Such men may have entertained thoughts of gunfighter glory, but they weren't suicidal.

This was the man who was on the cusp of becoming the 1860s equivalent of a matinee idol in a country whose Civil War glory was receding into history and was now looking west for new legends.

Chapter Seven

FRONTIER FAME

The unauthorized celebrity biography of today or the overnight fame achieved through social media has nothing on what was published in *Harper's New Monthly Magazine* in February 1867. The article took a plainsman with an emerging reputation as a superior scout and a sharp-eyed shootist and turned him, at just twenty-nine years old, into an American frontier legend.

True, even before the piece appeared, Wild Bill Hickok was no longer an obscure figure. Here and there, people had begun to pass around stories about him the way they had told tales the previous couple of decades about the frontiersmen Jim Bridger and Kit Carson. In the case of Carson, some of those stories, true or not, had been published, enchanting young boys like Jim Hickok on the family farm in Illinois. In the years to come, there would be stories printed in dime-store novels about Wyatt Earp, Jesse James, Bat Masterson, Buffalo Bill Cody, and a handful of other figures as the West was mythologized into an American *Iliad*. This would be true, too, on the big screen as motion pictures emerged as popular entertainment.

Beginning in 1903, when Edwin Porter released his silent film *The Great Train Robbery*, the western was a favorite among moviegoers. When Cecil B. DeMille took a train west from New York and stepped off at a place called Hollywood to direct the 1914 western *The Squaw Man*, the American film industry took root.

But no single published piece catapulted a man on the American frontier more than the George Ward Nichols article did for Hickok. *Harper's* was a very high-profile magazine, especially in the more-populated eastern states, where the literacy rate was much higher than in the West. Nichols may have cynically been trying to create a heroic character to sell copies, but most accounts suggest he was genuinely enamored of Hickok. His embellishments were true as far as Nichols (and apparently his editors) was concerned. Hickok did have real adventures in his life, including the behind-the-lines Civil War spying and the McCanles and Tutt gunfights. And he was a rather exotic figure in his features and the way he dressed and carried himself. He had exhibited an uncanny talent for gunplay and marksmanship. Add all this to the fertile imagination of a writer who could cash in on a sensational story and an outlet that offered that story to thousands of eager and mostly gullible readers, and America had its first postwar frontier star.

Nichols was no hack aspiring to be a better writer than he was. The former member of General Sherman's staff was a keen observer, and reading the article is like seeing a series of snapshots of the frontier in the immediate aftermath of the Civil War. While in Springfield that summer of 1865, Nichols had watched "men and women dressed in queer costumes; men with coats and trousers made of skin, but so thickly covered with dirt and grease as to have defied the identity of the animal when walking in the flesh. Others wore homespun gear, which oftentimes appeared to have been of lengthy service. Many of those people were mounted on horse-back or mule-back, while others urged forward the unwilling cattle attached to creak-ing, heavily-laden wagons, their drivers snapping their long whips with a report like that of a pistol-shot."

Nichols went on to observe about the citizens of Springfield loll-ing outside shops: "The most marked characteristic of the inhabitants seemed to be an indisposition to move, and their highest ambition to let their hair and beards grow."

Nichols was approached by the army officer Captain Richard Bentley Owen—the Captain Honesty in the *Harper's* article—who introduced Nichols to Hickok. From that day on, the reporter was a sponge, absorbing whatever Hickok recollected about his life on the frontier. In the absence of taped recordings and Nichols's notes, we can only conjecture, when reading the resulting article, where Hickok—or "William Hitchcock," as Nichols renamed him—ended and where the infatuated, easily impressed writer began.

An indication that Nichols did have an agenda of some kind was how he reported the way Hickok spoke. Though without a formal education, Hickok was an intelligent man who spoke like one. How-ever, Nichols offers, "I allers shot well; but I come ter be perfeck in the mountains by shootin at a dime for a mark, at bets of half a dollar a shot." Later in the article: "I am going out on the prarer a piece to see the sick wife of my mate. I should be glad to meet yer at the hotel this afternoon, Kernel." The use of such dialect by Nichols implies he was deliberately painting a more romantic or exotic portrait for his East Coast readers.

As copies of the *Harper's* article and word of it circulated and spread the rest of that winter, even the edge of the Great American Desert got wind of the tales told about the handsome, chivalrous, yet cold-eyed killer who roamed the prairie, a kind friend to children and a quick-drawing punisher of evildoers. The article proclaimed his code of behavior: "When the war closed I buried the hatchet, and I won't fight now unless I'm put upon."

Suddenly, Hickok had to contend with two strong and opposite realizations—he was a heroic figure, quite out of the ordinary compared to anyone he knew (except Kit Carson), and he was a marked man. The article had implied that Hickok had killed a couple of dozen men, if not more, and he was quick on the trigger, remorseless in a fight, he'd shoot first and ask questions later, and in this new kind of dueling, no one was faster to jerk out a six-shooter and fire with calm accuracy than Wild Bill. Inevitably, there would be those who would be willing to risk their lives to instantly gain such a reputation by killing this frontier demigod.

Thus, the *Harper's* article changed Hickok in dramatic ways. He made an effort to live up to the person portrayed in it, while allowing some of the stories to go undisputed. In fact, he began to repeat them in saloons and around campfires, living the life Nichols had partly been responsible for creating, becoming the famous Wild Bill the article celebrated, the kind of adventurer who could both endure and tame the American West. He also began to feel that bull's-eye on his back. As time went on, Hickok would make sure to keep his back to the wall, walk down the middle of a street instead of on the sidewalk, and develop a sixth sense for danger. For the rest of his life—less than ten years—he would experience the glory and tragedy of being Wild Bill Hickok.

Included in that was being the subject of more widespread press coverage. Newspapers in Missouri and Kansas were quick to pounce on the Nichols piece for the license it took. Tarred with the same brush, Hickok was held up for some ridicule. "The story of 'Wild Bill' is not easily credited hereabouts," intoned *The Leavenworth Daily Con-*

servative. "To those of us engaged in the campaign it sounds mythical. The scout services were so mixed that we were unable to give precedence to any."

The Springfield Patriot offered that the community "is excited" about the magazine article. "It has been so ever since the mail of the 25th brought *Harper's Monthly* to its numerous subscribers here. The excitement, curiously enough, manifests itself in very opposite effects upon our citizens. Some are excessively indignant, but the great majority are in convulsions of laughter." With a wry shrug, the writer concludes about the Nichols article, "If it prevents any consummate fools from coming to Southwest Missouri, that's no loss."

Naively, Nichols was unprepared for such criticism of the article and the ridicule for its author. Covering frontier figures quickly lost its allure. He wound up in Cincinnati and lived out the rest of his days—he died in September 1885—writing about music instead.

As if the sensation caused by the Nichols piece and reactions to it were not enough, in April 1867, Hickok met Henry M. Stanley. He was a reporter for *The New York Herald,* a daily newspaper, who had heard the siren call of the western frontier and found it to be a reservoir of good stories about colorful characters. His forays west of the Missouri River were not the first time he had traveled to seek excitement beyond the next horizon. Though only twenty-six, Sir Henry Morton Stanley—as he would later be known—had already enjoyed a life of adventure.

He had been born as John Rowlands in Wales. Orphaned very young, he lived in a variety of homes that included a workhouse for the poor. At eighteen, he managed to make his way to New Orleans and was taken under the wing of Henry Hope Stanley. The wealthy trader cared for the young man until he joined the Confederate army. The newly christened Stanley was captured during the Battle of

Shiloh in 1862, was released when he agreed to join the Union army, then was released to join the U.S. Navy, serving on the USS *Minnesota*. (He has the distinction of being the only man during the Civil War who served in those three military forces.) After the war, Stanley opted to organize an expedition into the Ottoman Empire, which turned out to be a bad decision when he was captured and tossed into prison. The Welshman had a silver tongue, though, and he charmed Ottoman officials enough that they released him. Early in 1867, he was in New York, working as a reporter for James Gordon Bennett's popular daily newspaper.

No doubt Stanley had read the *Harper's* article published three months earlier, and in May 1867, he sought out Hickok specifically when he arrived at Fort Riley. The restless frontiersman and the fearless reporter hit it off. The Fort Riley compound housed several sutlers' shops that provided liquid refreshment, and the two men frequented them together. They told tales of their most interesting experiences, and some of them were probably true. By this time, Hickok had digested Colonel Nichols's article whole. He may have repeated some of his adventures knowing they were embellished or entirely fabricated, or, especially as time went on, the line between fact and fiction narrowed until it became too thin for him to notice.

An example can be found in the article Stanley wrote that was published in *The New York Herald* soon after he left Kansas. Stanley reported that he had asked Hickok how many white men he had killed "to your certain knowledge." After seeming to give the question some thought, Hickok replied, "I suppose I have killed considerably over a hundred." Stanley marveled at the number and wondered if there had been good reasons for all those fatalities. Hickok assured him that he "never killed one man without good cause."

With Stanley's article appearing only a few months after the *Harper's* opus, and with no other frontiersman gaining a similar amount of attention, Wild Bill Hickok was further solidified in the minds of folks back east as the American westerner. He was busy blazing trails and defying savages so that Manifest Destiny could be fulfilled. If anyone got in his way and wasn't fast enough on the draw . . . well, that was good enough cause to meet a bullet.

After Stanley wrote up his article at *The Herald*'s office in New York, he was off on more adventures. He rode as a special correspondent with a British force sent to topple Tewodros II of Ethiopia, he was the first to tell the world of the fall of Magdala in 1868, he covered a civil war in Spain, and in his most famous outing, in November 1871 near Lake Tanganyika in Africa, he found a physician who had been reported missing and queried, "Dr. Livingstone, I presume?"

In today's celebrity-riddled culture, it may be difficult to comprehend the figure Wild Bill Hickok now cut in frontier society. Turning thirty, he was being talked and written about like adventurers Daniel Boone, Davy Crockett, and Kit Carson all rolled into one. When Hickok was staying in a town or just passing through, people elbowed each other and pointed and whispered, "There goes Wild Bill."

To his credit, the mounting fame did not turn him into an insufferable egotist. Several accounts written or relayed decades later insist that Hickok was a courteous and chivalrous man and that he did indeed have a particular fondness for children. He enjoyed talking to and sometimes playing with them. With other men, he never sought confrontations and had no need to prove his reputation. His outlook, expanding what had been quoted in the Nichols article, seemed to be one espoused by John Bernard Books in the novel by Glendon

Swarthout and subsequent movie *The Shootist:* "I won't be wronged. I won't be insulted. I won't be laid a-hand on. I don't do these things to other people, and I require the same from them."

This description illustrates a fundamental contradiction. Hickok knew that he had become a public figure thanks to the stories passed around the frontier coupled with the attention the *Harper's* article had generated from Kansas to New York and Boston. Being a public figure with a gunslinger reputation also meant being a marked man. It made self-preservation sense to blend into the background, to pass through the towns and along the trails as unobtrusively as possible. Yet that was not Hickok's way. He dressed and carried himself declaring to be Wild Bill. He did not invite trouble, yet he had the confidence to inflict damage on those who chose to cause trouble. No wonder that to this day, Hickok has been a hard man to understand.

Wild Bill Hickok's reputation may have had a brief shelf life if he had spent his days and nights loafing in towns gambling and telling tall tales. However, much of his time was spent on one trail or another in Nebraska and Kansas, especially the latter. For Hickok, there was much of Kansas still to be explored, and for the next couple of years, he would often do that as a scout and guide for the U.S. Army. The demand for guides and scouts was rising sharply, and being both reliable and a public figure with a dramatic reputation helped him to gain top dollar.

The postwar bloom of settlers and gold-seekers heading west was in full flower. Encounters with "hostiles," or "savages" as they were often labeled in the eastern press, were more frequent, and a downsized army was being called upon to do more to protect the white migrants. Ostensibly, officers and U.S. government emissaries, and their guides, some of whom also acted as interpreters, were sent out to persuade tribes to sign treaties. Few doubted that vast swaths of the former Great American Desert were going to be taken from the Indians anyway, but for those in the supposedly more civilized society back east, doing it legally, even with savages, was more justifiable under God.

Treaties were not all that hard to arrange. Many of the Indian leaders were not interested in making war and endangering their women and children. They might not understand white men, but they readily observed that there was an increasing number of them, carrying weapons far more sophisticated than lances, bows and arrows, and single-load carbines. Mostly, tribes wanted to be left alone to continue their traditions of hunting and raiding each other's camps to win horses and honor. Incredibly, though, after four years of death in the bloody Civil War, there appeared to be more white men than ever invading Indian lands.

One strategy, then, for Indian leaders was to let the white men pass on through. If they had somewhere to go farther to the west, let them go there as quickly as possible. But that wasn't working out well, either. The bulky wagons creaked and crawled along the rough, dusty trails, not making brisk progress across the hundreds of miles of flat prairie. Along the way, furniture, clothing, and other debris were tossed to the sides of the trails, and worse, to feed the white people, buffalo were being hunted with abandon. Indians found it fantastic and appalling that buffalo would be killed by the white man's long-range rifles to provide only one meal, and the next day when the wagon train moved on, carcasses still containing meat and tongues and hides were left behind to rot in the sun. If the stream of travelers trekking west continued, there would be no buffalo left in a corrupted landscape.

Worst of all, too many of the white men were choosing to stop and stay. They were setting up businesses in expanding towns and carving farms out of the rich prairie soil. To provide protection, the Bluebellies were building forts and other outposts. This was intolerable. But what to do about it? Resistance came at a high cost because of the firepower of the white soldiers. Perhaps treaties could be an alternative. Many Indians did not understand the concept of land-ownership, so it did not occur to them that they were giving anything away. If the government wanted to give them food and clothing and other gifts so it could do what it was going to do anyway, fine. Still, there were some leaders of the tribes who did fight and try to kill the encroaching white men—they saw no other way to protect their hunting grounds, families, and honor.

The excursions Hickok had guided, first with General Sherman and then with General Pope, into Nebraska in the spring of 1866 were just the beginning. It was a pretty good life for a plainsman. He was paid well, from seventy-five to one hundred dollars a month, and in between the journeys, he could spend time at the gaming tables in Kansas City, dressed in much finer clothes than on the trail. He enjoyed the ambience of saloons, the risks and rewards of gambling, the attention of the women (it did not matter that many were prostitutes), the alcohol, and dressing well. With a good-natured grin, Hickok tolerated the ribbing he received for being possibly the only man in Kansas City who bathed every day. When it was time for the next mission to kick off, it was back into buckskins and moccasins and being alert for hostiles.

One of his lesser-known exploits at this time was on a baseball diamond. In Kansas City was a ballfield at the corner of Fourteenth and Oak Streets. This was the home of the Kansas City Antelopes, the first baseball team in the city. It had been organized by the attorney D. S. Twitchell in July 1866, three years before the Cincinnati Red Stockings, recognized as the first professional team in the United

States. The Antelopes' park had no grandstand or scoreboard, and patrons had to sit on benches in the hot sun. Still, every Saturday afternoon, people filed in to watch this new sport. One of the spectators, when he was in town, was Hickok. He played pickup games with local youngsters before games, and one Saturday, he was asked to umpire an Antelopes game.

The reason Wild Bill, of all people, was asked was because the weekly contests had a habit of descending into brawls, especially if the umpire ruled on a play against the Antelopes. There was no gunplay—guns weren't allowed within the Kansas City limits—but fists, boots, bottles, and even the occasional knife were employed to dispute the call with fans of the visiting team and the cowering umpire. On this particular Saturday, the Antelopes were hosting the Atchison Pomeroys. The visitors had beaten the Antelopes on their home turf, and an attempt at a rematch in Kansas City had resulted in a riot, and the game was canceled. THE TOWN IS DISGRACED! blared a headline in *The Kansas City Star*.

A rematch of the rematch was arranged. Hickok agreed to be the umpire, and when the first pitch was thrown, he was behind the plate with what passed for umpire's gear then. Hickok also wore, thanks to a dispensation from the city fathers, his Colt six-shooters.

The game was played to its completion, and the pleased crowd cheered the 48–28 victory by the Antelopes. (Pitches were tossed underhand, making the ball easier to hit.) They cheered the umpire, too, who bowed to acknowledge their approval, then made his way to Market Square to take up that night's gambling entertainment.

Treaties or not, campaigns against the Indians were taking place more often with troops in the east freed up to be posted to hastily built frontier forts. Hickok routinely had to exchange his fancy frocks and other city duds for rough-and-ready outfits and to hit the trail once again as a scout. In this role, he met senior officers as well as up-and-coming ones, younger men looking to earn a reputation as an Indian fighter and ascend the ranks to the brevet levels they had enjoyed during the Civil War.

One of the officers Hickok encountered on expeditions against the Indians in the summer of 1867 was Arthur MacArthur, Jr. Born in Massachusetts to a man who would later serve as the governor of Wisconsin for just four days, the young MacArthur was only seventeen in August 1862 when he was commissioned a lieutenant in a Wisconsin infantry regiment. He somehow managed to survive the battles at Chickamauga, Stones River, Chattanooga, Missionary Ridge (where he ignored intense fire to plant the regimental flag atop the ridge), Franklin, and all the fights along Sherman's March to the Sea. When MacArthur stood down in June 1865, he was a lieutenant colonel.

But in the postwar army of the American West, he was back to being a captain. Over the years, he rose through the ranks again in campaigns against several Indian leaders (including Geronimo) and in the Spanish-American War. Lieutenant General MacArthur retired in 1909 as the highest-ranking officer in the army. He died at sixty-seven, having lived long enough to see his son, Douglas MacArthur, well on his way to a distinguished military career.

The articles by George Ward Nichols and Henry Stanley were still being circulated, or at least discussed, in frontier settlements, when Hickok was hired to be a scout in General Winfield Scott Hancock's campaign against Indians. Hancock had been a Union hero in the war and was the latest to think that what worked on a battlefield in Virginia or Pennsylvania would translate to success against the western tribes.

Hancock had a forty-year career in the U.S. Army, which included the Mexican-American War and distinguishing himself in many

Civil War battles, especially at Gettysburg, and had risen to commanding a corps in the Army of the Potomac. An important assignment for him immediately after the war was to hang those convicted of being part of the conspiracy to assassinate President Lincoln. He then served during Reconstruction in the South, but not very long because General Grant sent him west.

Officially, Hancock's mission, which got under way in the spring of 1867, was to negotiate treaties with elements of the Cheyenne and Sioux tribes. However, few saw it that way. S. J. Crawford, the governor of Kansas, recorded in his diary that April that "the plains were swarming with bloodthirsty Indians."

Hancock took the field with six companies of infantry and artillery, hardly appearing to be an emissary of peace. He was joined by Colonel George Custer, who led four companies of the Seventh Cavalry and an infantry company. Two more cavalry companies joined them at Fort Harker. Hickok and his fellow scouts—who, viewing treaties as worthless, did not have any faith in the mission being a success—guided Hancock's large force deeper into territory where the Indians were accustomed to roaming free and hunting.

The mission quickly devolved into a frustrating hunting expedition. Cheyenne bands conducted raids against Smoky Hill River settlements and stagecoach stations, making off with horses. Hancock had as much success at finding the fast-riding bands as he would have at grabbing running rabbits by the neck. Indians, he learned, did not stand and fight to the last man like Confederate troops did. Frustrated, he had his men set fire to Indian villages found along the Pawnee River. For Hickok, much of this was time wasted. He became frustrated, too, being mostly employed to carry dispatches, sometimes outriding Indians when they spotted him between Hancock's headquarters and one of his commanders in the field.

Hickok was relieved when Hancock essentially declared victory and returned to Fort Riley. The general was soon reassigned. Hickok remained in the field, attached to Custer's forces. The "boy general," as he had been nicknamed during the Civil War, was more suited to life in the field and not as easily frustrated by Indians, whom he found fascinating, though he had little respect for their culture.

While Custer's description of Hickok was not filled with as much blatant blushing as his wife's had been, he was also much impressed by the laconic plainsman. It's also interesting that Custer, already a legend in his own mind, would lavish such praise on another man, especially a rival for public attention. Noting that Hickok "always carried two handsome ivory-handled revolvers of large size," Custer recalled in his 1874 memoir, *My Life on the Plains.* "Whether on foot or on horseback he was one of the most perfect types of physical manhood I ever saw. Of his courage there could be no question. His skill in the use of the rifle and the pistol was unerring."

Custer continued, without irony, given his own behavior: "His deportment was entirely free from all bluster and bravado. He never spoke of himself unless requested to do so. His conversation never bordered on the vulgar or blasphemous. His influence among the frontiersmen was unchallenged." Custer reported that if there were quarrels among the scouts, all Hickok had to do was utter, "This has gone far enough," to calm things down. But if that wasn't enough, Hickok invited those in dispute to "settle with me," and that surely ended any conflict.

Custer and his cavalry and his scouts—with Hickok "the most prominent man among them," he would later state—embarked on a thousand-mile expedition that lasted well into the summer. They set out from Fort Hays and trekked through Kansas and Nebraska and back again to Fort Hays. Uppermost in Custer's mind was to capture

Pawnee Killer, the leader of the most active and violent band on the Plains, one that combined Sioux warriors with Cheyenne Dog Soldiers. This was not accomplished. Several times, Pawnee Killer surprised detachments and lone scouts, including Hickok, who was one of the few to escape with his life. By the end of July, the expedition was over.

Pawnee Killer, who had acquired his name for obvious reasons, would remain elusive. Ultimately, he died peacefully in his home on the Pine Ridge Reservation in South Dakota in 1895, at age sixty-nine.

Chapter Eight

LIFE OF A FRONTIER MARSHAL

When Charles C. Whiting was appointed U.S. marshal for the District of Kansas, he needed deputies. With Wild Bill Hickok now free from his scouting chores, Whiting hired him. He was a good man for the job, being by now very familiar with much of Kansas and being dogged in tracking down outlaws. His assignments from Whiting in 1867 took him as far as western Kansas and Nebraska to find army deserters. With many Bluebellies underfed, underpaid, and stuck at frontier outposts against their will, slipping away had become a frequent occurrence.

The occupation of federal marshal had been created in 1789 with the passage of the Judiciary Act, signed into law by President George Washington. It provided that the president appointed U.S. marshals and the Senate confirmed them. Officially, only crimes committed against the federal government or on government property fell under their jurisdiction, but on the frontier, where the next county sheriff or town marshal could be a hundred miles away, a U.S. marshal and the deputies he appointed often filled in the gaps. They had the weight and authority of the U.S. government behind them, so if a man committing a crime or on the run from one had to be arrested or shot, such actions were rarely challenged in court.

Deputy U.S. Marshal Hickok was kept busy trailing and apprehending horse thieves, catching counterfeiters, and even stopping illegal liquor sales and searching remote areas for woodcutters felling trees on federal property. Outlaws were not the most literate people on the frontier, but those who had at least heard of the daring and ruthless Wild Bill Hickok depicted in the two articles were intimidated enough by reputation alone not to resist when confronted by this lone-riding deputy U.S. marshal.

One adventure had Hickok riding to the Solomon River valley with a squad of cavalry out of Fort Riley—one of whom was young Sergeant Billy Cody—on the trail of an industrious band that had stolen as many as two hundred horses and mules from U.S. government facilities. Hickok found the animals but not the thieves, who had dispersed into the hills at the first sign of the armed soldiers. Realizing this, not long after getting the four-legged government property on the move east, Hickok doubled back to hunt alone. A few days after the horses and mules and their uniformed escort had arrived at Fort Riley, Hickok was back. *The Topeka Leader* reported that he had brought with him eleven prisoners "and lodged them in our calaboose."

Hickok rested up for part of 1867 in Hays City . . . after he had dallied in Ellsworth. Both towns were beginning to experience some success as cow towns. When Ellsworth was incorporated that year, the population had soared to two thousand people. This meant it was a place where a man like Hickok could have a choice of saloons and gaming tables to frequent.

It was also where he would find a new romance. Not too much is known about a woman who was dubbed "Indian Annie." According to Joseph G. Rosa's exploration, she lived in a small shack behind the Grand Central Hotel. She did various jobs for the hotel, including its laundry. She and Hickok kept company, and she was at least once identified in the Ellsworth newspaper as "Mrs. Wild Bill Hickok." The "marriage" was a short one, however, as the plainsman moved on to Hays City. Indian Annie did become a married woman, but her husband was a man named Ben Wilson, with whom she had a daughter, Birdie. Annie returned to doing menial labor and took up fortune-telling. She probably did not foresee her unhappy ending, which was dying in a poorhouse in 1883.

Earlier in 1867, Fort Hays had been established, and the tracks of the Kansas Pacific Railway were being stretched west toward it. A doctor named William Webb had been given the authority by the railroad company to establish town sites, and he went to work laying out Hays City after creating the Big Creek Land Company. Once the railroad arrived, the town took off, with hundreds of people settling there to establish businesses like the Gibbs House hotel and the Moses & Bloomfield general store. *The Railway Advance* newspaper began publishing. By the end of the year, the population of Hays City approached a thousand people.

However, it was an exception to quickly established towns along the railroad companies' paths in that Hays City did not become a cow town. Some trail drives did end there, and the cows were packed into railcars, but for the most part, the cattle trade bypassed Hays City in favor of other hubs like Abilene and, later, Dodge City. This did not save the town from its share of mayhem and unsavory characters, though, because there was still an abundance of saloons and whiskey and the women sometimes referred to as "soiled doves." At the very first official meeting of the board of commissioners of Ellis County, thirty-seven licenses to sell liquor were granted. Another important source of revenue was the wagon trains rumbling along the Smoky Hill Trail, which could be outfitted and resupplied in Hays City.

A particularly notorious example of the type of disreputable people who gave citizens second thoughts about living in Hays City during its early days was Jim Curry. Hailing originally from Ireland, he may have served in the Union army, or the Confederate army, or possibly both, before working his way west. He had little regard for human life and found a haven in Hays City. Curry had a particular hatred for black men and murdered them at will, tossing their bodies into a dry well. Even if some residents objected to the bigotry and killings, there was no law enforcement in the town. After murdering a man named Brady by slitting his throat, Curry threw the bloody body into a railroad boxcar, and nothing was done about it. Believing a nineteen-year-old named Estes had flirted with a girl he was interested in, Curry went up to the teenager on the street and shot him through the heart. Again, no recourse.

It was into this rough environment that Hickok rode during Hays City's first year. He did not stay long because of fresh scouting and guiding assignments as well as ones from Marshal Whiting. However, Hickok would later become a lawman in Hays City, his first significant frontier posting wearing a badge, charged with halting or at least slowing down the depravity. And he would have a memorable confrontation with Jim Curry.

For now, though, his focus was on being a federal marshal on a frontier where there was no lack of deserters and horse thieves. Hickok was back on the trail before winter could fully set in. Given the potential for violence in that occupation at that time, it would have been an achievement if Hickok made it to the end of 1867 without getting shot. But he had the misfortune on the afternoon of December 22 to walk into a rough-and-tumble crossroads saloon in Jefferson County, Nebraska. A dozen or so cattle herders had taken shelter from the early winter cold and were crouched against the sod walls. A tired and thirsty Hickok ordered a whiskey, which was drawn straight from a keg.

By this time in his life, though only thirty years old, Wild Bill had walked into hundreds of saloons, including remote ones like this, and encountered strangers without incident. On this day, probably working his way east back to Fort Riley, he expected to sip a whiskey, maybe two, then clap his sombrero back on and return to the cold and muddy road. It is not known if the other men knew he was a deputy U.S. marshal when they began to make remarks about the mud-covered stranger.

Hickok continued to ignore them as the remarks became more aggressive and personal. He knew the smart move was to knock back the rest of his drink and leave such an inhospitable shack. But one man, on purpose, bumped into Hickok. The whiskey he was about to finish off instead splashed on his face. Drops of it flew from his mustache as he whipped around and backhanded the man in his face, sending him sprawling across the dirt-strewn floor.

In an almost comical understatement, considering the hostility in the saloon and being so outnumbered, Hickok advised, "Now cut it out before this gets serious."

It got serious real fast. Several of the patrons went for their guns. Hickok shot one man but a moment later was shot in his right shoulder. If the others thought that would disable him, they did not know they were in a gunfight with Wild Bill Hickok, who now fired the Colt in his left hand. Two more men were hit. The man on the floor, now with a gun, was getting up, and Hickok shot off part of his jaw. Of the four men Hickok shot, he would be the only one to survive. By this time, as Hickok surveyed the dark interior of the saloon, the other men there had either not drawn their guns or had dropped them in a desperate plea for their lives.

Hickok backed out, got on his horse, and resumed his journey. He would stay in a Kansas City hotel until his shoulder had recuperated, allowing him to again draw and shoot with both hands. Hickok knew by now that not being a fully functional shootist was the kind of weakness that could get him killed.

Chapter Nine

BUFFALO BILL AND WILD BILL

Back in the saddle in the early spring of 1868, while passing through Junction City, Kansas, Hickok was reunited once more with the young scout now called Bill Cody. Though still only in his early twenties, Cody had just experienced two life-changing events—acquiring the name "Buffalo Bill," and getting married. His new wife, Louisa, in an effort to domesticate him, had cajoled Cody into becoming the proprietor of a hotel. In Junction City, Hickok learned that effort had not worked out too well.

Cody had been only eighteen when he first met Louisa Frederici. During the winter of 1864–65, he was with a Union army detachment stationed in St. Louis. There he encountered and became smitten with the beautiful young woman. After the war was over and he was discharged, Cody returned to St. Louis, and he later recalled, "I was not slow in declaring my sentiments to her." They became engaged, and satisfied enough with that, Cody was off to Nebraska to drive stagecoaches between Fort Kearny and Plum Creek. But Louisa proved too distracting, and in March 1866, Cody was back in St. Louis, where the wedding ceremony was held. The young couple then boarded a Missouri River steamboat for Kansas and Leavenworth. There, Cody's sister Eliza and her husband held a proper wedding reception, and soon after, he became the proprietor of a hotel he named the Golden Rule House.

The reason why Hickok found Cody in Junction City was the latter was by then fleeing the hotel business. Not surprisingly for a man who had packed a lot of adventure into a thus-far short life, the Golden Rule House "proved too tame employment" and Cody "sighed for the freedom of the plains." He had left Louisa behind—and come December, also a daughter, Arta—to find other work and was more than willing to ride again with Wild Bill. The two men traveled to Fort Ellsworth, where Hickok had been hired on as a scout. Cody came aboard in the same capacity, and together and separately, the two friends guided army units and sometimes wagon trains that had been provided with army protection.

Cody had acquired his nickname the year before. A pursuit of several business ventures had panned out as poorly as the hotel venture, so he took to buffalo hunting for the Kansas Pacific Railway. The company had twelve hundred employees working on laying track and related chores, and they had to be fed. There were plenty of buffalo around—estimates at the time were that millions of the beasts roamed the Kansas plains—but a hunter had to be a good shot to kill efficiently and be ready to encounter Indians angered by trespassers on their traditional hunting grounds. Cody had plenty of experience evading and outwitting hostiles, but it was his prowess with a rifle in killing the animals plus the sheer number of kills that had witnesses referring to Cody as "Buffalo Bill." The name stuck, and for the rest of his life, he would use it to promote whatever enterprise he was involved in, and especially himself.

If Cody is to be believed: "During my engagement as hunter for the company—a period of less than eighteen months—I killed 4,280 buffalo; and I had many exciting adventures with the Indians, as well as hair-breadth escapes."

In Junction City, Cody craved more of that rambunctious life. Hickok was happy to oblige. He had been given a new assignment by Marshal Whiting, this one to round up a gang of army deserters and thieves. Perhaps Buffalo Bill would like to join him?

He did, and the two friends set off. They were next seen in Topeka, with a familiar result to their lawman labors. As the March 28, 1868, issue of *The Topeka Leader* reported, "W.F. Cody, government detective, and Wm. Haycock, Deputy U.S. Marshal, brought eleven prisoners and lodged them in our calaboose on Monday last—a band of robbers having their headquarters on the Solomon, charged with stealing government property and desertion."*

That summer, with Cody having presumably returned to his family, Hickok signed on to scout for the Tenth Cavalry Regiment. Perhaps a little speculation is permitted here. Hickok may have been one of the few scouts who would take on such a task . . . or at least willingly. The regiment was made up of black troopers, who became known as "Buffalo Soldiers." Given Hickok's family history, being a guide for them did not pose a problem.

The Tenth U.S. Cavalry had been formed at Fort Leavenworth in 1866, composed of black enlisted men and white officers (there was no such thing as a black officer). By the end of July 1867, eight companies of enlisted men had been recruited from the Departments of

---

*If this sounds familiar, it is because there are actually several reports from different times of Hickok and Cody bringing prisoners to jail. However, no more than two of the tales are likely accurate.

the Missouri, Arkansas, and the Platte. They were under the overall command of Colonel Benjamin Grierson. The Pittsburgh native had been a music teacher before the Civil War, then had distinguished himself in battle, especially in what became known as Grierson's Raid, from LaGrange, Tennessee, to Baton Rouge, a pivotal part of General Grant's Vicksburg campaign in 1863. The following year, Grierson's cavalry force defeated that of General Nathan Bedford Forrest at the Battle of Tupelo. After the war, becoming head of the Tenth Cavalry could not have been the most coveted command, but Grierson championed the abilities of black soldiers—often putting him at odds with superiors—and he retained this position as commander of the Tenth for twenty-four years.

Because of the abusive behavior of the commander of Fort Leavenworth, Colonel Grierson wangled a transfer of his regiment to Fort Riley in August 1867. Soon after, the Tenth saw its first significant action at the Battle of the Saline River, about twenty-five miles northwest of Fort Hays. After a railroad work party was wiped out, patrols from the Thirty-Eighth Infantry Regiment accompanied by a Tenth Cavalry unit were sent out to locate the Cheyenne war party. Captain George Armes and his Company F of the Tenth Cavalry were following an active trail along the Saline River when suddenly they found themselves surrounded by about four hundred Cheyenne warriors.

Briskly, Armes formed a defensive "hollow square" with the cavalry mounts in the middle. Seeking better defensive ground, Armes walked his command while maintaining the defensive square. After eight hours of combat, two thousand rounds of defensive fire, and fifteen miles of movement by Company F, the frustrated Cheyenne finally gave up and rode away. The black soldiers, without reinforcements, concluded 113 miles of movement during the thirty-hour patrol, riding the final 10 miles back to Fort Hays, with only one trooper killed in action. Among the surviving wounded was Captain Armes, who had been struck in the hip by a bullet.

Hickok spent much of the summer and fall of 1868 as a scout and dispatch rider for the Tenth Regiment.* In between such chores, he continued to tackle missions as a deputy U.S. marshal. One assignment brought him into contact with a twelve-year-old who would go on to have a long career as a western lawman.

On the trail of a horse thief that summer, Hickok rode into Atchison, Kansas. He encountered a group of boys and girls, one of whom was William Tilghman, who was immediately impressed by the mounted stranger. Hickok was atop "a sturdy government mule" and "rode with the easy grace of a Plainsman," Tilghman wrote years later. "Tall, he was over six feet, splendidly built, and his face as handsome as his form, with strong clear-cut features and keen dark blue eyes, long drooping mustache and hair curling upon his shoulders." Speaking in "a slow assured manner," Hickok queried the youngsters about the suspect. Tilghman would contend that this one meeting with Wild Bill inclined him toward a career in law enforcement, which would include serving with Wyatt Earp and Bat Masterson and other lawmen in Dodge City and later in Oklahoma. Tilghman was still wearing a badge at seventy years of age in 1924, when he was gunned down.

With General Sherman's okay, General Ulysses S. Grant (soon to become President Grant) had appointed General Philip Sheridan to head the Department of the Missouri. The saying "The only good Indian is a dead Indian" was mistakenly attributed to him, but there

---

*The Tenth Cavalry Regiment would continue as an African American unit until deactivated during World War II in 1944.

was no mistaking Sheridan's aggressive attitude toward making the frontier safe from hostiles.

True, Sheridan was, like Hancock, another in a series of Civil War heroes sent west to succeed where previous commanders had failed. But at least Sheridan had served on the frontier as a young officer and had some experience with Plains Indians, once describing them as "the best light cavalry in the world." And Sheridan was accustomed to winning, having campaigned successfully against J. E. B. Stuart and Robert E. Lee, and Sheridan's successful Shenandoah Valley campaign in 1864 had greatly weakened the rebel resistance.

Sheridan was also smart enough to recognize that the western tribes were not dumb savages waiting to be wiped out or herded onto reservations. Unlike previous commanders, he was not about to underestimate his adversary. He had about fourteen hundred men under his command, and he expected the number of warriors the tribes could put on the warpath was three times that. Plus, the natives knew the landscape better than anyone. For some tribes, this area had been their home for generations. To have any chance, Sheridan had to have the best scouts federal funds could buy.

That is where Wild Bill Hickok and Buffalo Bill Cody, as well as several other plainsmen, came in. Being outnumbered, Sheridan's various detachments could not afford to be surprised. Scouts would have to take the risks necessary to track the movements of Cheyenne, Sioux, Comanche, and whatever other tribes were resisting the soaring number of westbound travelers and relentless fort-building.

In July 1868, the Cheyenne and Comanche began attacking settlements in Kansas. Farmers, ranchers, and emigrants on the trails were killed, many of them scalped and mutilated in unspeakable ways. Sheridan ordered troops into the field to track down the war parties, especially Cheyenne raiders led by Roman Nose. Still bitter over the

Sand Creek Massacre in Colorado four years earlier, the Cheyenne were spoiling for a fight.

The second week of September found Hickok with the Tenth Cavalry at Fort Lyon in Colorado for what he thought would be a break from outriding Indians while carrying dispatches to and from General Sheridan. But reports were coming in about Cheyenne war parties nearby, and Hickok was sent out to see if this was true, and if so, where they were before the hostiles simply showed up outside the fort.

That Sunday afternoon, he arrived at Kiowa Creek and found on one bank a burned-out wagon and several bodies. He kept riding to find a town and round up a burial party. That turned out to be Gomerville, fifty miles southeast of Denver. There, Hickok learned that the burned wagon had been part of a wagon train that had been attacked by Cheyenne, and some residents of Gomerville were preparing to go after the warriors before they could do more harm. Given his experience, they asked Hickok to lead the way.

He and the thirty-four men of the improvised militia unit searched for days between the Republican River and Kiowa Creek without turning up a single Cheyenne. But one afternoon when they were returning to Gomerville, a large war party found them. Hickok's group was dangerously exposed. Atop a sunbaked mesa, they dug in as best they could, using tin plates and spurs. They had barely begun making headway when the Indians attacked. Hickok and the other better shooters picked off as many as they could while the rest kept digging. Finally, a sufficient series of trenches and holes was dug to offer some protection. In the interim, though, many of the militia's exposed horses had been killed. The Cheyenne wanted to make sure no one escaped.

As it turned out, the warriors were the ones who had to do the escaping. They had not cornered a bunch of shopkeepers or an inexperienced army patrol but hardy frontiersmen who could shoot fast and well. Warriors were repulsed by a barrage of bullets, and even after they retreated, they were shot off their horses while figuring out what to do next. Frustrated, they continued to move away to what they hoped was a far enough range. If they planned next to wait until the white men were weak from hunger and thirst, they could not have known how effective this strategy would be. After eight days on the trail, Hickok and the Gomerville residents were already worn out and were low on food and water.

That night, Hickok rode down the slope of the mesa and aimed his horse in the direction of Gomerville. Startled Indians fired rifles, but quickly Wild Bill was beyond them and galloping too fast for anyone to chase. His experience with the rough country coupled with the desperate situation of the men left behind spurred him on to make the night ride without a mishap. When Hickok arrived, he roused the residents of the town. Twelve armed men rode with him when he left.

Shortly before dawn, the rescue party arrived. They crept quietly up behind the Indians, then let out loud yells and began shooting. The men under siege began shooting, too. The frightened Indians, believing that they had suddenly been surrounded by army cavalry, grabbed their mounts and took off. After one more trip to Gomerville with the men making a triumphant return, Hickok continued on his way to Fort Lyon.

This siege and its outcome were harbingers of a similar but bigger one that happened almost simultaneously. By 1868, Roman Nose was a veteran fighter. "Perhaps no other chief attacked more emigrants going west on the Oregon Trail between 1860 and 1868," writes the American Indian historian Charles A. Eastman. He was a Cheyenne whose command of warriors included Oglala Sioux, who had fought in Red Cloud's War the previous two years, as well as Cheyenne Dog Soldiers.

In this instance, Roman Nose allowed Sheridan's troops to chase him until he reached the Arickaree Fork of the Republican River in Colorado. There, in mid-September, the Sioux and Cheyenne turned to fight, and abruptly, the pursued had the pursuers at a disadvantage. Roman Nose commanded several hundred warriors as opposed to only fifty or so led by Major George Forsyth. However, what was unique about this "army" force was that it was made up of experienced scouts, not regular troopers. Sheridan had ordered Forsyth to lead a smaller, more mobile, more experienced, and presumably tougher contingent than typical troopers. The thought was these white men could beat the Indians at their own game.

This was innovative thinking by the top general on the Plains. However, Roman Nose was not inclined to be outwitted or outfought. At dawn on September 17, he attacked Forsyth's camp. Almost immediately, the scouts were surrounded. But they did not panic, even after recognizing that no escape route was open. Having managed to turn back warriors trying to stampede their horses, the scouts took to their mounts and hurried to a sandbar in the middle of the Arickaree (later to be known as Beecher Island). This provided some cover as the Indians attacked. There were at least two hundred of them, with later (and probably less accurate) estimates being as high as six hundred warriors.

The initial assaults by the yelling and whooping combination of Sioux and Cheyenne riders were intended simply to overwhelm the outnumbered scouts. But their ranks were shredded by the sharp-shooters and their Spencer rifles. The next tactic was for small groups of Indians to make sudden dashes at the sandbar to kill just one or two scouts at a time and win the battle by attrition. The scouts shot the horses first, then their riders after they got up and were figuring out which way to go. Between these attacks, the scouts dragged the dead horses back to the sandbar to use as breastworks, and thus they were better protected as the day went on. This allowed them to scan the shore and aim at individual Indians before they could form an attack. The accuracy was disconcerting to the Indians, even more so when a bullet found Roman Nose, who was killed.

The scouts survived the night. Before dawn, two of them, Jack Stilwell and Pierre Trudeau, slipped away from the river. Their destination was Fort Wallace, seventy miles away. They crawled through the tall September grass the first three of those miles, then began walking. They traveled only at night, hiding from Indians during the day. After four days, the exhausted duo found Fort Wallace. Meanwhile, the scouts at the Arickaree Fork continued to fend off attacks, with both sides paying the price. Seven scouts were killed and at least fifteen wounded, including Major Forsyth, who was shot twice and was not expected to live. Eventually, none of those under siege expected to live because in addition to the relentless Indian attacks, the men had nothing to sustain them but muddy river water and rotting horseflesh. And they assumed Stilwell and Trudeau had by now been killed, their horribly mutilated bodies left in the tall grass.

At dawn on September 25, Troops H and I of Hickok's unit, the Tenth Cavalry, swooped down on the entrenched Indians and routed them. The scouts, very much weakened by the ordeal, may at first have thought that Lieutenant Colonel Louis Carpenter and his Buffalo Soldiers were a mirage. The rescuers found at least fifty dead horses and Forsyth still alive and in command. Two days later, after the more severely wounded were able to travel, the combined units set off for Fort Wallace. Because of his ability to find the remote location of the besieged scouts, his actions during the battle that defeated the Indians encircling the sandbar, and his care of the wounded, Carpenter was awarded the Medal of Honor.

Since the French and Indian War over a century earlier, winter in the United States had been a time for armies to dig in and plan their spring campaigns. That had remained true on the Plains, with the tribes repairing to remote camps that afforded some protection from the elements and army units holing up in forts. General Sheridan thought that such idleness was a waste of time. With a good supply of experienced plainsmen like Hickok and Cody, the winter encampments of the Indians could be located, and the cavalry could attack when the inhabitants least expected it and were most vulnerable. As fall waned, Sheridan ordered three columns, led by Colonels George Armstrong Custer and A. W. Evans and General Eugene Carr, out into the field. They were to converge at the headwaters of the Red River, where it was believed there was a large concentration of Cheyenne.

Though Hickok was reunited with Custer from time to time during the campaign, especially as he outrode war parties carrying dispatches between the army column commanders and Sheridan, he was not present for the most notorious event of the fall actions against the Indians. What happened at the Washita River, where Custer's troopers destroyed an Indian village, was a terrible reminder of the despicable actions of Colonel John Chivington's troops almost four years to the day earlier at Sand Creek.

As Hickok and most scouts and military men on the Plains knew, Custer had gotten into hot water with his superiors the year before, and it was something of a miracle that he and the Seventh Cavalry were part of Sheridan's early-winter campaign at all. In a bizarre series of events, during a campaign in 1867, Custer had overmarched his men and summarily hanged several of them for desertion; then he himself deserted, detouring to meet his wife, Libbie, at Fort Harker. He had been tried in a military court and found guilty. The punishment was a one-year suspension from command. However, Sheridan, needing leaders of courage and initiative, petitioned Grant to allow Custer to return to the field two months early. Always inclined to fight anyway, the former boy general (still only twenty-eight) recognized that a victory in battle would best restore his reputation. Unfortunately for a Cheyenne leader named Black Kettle and his band, they were on the road leading to Custer's redemption.

On November 26, scouts located a Cheyenne village near the Washita River, near what is today Cheyenne, Oklahoma. The Indians had no cause to be alarmed when they first saw white men. They had recently visited Fort Cobb to receive food, had been guaranteed safety by the commander there, and were on Cheyenne reservation land. Custer knew none of this—apparently, not even the white flag that flew atop one of the lodges made him pause. He saw only a necessary and convenient target.

At dawn the next day, with the regimental band playing "Garry Owen," four columns of soldiers streamed into the village, firing rifles and pistols. A few startled warriors managed to fight back, but there were not nearly enough of them; the majority of the village population was women and children. By the end of the action, the destroyed village was littered with 103 bodies, one of them being Black Kettle's. As reports made their way to nearby military outposts and then to Washington, D.C., and other points east, the Battle of Washita River was hailed as a stirring victory.

Instead of being with Custer, Hickok's part of Sheridan's campaign as fall gave way to winter was being the guide for a contingent of three hundred men under General William Penrose who were the advance guard for the main column commanded by General Carr. Their route was through the Raton Pass. This trek turned into an ordeal that was almost catastrophic.

Snow had fallen regularly at the higher elevations since early November, and that made for slow going to the supply wagons, which kept threatening to slide down the slopes. Sudden squalls blinded the men and their horses, and Hickok struggled to keep everyone on a narrow path worn over the decades by hunters. Frostbite attacked hands and faces. Campfires flickered before being doused by snow or extinguished by gusting winds. Supplies meant to last the entire journey were dwindling. The contingent finally made its way down to the Cimarron River, then turned south toward the Canadian River. By then, Penrose's men were frozen and exhausted and starving. The surrounding countryside was barren and bleak and covered with snow and ice.

The only reason why Hickok might have been a little less concerned than the army troopers was he knew who was guiding the Carr column. If anyone could get those men and their supply wagons through, it was Buffalo Bill Cody. When the advance guard reached Polladora Creek, the soldiers set up camp. It made sense to give Carr an opportunity to find them—plus, with their food almost gone and most of their mules now dead, they could not go much farther.

Day after freezing day, the plight of Hickok and the soldiers grew more desperate. A rescue party had been dispatched, but it was slow going. "We followed the trail very easily for the first three days, and then we were caught in Freeze-Out canyon by a fearful snow storm, which compelled us to go into camp for a day," Cody recalled. "The ground now being covered with snow, we found that it would be almost impossible to follow the trail" left by the advance guard. Carr picked Cody to lead a small contingent of men to try to follow the trail, and the entire column would do its best to keep up.

After a few more days, true starvation loomed. Hickok scanned the white, bleak landscape for any sign of life. Finally, he spotted one . . . and as it grew closer, he realized it was Buffalo Bill at the head of a squadron of troopers leading fifty mules loaded with supplies. The young man had sure repaid Wild Bill for confronting that bully years before. "The camp presented a pitiful sight, indeed," Cody observed. "About the first man I saw after reaching the camp was my old, true and tried friend Wild Bill. That night we had a jolly reunion around the camp-fires."

Their happy reunion was about to become even happier. Once the men were sufficiently recovered and the rest of Carr's force had arrived, they set out, guided by Hickok and Cody, for Fort Evans, a new supply depot that had been established by an army force originating in New Mexico. After arriving there and setting up camp outside the fort, the scouts learned that supply wagons carrying beer brewed in Mexico were on their way. Cody reported that he and Hickok went out that night and intercepted the apparently poorly guarded barrels of beer. Ownership of them changed hands. The barrels never made it to the intended customers inside Fort Evans but were tapped and enjoyed by General Carr's men. And the scouts slaked their thirst as well: Cody wrote that the beer bacchanal was "one of the biggest jollifications it has ever been my misfortune to attend."

Chapter Ten

---◆◆◆---

"THEY KILLED ME"

Most likely, Hickok would not have been stuck starving and freezing to death in the middle of the Raton Mountains if the previous fall he had managed to win an election. A better outcome would have allowed him to be comfortably sitting in the stove-heated office of the sheriff of Ellsworth County.

Fort Ellsworth had been established in August 1864 by soldiers of the Seventh Iowa Cavalry, named for their commander, Lieutenant Allen Ellsworth. After the war, it was rechristened Fort Harker. The town of Ellsworth was founded in February 1867, in almost the center of Kansas and near the Smoky Hill River and the Santa Fe Trail. The town began to prosper after the Kansas Pacific Railway arrived, with the population growing to a thousand. Prosperity was short-lived, however—soon Ellsworth suffered a triple dose of bad luck: a swollen river poured over its banks and flooded the town, Indian war parties killed some residents and frightened some others away, and there was an outbreak of cholera. Within months, there were only about a hundred residents left.

One of those of stubborn stock who remained was Arthur Larkin. Accepting that the river could not be moved and he couldn't cure cholera (the hostiles would have to be the army's responsibility), Larkin, in the fall of 1867, coordinated an effort to take what was left of the town and rebuild it on higher ground. He constructed a hotel and opened a general store. Ellsworth rebounded and became a popular destination for the cattle drives up from Texas. Saloons and brothels blossomed, and inevitably, violence became rampant as drunken cowboys took advantage of a lawless environment.

By the end of the summer of '68, citizens in and around Ellsworth were all for law enforcement. It is not known what motivated Hickok to run for county sheriff—perhaps the steady (though modest) paycheck or the challenge. His opponent was E. W. Kingsbury, who had been a Union officer during the war. Despite the reputation of being a good man with a gun that Hickok had brought with him to Ellsworth—or because of it—voters sided with Kingsbury.

There was no further reason to hang around Ellsworth. The open prairie and an army scout's paycheck awaited. And more adventures outriding Indian war parties and surviving to ride another day.

For years, until too many people had heard it, Hickok told a story of being discovered by such a war party while on the open prairie and making a desperate ride for shelter as the whooping hostiles, shooting arrows and rifles, rode hot on his horse's heels. No one in his audience at whatever saloon or campfire doubted such a tale because Hickok, as a wagon driver and an army scout and all-round plainsman, had had many encounters with Indians and, obviously, had survived them. In this particular story, though, Hickok, his expression dead serious, described finding a grove of tall boulders that offered some protection.

The Indians would not be thwarted, however. They rushed through the rocks, and as they showed themselves, Hickok, backed up against a cliff wall, killed them one by one. When he was out of ammunition, he took out his bowie knife and continued to fight as more of the emboldened hostiles pressed forward. Wild Bill was in a tight spot for sure.

There was a pause in the story. "Darn it, Bill, what happened?" his listeners demanded.

"Well, boys," he finally drawled, "they killed me." The stunned silence that followed was broken by Hickok's loud laugh.

Wild Bill was not laughing in March 1869, when it looked like his punch line could come true. He had parted ways with the stolen beer and Buffalo Bill. In an odd overlap, by this time, Hickok was appearing as the title characters in pulp stories about his Indian adventures. The first one, *Wild Bill, the Indian-Slayer,* had appeared eight months earlier.

Riding the prairie as a courier between Fort Lyon and Fort Wallace, Hickok was spotted by a roving band of Cheyenne. Unwisely, after killing a buffalo, he had stopped by the side of a stream and built a fire to roast the meat. The smoke and possibly the aroma had attracted the hunting party's attention. With stays in winter camps ending, most likely the Cheyenne had little food left and were anxious to find buffalo and game. Here was a lone white man providing a cooked meal and, soon, his scalp. As the Indians drew closer, they observed what a long and silky scalp it was.

Hickok had not cultivated his luxurious locks with the intention of passing them on to anyone. He climbed onto his horse just as the Cheyenne hunters arrived at a cut bank above him. Hickok fired his repeating rifle, and four of the Indians were knocked from their ponies. The other three attacked, and one of them plunged a spear into Hickok's thigh. Now with his revolvers out, he began firing. Another

Indian with a spear was hit, but not before striking Hickok's horse, which went down. He rolled away from it, firing, and another Indian was hit. The seventh one rode away from the creek, and a wounded Hickok let him go.

Using one of the Indians' ponies, after shooting his own disabled horse, Hickok rode as best he could to Fort Lyon. Along the way, he had yanked the spear out, but the spearhead remained embedded in his thigh. As it happened, Buffalo Bill Cody was at Fort Lyon. He later reported that several woodcutters working a few miles from the fort saw Hickok riding down the trail from the north. He was barely staying upright, and the woodcutters reached him just as the rider was about to fall off the pony. Hickok was placed in the back of a wagon and brought to the fort, where a concerned Cody greeted him. Hickok still had the rest of the spear, and he presented it to his friend.

The fort surgeon—who in civilian life may have been the town barber or undertaker—could not manage to get the spearhead out without severing a major artery. He insisted that amputation was the only answer. Otherwise, gangrene or a similar potentially fatal infection was likely.

This was as good a time as any to go home. Hickok had been meaning to head east soon anyway, because letters from siblings had mentioned his mother being ill. Illinois, he recalled, had real doctors, ones who had actually been to medical school, and having the leg looked at by one of them was a more appealing idea than having it chopped off.

How he survived the journey there with such a grievous wound does call the story into question, but an account of the operation performed to dig the spearhead out and patch up his thigh appeared in a Chicago newspaper in 1896, written by one of his sisters. According to Lydia, by the time her brother arrived, the wound was indeed infected. A doctor had to lance it. He drew the flesh back to scrape the bone. Not only did Hickok endure this without flinching, but when Lydia grew faint, he said, "Here, give it to me," taking the lamp from her and holding it for the doctor until the procedure was completed.

James, as he was again called, was back at the Hickok homestead in the rechristened Troy Grove for the first time since he had left as a teenager. He was now approaching his thirty-second birthday. He was, as Joseph G. Rosa commented, "a man whose name was second to none on the frontier. Of all [Polly's] sons, her youngest was the man of destiny."

James remained with his family for the rest of March and through April 1869. There, he was reunited with Horace, who had married Martha Edwards, a woman who had been smitten with his younger brother a decade earlier, and sisters Celinda and Lydia, both also married. Oliver had never returned from the sojourn in California, preferring to settle there, and Lorenzo was still hauling freight in Kansas and Nebraska. (He would soon return to Troy Grove for good, sharing farming duties with Horace.) Though not in robust health, their mother, Polly, was now in her sixty-fifth year.

The contrast between James and the other Hickoks could not have been more apparent. Whether in buckskin or one of his in-town fancy outfits, James Butler would have been dressed differently from small-town farmers. Their world was Troy Grove, where everyone knew each other, and many residents intended to live the rest of their lives there.* His world was the expanding frontier and its wide variety of

---

*James Butler is the only member of the Hickok family not buried in Troy Grove, Illinois. Perhaps one indication of how close the family was is that three of James's siblings died within months of each other in 1916, a full forty years after Wild Bill's violent death.

people and experiences. Quite possibly, no other member of the family had ever killed anyone, while James, counting victims during the Civil War and encounters with Indians, might have killed dozens of men. One wonders if the family now viewed James as a romantic figure from a mythical land or as an unfortunate who had chosen a rough, dangerous life over home and hearth . . . with a hint of menace.

In any case, as May began, he chose the frontier life again. He bid farewell to his family and Troy Grove and being known as James Butler Hickok. He put back on the badge of a deputy U.S. marshal and was Wild Bill again.

The orders from his boss, Marshal Charles Whiting, were to head to Fort Wallace and find two men who were stealing army mules. It wasn't long before Hickok was on a train with two prisoners to stand trial in Topeka. There, he learned he could be fired.

It was not for anything he did wrong. Back in Ellsworth, there had been more trouble. It was a federal matter because several Pawnee had been killed, and rumors had spread that deputy U.S. marshals had done the killing. The first head to roll, though, was Whiting's, for not having control of his marshals. Taking his place was Dana Houston, who in Leavenworth interviewed all of the former marshal's deputies. Hickok was summoned to Leavenworth, too, but when the hatchet fell, Houston asked him to stay on. This may have been because Hickok truly had nothing to do with murdered Pawnee, but a factor had to be that Wild Bill was an especially effective and intimidating lawman.

His next assignment brought him back to Hays City. Hickok by now was quite familiar with it. In December 1867, the Atchison newspaper editor Frank Root had reported that during a previous visit to Hays City, he had "formed the acquaintance of Wm. Haycock, better known as 'Wild Bill.' He is a man about thirty years of age, over six feet high, straight as an arrow, with long hair hanging over his shoulders. He is in the employ of the Government as a detective and is probably better acquainted with the plains than any other man living of his age."

This time, though, after just a short stay, Hickok again had to leave Hays City behind because of various army scouting adventures and deputy marshal labors that Whiting assigned him. One of the acquaintances whose company he could no longer enjoy was one of the more eccentric residents in a town that had its fair share of characters.

David Morrow hailed from upstate New York, had served in the Union army during the war, and as a cavalry trooper had been part of campaigns against Navajo and Apache bands in Arizona and New Mexico. When he had enough soldiering, Morrow mustered out and found work hunting buffalo in the Hays City area. From time to time, he was residing in the city itself when a glut of buffalo meat on the market—Buffalo Bill was not the only efficient killer on the prairie—meant the cost of hunting outweighed the revenue. It was during one of these periods that Prairie Dog Morrow earned his nickname. A few years later, he would take it with him to Dodge City, where he served as a part-time deputy to Wyatt Earp, Bat Masterson, Charlie Bassett, and other lawmen.

As was true with many settlements in Kansas, Hays City was surrounded by thriving prairie dog communities. Officially, they were short-tailed ground squirrels, but their calls sounded like barking dogs, thus the name. Checking for any danger before searching for food, a prairie dog's head popped up and down from the crater housing its underground burrow, which typically had several entrances. The burrows were connected by tunnels, and at the end of these subterranean corridors would be its nest, well protected from whatever weather or human havoc was above the ground. During some downtime in Hays City, Morrow captured two prairie dogs. Instead of killing them, it occurred to him to train them as performing pets.

It should be mentioned that Morrow was a storyteller, so it was not unusual for him to be waiting at the railroad station to regale disembarking passengers with tales of his and others' adventures on the frontier, the true ones mixed in with the fabrications. One particular day, though, travelers were presented with the two prairie dogs Morrow plucked from his pockets, along with descriptions of all the remarkable tricks they could do. A persuaded passenger purchased the animals for five dollars. This was all the encouragement Morrow needed.

After pondering the landscape right outside the city, Morrow created a prairie dog trap. It was a simple apparatus—a barrel of sand placed open-end down over a hole. To not become trapped, a desperate prairie dog climbed up through the flowing sand into the barrel. Trapped there, it could not escape because by then, sand had filled and covered the hole. Every day, Morrow made his way through the cratered community, carefully upending barrels and placing prairie dogs into a sack. Very soon, Hays City residents dubbed him Prairie Dog Dave Morrow. Alas, the town had its share of loafers who were copycats looking for a quick and easy buck. They, too, became collectors, and crowded the train station with their barking wares. Once the price of a pair of prairie dogs went from five dollars to fifty cents, Morrow grabbed his rifle and returned to where the buffalo roamed.

In July 1869, after months of working for U.S. Marshal Houston, Hickok was back in Hays City. Its citizenry was in need of his peacekeeping abilities. The year had begun with three black soldiers in the local jail for minor offenses being dragged out by a mob and hanged. During the year, patrols from Fort Hays entered the town to temper the rowdyism a bit, but it resumed as soon as they rode out. That summer, with violence in the city reaching new levels, several business leaders petitioned Kansas governor James Harvey to appoint R. A. Eckles as the county sheriff. The mystery here is that there already was a county sheriff, and Hickok may have known the man, Isaac Thayer, because he was one of the scouts who had survived the attacks by Roman Nose's warriors at the Battle of Beecher Island. But by the second week of July, Thayer was nowhere to be found. He was the third sheriff in eighteen months to suddenly crave new employment.

Considering that in the weeks before there had been several murders, at least three lynchings (in addition to the one in January), and numerous brawls between civilians and soldiers stationed at Fort Hays, the sheriff may simply have thrown his hands up and escaped while he could. Another possibility is that some prominent residents, appalled by the escalating violence, had formed a Vigilance Committee, headed by Alonzo Webster.* The committee, seeing how ineffectual Thayer was, may have pressed upon him a one-way ticket out of town, then endorsed the petition to the governor.

But Harvey balked at becoming involved in the circus of mayhem that was Hays City. He contended he did not have the authority to appoint a sheriff and that it was up to Hays City residents to elect one. The problem was, the next election was not until November, and no one knew how to go about scheduling one earlier. Plus, who would want to be in Thayer's boots? Then the answer ambled into town: Wild Bill Hickok. That July, he became marshal of Hays City.

---

*Readers of *Dodge City* will recall that Webster would relocate to Dodge City, serve four terms as mayor there, and become a central figure in the Dodge City War of 1883.

There has long been confusion about how legitimate a peace officer Hickok was there. It seems that initially he was the marshal because the desperate Vigilance Committee said he was, an action that had no official stamp to it. Hickok served as marshal with this dubious imprimatur for a few weeks. Then, *The Leavenworth Times and Conservative* reported that an election had been held in Hays City on August 23 and Hickok had been voted in as sheriff of Ellis County. In essence, he held two law-enforcement offices at once. The governor, finally doing something, declared that Hickok's status was illegal, but this time, no one paid attention to him.

Just as well, because by then, Hickok had already been quite busy, as there was no lack of lawing to be done in Hays City in the summer of 1869. On July 23, Samuel Strawhun,* one of the city's residents who had unsuccessfully petitioned Governor Harvey, accompanied by Deputy U.S. Marshal Joe Weiss, walked into a store owned by Richard Evans and there encountered Webster. Whatever the confrontation was about, Webster felt threatened enough that he pulled out a pistol and shot and killed Weiss as Strawhun fled. Webster and the store owner went outside to summon members of the Vigilance Committee to assist if Strawhun returned with reinforcements.

One of those answering the call was Hickok. Once inside Evans's store, he pointed to his two Navy Colts and said, "Let them come. We are ready for them." It would appear that the death of the unfortunate deputy marshal was not avenged and Webster did not even see the inside of a courtroom. (Possibly, Hickok informed Marshal Houston that he would take care of the situation—which he ended up doing.) One of the challenges Hays City had at the time was the

---

*This is just one of several variations of his name, with Strayhun and Strawhim being used frequently, too.

lack of even a rudimentary justice system. Hickok could keep busy rounding up rowdy cowboys and others breaking the few laws the city had, but not much happened after that. As one newspaper account put it, "If Wild Bill arrests an offender, there is a log jail to receive him, but no justice to try the case."

Nevertheless, Hickok had little spare time to enjoy the gambling and other pleasures of Hays City. He was fine with those who did, as long as they did it without fighting, especially gunplay. Every night, when he interrupted the activities of lawbreakers, Hickok offered them three courses of action. One was to head over to the train station and get on the first eastbound that arrived. The second was to take the first westbound train out of Hays City. The third was to "go north in the morning." The cemetery was to the north, and the miscreant knew that if he hadn't left town by then, Wild Bill would come gunning for him. No surprise that the railroad's business in Hays City increased, and the marshal saved money on bullets.

Sometimes, just a piece of wood was enough to keep the peace . . . and generate a few laughs. Simon Motz, a future Kansas state senator—and, ironically, a supporter of Hickok and his aggressive efforts—owned a shop in the middle of town. One night, he went to reopen the front door and realized he had forgotten his key. Motz pried open a window, stepped inside, got what he'd come for, and was on his way back out the window when a board connected with his head. When Motz came to, there was the marshal looming over him. Hickok was a tad embarrassed about capturing the "burglar."

There is always at least one in every crowd, however, who is not big on law and order, and in Hays City, it was Bill Mulvey. Some men are driven mad by alcohol, and one night in September, it was Mulvey's turn. Liquored up, the Missouri man—whom the press described as an "intoxicated rough"—went on a rampage that included staggering from one saloon to another and shooting up whiskey bottles, lamps, and mirrors. When warned that the marshal was on his way, Mulvey declared that he "had come to kill Wild Bill Hickok." This caused some alarm because Miguel Otero, one of the witnesses to what followed, knew of Mulvey as "a handy man with a gun."

That opportunity presented itself when Mulvey was en route to the next saloon, this time atop a horse and with a cocked rifle in hand. When he rounded the corner, Hickok could have shot Mulvey on sight, but for some reason—not a very prudent one—he waved at the rider, perhaps trying to calm him down. The roaring-drunk Mulvey was not inclined to be calmed. Hickok then called out, "Don't shoot him in the back, he's drunk."

Fearing a bullet from that direction, Mulvey wheeled his horse around. He glanced this way and that, the rifle ready. Probably realizing it was a ruse, he was in the process of turning back and finishing his business with the marshal when Wild Bill whipped out one of his pistols and jerked the trigger. Shot through the temple, Mulvey died instantly.

He would not be the last man Marshal Hickok killed to keep the peace. It would later be attributed to him that he said, "There is no Sunday west of Junction City, no law west of Hays City, and no God west of Carson City." If it took both of his Colt six-shooters, for as long as he wore a badge, Wild Bill would make sure that there was law in Hays City.

Chapter Eleven

THE MAN-KILLER

The killing of Bill Mulvey sent a message, or perhaps a known gunfighter with a badge was message enough, because a reporter visiting Hays City wrote back to readers of *The Topeka Commonwealth* that the city "under the guardian care of Wild Bill Hickok is quiet and doing well."

Apparently, Hickok believed that dressing well would enhance his peacekeeping efforts. He patrolled the streets not only well armed, with a sawed-off shotgun complementing his Colt six-shooters, but also attired as fine as any Hays City leading citizen. Another reporter, this one having been dispatched by *The St. Louis Republican*, included in his article a description of Hickok that had not changed from ones written the last few years ("In physique he is as perfect a specimen of manhood as ever walked in moccasins"). But he added a few details that reflected the impression the marshal made on his new jurisdiction: "Bill is a dandy at all times in attire—a regular frontier dude. . . . There is nothing in his appearance to betoken the dead shot and frequent man-killer, except his tread. He walks like a tiger and, aroused, he is as ferocious and pitiless as one."

Because trouble could occur at any moment, during his lawman stint in Hays City, Hickok sometimes went on patrol on horseback, the better to see his surroundings from a higher vantage point. When on foot, adhering to his previous practice, he strolled in the middle of the street rather than on the wooden sidewalks. If someone was foolish or ambitious enough to jump him, Hickok wanted to see him coming.

The St. Louis scribe informed his readers about such a confrontation that demonstrated that even with precautions, the sheriff's life hung on a slender thread. Hickok was patrolling an unsavory section of the city—such sections at that time were in the majority—when a short man known as Sullivan suddenly appeared in the street brandishing a pistol. For some reason, he aimed to harm Hickok. "I've got you. Hold up your hands!" Sullivan shouted. "I'm going to kill you."

There may have been some newspaperman himself in Sullivan because the diminutive gunman began to compose out loud the type of article he expected would be published about the death of Wild Bill. Onlookers were gathering, and Sullivan regaled them with increasingly colorful adjectives. His fatal mistake was not only forgetting who his intended victim was but forgetting him altogether. Hickok stood still, his eyes gazing at the loquacious gunman, but his hand slowly crept toward his right holster. Sullivan was between one syllable and the next when he died.

As Hickok put his pistol away, he remarked to the crowd, "He talked his life away."

As if keeping the peace in Hays City weren't handful enough,

Hickok doubled as a sort of one-man employment agency. There are enough tales of him helping young men find jobs that at least a few must be true. One of them came from Harry Young, who many years later wrote about his first encounter with Hickok, in Hays City.* He had come to town with $40 in his pockets. By the end of a night's entertainments, Young was left with $1.50.

Rather morosely, he was swaying on the sidewalk when he felt a tap on the shoulder. "I turned and found myself face-to-face with the finest-looking man I have ever seen or expect to see," Young recalled. He noted the "long auburn hair and clear blue eyes—eyes that showed kindness and friendship to all except the evil-doer, to whom they meant the reverse."

In answer to the lawman's question, Young explained that he had just frittered away his pay from a construction job, and now being pretty much broke, he hoped to find work in Hays City. Hickok told him there were jobs hauling freight for men who could drive a six-mule team and could tie "a government ham-string." Hickok taught him this knot and told him to meet him the next morning. Young did, and the two rode out to Fort Hays.

According to Young's recollection: "There we met the corral boss, and Wild Bill asked him to put me to work." After demonstrating that he could tie the ham-string knot and passing a few other rudimentary tests, Young was hired. He worked the job for six months to get back on his feet and "saw a great deal of Wild Bill." After Hickok moved on from Hays City, he and Young would meet each other once more, in Deadwood.

Sometime during his service as a lawman in Hays City, Hickok met a man who would later play a role in his "career" as a stage actor.

---

*He was also known as Sam Young or Harry "Sam" Young.

John Omohundro was born in July 1846 in Palmyra, Virginia. He was just seventeen when he enlisted in the Confederate army, and until the war ended, he served in the Fifth Cavalry Corps commanded by J. E. B. Stuart. After the surrender, rather than return to his family in Virginia, Omohundro set off for Texas, where he spent three years as a cowboy in a reviving cattle industry. During one drive into Tennessee, he acquired the nickname "Texas Jack."

Late in the summer of 1869, Omohundro was at Fort Hays, where he met California Joe, who in turn introduced him to Wild Bill Hickok. Moses Embree "California Joe" Milner was a veteran plainsman and scout who had crossed paths with Hickok several times. When George Armstrong Custer had been assigned to the West after the Civil War, Milner looked like a good candidate to lead a new unit of civilian scouts. "He was a man about 40 years of age, maybe older, over 6 feet in height and possessing a well-proportioned frame," the lieutenant colonel wrote in *My Life on the Plains*. "His head was covered with a luxuriant crop of long, almost black hair, strongly inclined to curl and so long as to fall carelessly over his shoulders. His face, at least so much of it as was not concealed by the long, waving brown beard and mustache, was full of intelligence and pleasant to look upon. His eye was undoubtedly handsome, black and lustrous with an expression of kindness and mildness combined."

Milner had been born in Kentucky in 1829 to parents who had emigrated from England. At fourteen, he ran away from home and in St. Louis joined a hunting and trapping expedition. He served with Brigadier General Stephen Kearny in the war with Mexico and returned to marry a thirteen-year-old, and the couple moved to California. Milner toiled as a prospector. When gold did not appear in his pan, he and his wife, Nancy, bought a ranch in Oregon and raised four children. He was known as a man of decisive action: when one of his horses was stolen, Milner tracked the thief down, shot him in the head, and left him on the side of a road with a note pinned to his coat warning other thieves the same fate awaited them.

In the 1860s, he was on the move a lot because of his abilities as a scout and a handler of mules. In a saloon in Virginia City, Montana, when miners asked him where he was from, Milner responded, "I'm from California, where most of the gold is, and my name is Joe. That's enough for you to know." He was christened California Joe. He scouted for Custer and the Seventh Cavalry for close to a decade. In the 1941 film *They Died with Their Boots On,* California Joe is portrayed by the character actor Charley Grapewin and is shown dying next to Errol Flynn's Custer during the Battle of Little Bighorn. However, Milner was not on that expedition; he was prospecting in the Black Hills.

After meeting up in Hays City that fall of 1869, Wild Bill, California Joe, and Texas Jack enjoyed each other's company in the saloons, with the young Omohundro being an eager audience for the plainsmen's tales of adventure on the prairie. When Texas Jack moved on sometime that autumn, he encountered Buffalo Bill. Cody was scouting for the Fifth U.S. Cavalry stationed at Fort McPherson in Nebraska. He invited Texas Jack to sign on, and the two became good friends. In their future was a production titled *Scouts of the Plains,* which would, improbably, feature Hickok as a member of the cast.

When that time came, it could be said that Hickok had some experience as a showman because, as he had done in previous stops, he enjoyed putting on shooting exhibitions. Most likely, there was a good public relations angle for such demonstrations—bad guys or even just rowdy cowboys had better think twice about carrying a weapon in town and risk being confronted by the marshal. But it also seems Hickok had fun awing onlookers.

"I saw him draw his pistol in front of the old depot, throw it over his first finger, cocking it with his thumb as it came around and keep a tomato can jumping for a whole block down to Riley's saloon on the next corner," remembered Joe Hutt, a former buffalo hunter, about Hickok. "He was not a drunken, quarrelsome man-killer, but picturesque and a fine shot. It was not always the blustering bullies that were the bravest men in a western town."

Time for Jim Curry to reappear in these pages. Inevitably, as a patrolling peace officer, Hickok would come up against the dangerous desperado. Perhaps trying to spurn his violent past, by the fall of 1869, Curry was a fairly successful saloonkeeper. However, he still believed the law did not concern him. The marshal did not share that belief. In an article published in the June 15, 1913, edition of *The Kansas City Star*, C. J. Bascom, a young resident of Hays City forty-four years earlier, recalled that Hickok "was ruling the town with an iron hand. It was something unusual and unexpected. They did not know just what to think nor how long this rule would last." Bascom himself witnessed what was almost the end.

Curry, apparently, was outgoing and friendly when he was of a mind to be. On a lovely late-summer day when Bascom entered Curry's establishment, the proprietor suggested they take a walk. When they came to a saloon owned by Tommy Drum, they decided to go in for lunch. When Curry spotted Hickok playing cards at a table at the back of the saloon, a switch was thrown. Remembering or imagining all kinds of slights, Curry snuck up behind Hickok, then pointed the barrel of his cocked pistol at his head. "Now, you son of a gun," Curry whispered, "I've got you."

Enhancing his reputation of being fearless, Hickok remained still for several seconds, then, as if remarking on the weather, he said, "Jim, you would not murder a man without giving him a show."

"I'll give you the same show you would give me," Curry hissed, adding, "you long-haired tough." (We can assume the newspaper version of this event was sanitized for general consumption.)

Hickok considered this unpleasant option, then suggested, "Jim, let us settle this feud. How would a bottle of champagne all around do?"

There was another shift in Curry's brain because his reaction was to burst out laughing, and nervous onlookers followed suit. Drum began popping open pint bottles of bubbly. Hickok and Curry shook hands and poured a couple of glasses each down the hatch.

Unfortunately, the peaceful outcome to the confrontation with Jim Curry did not put an end to the killing in Hays City. The next man to take on Hickok was Samuel Strawhun, and this showdown had a much different ending.

Only twenty-four in September 1869, Strawhun already had a reputation as a man-killer, though his actual occupation was cowboy. In Hays City, he'd already caused considerable trouble that summer, particularly his connection to the shooting death of the deputy U.S. marshal Joe Weiss. Yet Strawhun had been one of the men who had petitioned Governor Harvey to appoint a new sheriff of Ellis County. Still, his behavior was such that the Vigilance Committee had ordered him to leave. His response was to confront Alonzo Webster once again and this time to pistol-whip him, and no one had done anything about it. However, when Hickok was hired as marshal, Strawhun left town. There was a collective sigh of relief, and it was presumed he would not return to Hays City as long as Wild Bill patrolled its dusty streets.

Thus, there was fear and disappointment when on the twenty-sixth of September, Strawhun was back and had brought eighteen cowboy colleagues with him. They didn't care who was in charge; it was simply time to raise hell. They got off their horses and parked themselves in John Bitter's Leavenworth Beer Saloon, determined to cause as much of a ruckus as they could while drinking it dry. Strawhun was heard to declare, "I'm going to kill someone tonight just for luck."

As *The Leavenworth Times and Conservative* would report, "It appears that Stranghan [*sic*] and a number of his companions being 'wolfing' all night, wished to conclude by cleaning out a beer saloon and breaking things generally. 'Wild Bill' was called upon to quiet them."

It was close to 1 A.M. on the twenty-seventh as Hickok approached the saloon. Glasses were flying out into the street, tossed by Strawhun and his cowboy pals. There was quite a commotion inside the saloon; as *The Leavenworth Daily Commercial* reported in its October 3 edition, "The noise was fearful, all the men crying at the top of their voices, beer! Beer! And using the most obscene language."

Hickok picked up several of the glasses that had not broken and carried them inside. Sizing up the situation, he said, "Boys, you hadn't ought to treat a poor man in this way." When Strawhun vowed to take the glasses from Hickok and throw them out into the street again, the marshal replied, "Do, and they will carry you out."

Strawhun made a sudden move, either for a glass or for his gun. In any event, suddenly blood gushed from his neck, spewing from the hole Hickok's bullet had left. He would be buried later that day in the city's cemetery. Though severely outnumbered, Hickok, with both pistols now out, went unchallenged as the crowd inside the saloon backed down.

A coroner's inquest was held at nine o'clock that morning. There was some contradictory testimony, probably owing to many of the witnesses having been inebriated when the shooting occurred. Hickok's terse defense was he had "tried to restore order." The jury agreed, declaring the death of Samuel Strawhun justifiable homicide. The *Leavenworth Daily Commercial* concluded its account: "Too much credit cannot be given to Wild Bill for his endeavor to rid this town of such dangerous characters as this Stranhan [*sic*] was."

The news of such quick and rough justice spread fast, and during the following weeks, there was no more gunplay in the county. Still, Hickok had to be constantly on the alert for an ambush. For those who disapproved of Hays City becoming less rowdy and lawless, the easiest solution would be to get rid of the marshal. The eyesight that made him such a good marksman was in full use as he strode down the middle of the street. Few were allowed to approach him, especially from behind. If it sounded like activities in a saloon were getting out of hand, Wild Bill Hickok pushed through the doors, then, with his back to the bar, calmly said what he wanted to say. With his hands poised near the handles of his Colts, he passed back through the crowd to the street.

There was to be an election in November 1869. One would think, given his mostly successful efforts at bringing some law and order to Hays City, that Hickok would be more officially elected marshal of Hays City or sheriff of Ellis County or possibly both. The people who hired him appeared to approve of his very direct methods. In his book *Buffalo Land*, published just four years later, William Webb, one of the founders of the city, described Hickok as "very quiet and gentlemanly, and not at all the reckless fellow we had supposed. His form won our admiration—the shoulders of a Hercules with the waist of a girl."

It is interesting to note that some people who encountered Hickok saw almost a feminine quality to him. Part of this had to do with his physique and perhaps also because of his dress and an unusual practice at that time on the frontier. As Joseph Rosa explained, "Hickok's passion for taking a bath every day, at first frowned upon by the wild men of Hays, soon started a tradition, and many of them made regular trips to the bathhouse." (In more ways than one, Wild Bill cleaned up the city.) When he dressed for the day, the lawman left buckskins behind and stepped out wearing a Prince Albert coat.

His opponent on Election Day would be Rattlesnake Pete Lanahan. Hickok may have first made his acquaintance during the Civil War. Lanahan spent those years working in the quartermaster's department at Fort Hays and stayed on afterward as the town was being established. In February 1868, during an early effort at peacekeeping in Hays City, town fathers hired Lanahan as a city policeman. This lasted only a few months patrolling what *The Junction City Weekly Union* dubbed the "Sodom of the Plains"; then Lanahan sought the safety of the fort, returning to work there. When Hickok was placed in control in August 1869, one of his first acts was to appoint Lanahan as a deputy.

He had proven to be a good lawman. And Lanahan, running on the Democratic line, proved to be a good candidate, too. Hickok, listed as Independent, lost the election 114–89. His defeat could be attributed to more citizens fearing Hickok than liking him, or he was simply a victim of numbers, as most voters in Ellis County were registered Democrats.

Especially since his trusted deputy had won, Hickok must not have had any hard feelings about losing yet another election, because instead of mounting up and moving on after the last vote was counted, he agreed to serve through the transition to Lanahan's taking office. For Lanahan's sake, too bad Hickok didn't stay on longer. Lanahan was not the feared shootist Wild Bill had been, and while that was fine with solid citizens, the rowdier element saw opportunities. Lanahan found it harder and harder to keep the peace, and one night in July 1871, he lost his job . . . permanently.

It was a setup. Several men began fighting in a Tenth Street saloon. When Lanahan arrived to break up the brawl, he was greeted with two bullets in the chest. Lanahan lingered for a couple of days in his room at the courthouse building, then died. One of the men who fired at him was Charles Harris, the saloon's bartender. Rattlesnake Pete had some satisfaction that he had managed to get off one shot, striking Harris in the head and killing him.

Back before Lanahan's tenure began, Hickok had to think December 1869 would be quiet, even in Hays City. He had not counted on a fighter named Patterson and his boxing ring. He was as professional as a boxer could be in the late 1860s and had come to introduce what would later be called the "sweet science" to the frontier. He set up a ring in Hays City and began to demonstrate the art of pugilism and its advantages over barroom brawling. When spectators were not impressed enough to pay real money to witness these demonstrations, Patterson decided he had to raise his profile. He had noticed the slender, long-haired marshal and figured without his guns he would be an easy conquest.

He approached Hickok in Drum's saloon and challenged him to a fight. The marshal was puzzled, with his adversary not wearing any weapons. Patterson explained, "I'm told you're the toughest man on the frontier. I'll prove you're not, with my bare hands."

Grinning, Hickok sized up the larger man, then invited him to step outside. Those in the saloon followed them out and were immediately joined by other onlookers. Patterson went into something of a crouch, what passed then as a boxer's stance. (It would not be until 1889 that the Marquess of Queensberry Rules were used in the United States.) When Patterson began to advance, Hickok assumed the fight had begun. It lasted less than five minutes and was deemed over when buckets of water from the nearest horse trough were splashed onto

Patterson to revive him. He was soon plying his brand of pugilism elsewhere on the frontier.

The Topeka House was a hotel in the capital of Kansas, and Hickok went there when he left Hays City. With a new decade about to begin, the thirty-two-year-old man-killer and ex-marshal had to ponder what would be the next chapter in his life. He could not have known that his experience in Hays City of being a lawman in a lawless town had been a sort of a dress rehearsal for being a lawman in Abilene.

Chapter Twelve

THE TWO-FISTED MARSHAL

When the construction of Drovers Cottage was completed in 1868, it represented Abilene's potential as a cow town. That potential was fulfilled, but at a cost. Abilene also came to represent the lawlessness and violence of the Kansas cow towns that put prosperity above peacekeeping. When the latter became a priority for the citizenry, the way was paved for two lawmen to take over a daunting responsibility. One of them was Wild Bill Hickok.

As mentioned previously, Timothy Hersey deserves much credit for the founding of Abilene, but it was Joseph McCoy who set it on the road to being a boomtown. In the fall of 1867, he and his two older brothers arrived in what was then a rather sleepy settlement. Though still young men, they had experience in the cattle trade, running their own business in Springfield, Illinois. Joseph McCoy, in particular, was a visionary. He added together the facts that there were tens of thousands of cattle in Texas and the Kansas Pacific Railway was working its way west, and the sum was somewhere in Kansas there was a place that would generate huge profits.

Earlier that year, McCoy had visited the offices of Kansas Pacific in St. Louis. He tried to persuade executives there to relocate the company's stockyards from Sedalia, Missouri, to Kansas. McCoy offered two sensible reasons, the first being a combination stockyards and a railroad station in Kansas made for shorter cattle drives up from Texas, and that meant less wear and tear on the beef. The other reason was a tad more complicated.

Though the Civil War had ended two years earlier and the free state versus slave state issue was thus rendered moot, Jayhawkers still existed. Most of them were men mustered out of the military who were unable or unwilling to find gainful employment. Instead, groups of Jayhawkers patrolled the prairie for cattle being driven north and east, and they exacted a form of protection. Trail bosses were offered safe passage in exchange for tribute, the exact amount determined by the size of the herd or the number of guns backing the boss up. A shorter and more direct route to a rail hub would make it easier for the trail drovers to protect themselves, and the Jayhawkers would eventually, finally, fade away.

To his surprise, McCoy's proposal was rejected. The executives did not trust the young stranger enough to make such an expensive move, and they feared the jilted Jayhawkers would turn their attention to the railroad itself. Plan B: McCoy bought a Kansas Pacific ticket and rode the rails until they ended, which at that time was at a water station in Ellis, Kansas. There he gathered what maps he could and saw that the small town of Abilene 130 miles to the east was directly north of Caldwell, the first stop in Kansas on the Chisholm Trail. He had actually passed Abilene on his way west and recalled it did not have a station; the train had slowed only to toss out a bag of mail. It may have taken a few dollars, but during the return trip, McCoy persuaded the train crew to stop and let him off on the side of the tracks in Abilene.

According to the historian Robert Dykstra in *The Cattle Towns*, McCoy was "a slender figure in unpretentious garb—heavy boots, short topcoat, black slouch hat—the goatee that hid a weak chin lending age to his twenty-nine years, his bland, ascetic visage concealing qualities both good and bad: a brilliant entrepreneurial imagination, a tenacious fixity of purpose, but also a somewhat undisciplined ego that frequently impelled him to an overconfidence in his personal mastery."

The townsfolk were polite enough to the stranger, and McCoy was directed to the home of Timothy Hersey. It was something of a passing-of-the-baton meeting. Hersey took his visitor on a ride south to the Smoky Hill River. There, McCoy observed bottomland bursting with buffalo grass, an easily fordable river, and pure drinking water. By July, he was a landowner on the east side of the Smoky Hill.

With some urgency, before someone else had the same idea but for a different town, McCoy set about having stockyards constructed. Lumber arrived from Hannibal, Missouri, and the Kansas Pacific was happy enough to take his money for railroad ties. While this project was progressing, the brothers James and William McCoy went south to Texas to spread circulars, take out advertisements in newspapers, and personally visit ranchers to let it be known that Abilene was the place to send and sell their cattle. From Abilene, Joseph McCoy dispatched a work crew to extend and mark the Chisholm Trail from Caldwell north.

Next on his to-do list was to build Drovers Cottage.* The name does not do justice to McCoy's plans—it would be for drovers as well

---

*Aside from Hickok, Abilene's most famous resident was Dwight D. Eisenhower. Though born in Denison, Texas, the thirty-fourth president grew up in Abilene and worked at the Belle Springs Creamery, the site of the former Drovers Cottage. Eisenhower's connection to Abilene continues in that he and his wife, Mamie, and

as other businessmen, all right, but would hardly be a modest cottage. There would be eighty rooms, a spacious dining room, and a saloon with comfortable furnishings and the best liquor, certainly not any sod-house swill. McCoy wanted Abilene to be ready, willing, and able to accommodate the expected herds of prime beef from Texas.

He miscalculated, in the sense that his vision was realized too quickly. When cattle began to arrive, the construction projects remained incomplete and buyers from the big cities had not yet come to town. Tents and other temporary structures were erected to contain the first hundreds of head of cattle. Then a bigger herd arrived, owned by Colonel O. W. Wheeler, who was from California but was partnered with two Texans. Their original plan had been to take the cattle bought in the Lone Star State and drive them to Kansas, then make a left turn and head west to California. But along the way, the cattlemen were bedeviled by horrible weather, Indians, and a cholera outbreak. When Wheeler and his partners, in a sour mood and ready to abandon their plan, got to Caldwell, they were told about what the McCoy brothers were trying to do in Abilene. Wheeler went there to see if the herd could be sold.

By the time he arrived, so had buyers. Wheeler was wined and dined in what was a partially completed dining room in the Drovers Cottage. His nightmare was over. He sold his herd, and on September 5, 1867, the train that headed east from Abilene carried car after car of cattle. By the end of the year, thirty-five thousand head were shipped. The McCoys had a financial piece of every cow.

---

their firstborn son, Doud Dwight, are buried on the grounds of the Dwight D. Eisenhower Presidential Library, Museum, and Boyhood Home.

During the next three years, there were some setbacks, including the flooding of the town caused by an overflowing Mud Creek, fears of "Spanish fever" that made some buyers look elsewhere for beef,* and periods of drought and dust storms. But otherwise, Abilene prospered. Through 1870, there was a steady stream of Texas cattle going from the trail to the stockyards in Abilene, then onto train cars taking them to the eastern markets. Abilene was by no means the first Kansas cow town, but it became the busiest one as saloons and boardinghouses and dance halls and various shops blossomed. The previous year, 1869, saw 160,000 head of cattle be shipped out of the city.

And all that beef was escorted north by cowboys, who became increasingly trail-weary and thirsty as they went. In his *Historic Sketches of the Cattle Trade of the West and Southwest,* Joseph McCoy offers a vivid portrait of this particular human species based on his Abilene observations:

> *He lives hard, works hard, has but a few comforts and fewer necessities. He has but little, if any, taste for reading. He enjoys a coarse practical joke or a smutty story; loves danger but abhors labor of the common kind; never tires riding, never wants to walk, no matter how short the distance he desires to go. He would rather fight with pistols than pray; loves tobacco, liquor and women better than any other trinity. His clothes are coarse and substantial, few in number and often of the gaudy pattern. The "sombrero" and large spurs are inevitable accompaniments.*

---

*Also known as "Texas fever" in Kansas, this was a tick-borne scourge that could be transmitted to Kansas livestock and prompted some communities to ban cattle coming from Texas altogether.

Appropriately, Texas Street—more a section of town than a single street—was the epicenter of exuberant cowboy merriment. The whiskey and the women were cheap, and there was plenty of the former. Alas, before long, life was considered cheap, too. With guns as readily available as shots of whiskey, confrontations quickly escalated. This could be bad for business. Drovers Cottage had been finished and was regarded as the best hotel to be found west of Kansas City until Denver, and it was seeking to cater to a moneyed clientele. However, Abilene's reputation was more based on its being an anything-goes oasis for parched and lusty men who had spent weeks in clouds of dust and insects on the trails up from Texas.

According to Stewart Verckler in *Cowtown Abilene*, the typical Texas cowboy in town

> *gulped his whiskey straight at the bar of the many saloons. He was quick to anger and argue, having a short temper, but would side quickly with another who had ridden the trail with him. He did not get a large sum of money for riding the trail [; his] salary would vary from fifteen to twenty dollars per month. His money was gone in less than a week, and there was always another trail herd on the way, the merchants and saloonkeepers thought. The cowboy would have no regrets about shooting up a saloon. They had courage, six-gun courage.*

Joseph McCoy, T. C. Henry, and other business and civic leaders were having some misgivings about what they had created. Sure, they were making money hand over fist, but such prosperity would be short-lived if a pile of dead cowboys persuaded trail bosses to take their herds elsewhere. The ongoing westward extension of the railroads was creating other candidates. And cowboys killing cowboys was one thing; worse would be the violence getting so out of hand that everyday citizens, even women and children, were becoming caught in the cross fire.

The local government, with Henry as mayor, desired law enforcement. However, the first two marshals hired were chased out of town by gleeful cowboy gunfire. Chaos continued to threaten to reign, with each herd arriving bringing with it cowboys seeming to be thirstier and rowdier than the last batch. But there would soon be a new marshal in town: one day in the spring of 1870, Tom Smith rode into town and tied up his two matching gray horses in front of T. C. Henry's real estate office.

Thomas "Bear River" Smith had earned a good reputation as a bare-knuckled battler of crime in the New York City Police Department, with his beat including the brutal Bowery section. It sounds like a bit of blarney, but an account offered by the Abilene historian Henry Jameson contends that sometime during the Civil War, Smith was chasing a teenage robber down an alley, and when he stumbled, his gun discharged, killing the boy. Feeling guilt over this tragedy and shying away from the resulting headlines, and mourning the recent death of his mother, Smith—who had also been a prizefighter known as the "Slugging Newsboy"—decided to start over away from New York and its mean streets. Whatever the real motivation was, Smith left New York and wound up in Wyoming, Utah, and Colorado as a freight hauler. His nickname was earned when working construction for the Union Pacific Railroad in the Bear River area of Wyoming in 1868.

In the towns there, off-duty railroad workers could be like the rowdy trail riders in the Kansas cow towns. In some settlements, vigilance committees were formed to apprehend the most drunk and belligerent. One day, three railroad workers were nabbed, and preparations were under way to hang them. Smith led a sort of vigilante group of his own, which freed the workers, burned down the jail, and apprehended several committee members. Things escalated to gunfire between the two sides, with fourteen men being killed and Smith wounded by a man named Nuckles. Peace was restored only after army cavalry arrived.

A recuperating Smith was appointed marshal of the Bear River settlement. The following year found him as marshal of a town named after Kit Carson in Colorado. What he had learned from his previous experience was that pistols provoked more violence than they prevented, so he no longer wore a gun, but the former pugilist did his policing with his fists.

It is not known how Smith came to stop in at Abilene in 1870. He may have visited remaining family back in New York the previous fall and was moseying west when he heard of Abilene's troubles and applied for the job of peace officer. Smith seemed to be a man who relished a challenge.

That he was not immediately appointed marshal demonstrated the city's dysfunction. Going from east to west, Smith had spent the winter in St. Louis, then in Kansas City. His aim was to continue west and discover more of what the Great American Desert was all about. But in Abilene, he walked inside Henry's office and applied for the job. He then met with the board of trustees. They liked him a lot . . . which was a big reason why Smith was rejected. Mayor Henry explained that with the short life expectancy of Abilene marshals—which would be even shorter for one who didn't carry a gun—they didn't want him to get killed. Best he continue on his journey west and stay healthy.

Smith replied he was on his way to visit friends in Ellis, and he could be reached there if the trustees changed their minds. It did not take them long to do so. The simple version of a convoluted tale is that optimistic lawmakers in Abilene had a jail erected. It was just a stone-walled single cell with two barred windows, but to the cowboys, it still was like waving a red towel in front of a bull. Soon after construction finished, cowboys gathered and tore it down. To further emphasize their displeasure, they distributed the stones all over town. After this happened again to a second jail, Mayor Henry sent a wire to Ellis.

Smith returned, to a hefty salary of $150 a month plus bonuses for the convictions of men he had arrested for serious crimes. The citizens of Abilene found their new marshal to be a thirty-year-old, soft-spoken, slender man just under six feet tall, whose speech reflected the Ireland his parents had emigrated from. He had auburn hair, a thick mustache, and strong shoulders and hands from his recent years of labor and being a good boxer. Smith was a devout Catholic and did not curse or drink alcohol. And he still wouldn't display a gun, though he agreed to keep one concealed under his coat. Some of those citizens wagered on how long Smith would last, with the shortest tenure getting the best odds.

His first act was to repost signs the cowboys had taken down declaring no firearms were allowed within the Abilene city limits. Next, he climbed on one of his two gray horses and rode to the Texas Street section. Watching him go, Mayor Henry, Joseph McCoy, and others wondered if Smith would even last until sundown. But the new marshal had a new strategy—given that he had no staff, he would sort of deputize the saloonkeepers. He persuaded them, and hotel managers, to put up signs telling patrons to deposit their guns with the proprietors. Cowboys and other customers might still get drunk

WILD BILL · 161

and rowdy, but gunplay would not be involved. Surprisingly, everyone agreed to the new system.

However, it wasn't long before it was challenged. J. B. Edwards, an Abilene resident until his death at 106,* recorded in his diaries a confrontation that took place in 1870. A cowboy known as Big Hank, wearing two six-shooters and backed "by a gang of gun-swinging, smirking cronies," accosted Smith on the street, with Big Hank boasting that no one could ever disarm him.

"Look, mister," Smith responded, "I am employed as marshal and shall try to maintain order and enforce the law. Be sensible about this and don't make any trouble." He added, "I must trouble you to hand me your gun."

"The hell you say," Big Hank said. "No redheaded SOB wearing a tin badge is going to take my gun!"

Seconds later, the big Texan was crumpled in the street. At first, he was unaware that he had been introduced to Smith's pugilistic prowess. When he came to, he needed little persuasion to get on his horse and ride away. His "cronies" were allowed to stay, after they turned in their guns. The marshal explained his philosophy of policing to Mayor Henry: "Anyone can bring in a dead man, but to my way of thinking a good officer is one who brings them in alive."

The felling of Big Hank did not stop the challenges; in fact, it led to another within a couple of days. The "unfair" treatment the visitor to Abilene had received was discussed at the cowboy camps, and deciding

---

*Edwards would claim to be the last man alive who had known Tom Smith and Wild Bill Hickok personally. For an obvious reason, no one stepped or was wheeled forward to challenge him.

to do something about it was a fellow known as Wyoming Frank. Wearing his guns for all to see, Frank paraded up and down the main street until Marshal Smith appeared and walked toward him.

The intensity of Smith's gaze had Frank stepping backward, but he did refuse the request to hand over his six-shooters. Smith kept backing him up until Frank felt the doors of a saloon behind him. A crowd gathered around, a few covering their ears as Frank used a few choice words to refuse another request. Smith punched him in the face twice, then took Frank's guns and beat him over the head with them. After being told to leave town, with a return to Wyoming being a good option, Frank staggered to his feet, found his horse, and was woozily on his way.

Awed by the dynamic display, the crowd was in stunned silence. Suddenly, the saloonkeeper emerged and said to Smith, "That was the nerviest act I ever saw. Here is my gun. I reckon I'll not need it so long as you are marshal of this town."

According to Edwards's diaries, Smith practiced this peacekeeping technique in other confrontations almost identical to the ones with Big Hank and Wyoming Frank. "Smith was the master," the Abilene historian Henry Jameson declared. "He became popular with the merchants, gamblers, citizens, saloonkeepers, and even most of the cowboys. Now and then he had to clip a newcomer—once slugging a guy so hard it cut his tongue in half."

So how was it there was an opening for Wild Bill Hickok in Abilene? Marshal Smith did some moonlighting as a deputy U.S. marshal, and on November 2, 1870, he was asked by James McDonald, the sheriff of Dickinson County, to help serve a warrant on Andrew McConnell and Moses Miles. The Scottish farmers were not known for their hospitality, and McConnell's record included being tried for murder, though being acquitted for self-defense. McDonald had once been Smith's deputy, and he asked the Abilene marshal to go along on the job in his capacity as a federal officer.

McConnell and Miles saw the two men riding their way, and instead of waiting to hear the charge (it was a minor one), they barricaded themselves in the dugout that was their residence. McDonald kept asking them to come out. Finally, an impatient Smith grabbed the warrant and busted the door open. McDonald followed him in, and soon there was a brawl involving all four men. The sheriff was not nearly the fighter Smith was, and at the first opportunity, he fled the dugout. Miles, now free, grabbed a rifle and shot Smith in the chest. This did not kill him, and he and McConnell continued to struggle. Miles exchanged the rifle for an ax and brought it down on Smith, nearly decapitating him. The two Scotsmen left the dead marshal where he was, and they took off even faster than McDonald had done.

A posse eventually found McConnell and Miles. They were tried and convicted and sent to prison. Smith was buried in a small cemetery. In 1904, the grave was relocated and a large granite boulder was erected that proclaimed Tom Smith a "Fearless Hero of the Frontier Days."*

Abilene was not quick to replace its marshal. This probably had to do with the time of year. Smith died at the time when the cattle trade was winding down. With policing not a priority and business in general slow during the winter months when whiteout blizzards burst out of the Plains, the local government preferred to save the $150 a

---

*Presidential historians might be interested in this connection: In one of his last roles as an actor, Ronald Reagan played Tom Smith in "No Gun Behind His Badge," an episode in the *Death Valley Days* TV series. The following year, 1966, Reagan ran for and was elected governor of California.

month. As spring of 1871 approached, though, saving salary was not as important.

Given the grisly fate of his predecessor, why did Hickok take the job? Boredom was one reason. As dangerous as the Hays City position had been, it was also exciting. Gambling and dalliances with dancing girls were fine, but they weren't occupations; they were interludes between more interesting and meaningful pursuits. They also did not provide a steady income. Hickok calculated, correctly, that an overture from a troubled town like Abilene would be backed up by some good pay. Hence, he would again wear a peace officer's badge, for the same salary as Smith received.

One more reason: by the spring of 1871, Wild Bill had grown accustomed to being the most famous figure on the American frontier. True, being a target of ambitious or simply psychotic gunslingers came with that, but Hickok was used to this by now. He took the proper precautions, and no one had gunned him down yet. Taming a town that was becoming infamous for violence and debauchery would be a huge achievement for any lawman, but if he did it—and survived, unlike the unfortunate Tom Smith—the legend of Wild Bill would eclipse all others. Add a dash of ego: after Smith, the next marshal of Abilene had a lot to live up to, and only Wild Bill Hickok was the man for the job.

That spring, Joseph McCoy was elected mayor to replace T. C. Henry. The sordid scenario that had played out in the city before Tom Smith arrived was still vivid in McCoy's mind. "We were used to seeing men killed because someone disliked their looks, the color of their eyes, the cut of their clothes, or the refusal of a drink, or because they danced too much with one girl," he wrote in *Historic Sketches of the Cattle Trade*.

So, on April 15, the new mayor swore Hickok in as the new marshal. In addition to his salary, Hickok would earn 25 percent of all fines collected. Before long, the pot was sweetened when the new top peace officer was paid an additional fifty cents for every stray dog deemed worthy of execution.

Chapter Thirteen

THE STREETS OF ABILENE

As the few existing photographs attest, Wild Bill Hickok's appearance had changed little from the first descriptions of him. Henry Jameson, using J. B. Edwards's diaries as a source, reported that Hickok's appearance in Abilene was "striking and impressive. He stood six feet, one inch, weighed 175 pounds and his graceful, straight figure, brown, wavy hair down to his shoulders, piercing gray blue eyes, fair complexion, aquiline nose, flowing mustache and always expensive dress, made him a figure to attract attention." His in-town attire of a Prince Albert coat, checked trousers, an embroidered waistcoat, and sometimes a cape lined with scarlet silk was topped off by a low-crowned, wide black hat.

Citizens of Abilene immediately noticed that not only did Hickok openly wear guns, but did so in a peculiar way. The Colts were fitted in smooth open holsters that were not worn low or tied down on the thigh but were positioned around the waist with the butts leaning forward. This allowed Hickok to cross draw or use a reverse draw with either hand. This worked well when the gunfighter wore a coat, which

Hickok routinely did. In a cross draw, the hand brushes the coat away during the movement of jerking the pistol out of the holster. Also causing comment was that from time to time when the marshal put on exhibitions, onlookers marveled at his accuracy with both hands.

As marshal, Hickok returned to familiar habits. In a saloon or restaurant, his back was to the wall, and he sat or stood facing the door. When he slept, a pistol was within easy reach. Whenever he entered a building, one hand was on a gun. On the street, he used the same caution he had in Hays City. And he often had a shotgun to complement his Colt six-shooters, derringer, and bowie knife.

A man named John Conkie was employed as the city jailer. Though this was certainly not a full-time occupation given the size of the calaboose in Abilene—it had been built a third time during Tom Smith's tenure—Conkie did get to know the marshal. One of his recollections was spotting Hickok "sitting in a barber's chair getting shaved, with his shotgun in hand and his eyes open."

Hickok found in Abilene a small but vibrant city surrounded by vast swaths of brown cattle. Stewart Verckler writes, "Wherever anyone looked, tremendous herds of longhorn dotted the spacious plains. Cattle covered every available acre of grazing land." In what would turn out to be Abilene's last year as a booming cow town before it gave way to Dodge City to the west and south, close to 121,000 head would be shipped out. One result: "The cowboys were wilder this year than they had ever been in the short history of Abilene."

The Texas Street area saloons stayed open all day and night and never lacked for business. They offered a steady diet of whiskey and beer and gambling and women, and a few saloons provided musical entertainment. Wisely, Hickok continued to enforce Smith's ban on weapons within the city limits, so gunplay was rare. Hickok may not have been quite the boxer Smith was, but he was quick and strong, and most of the men who wound up in the small jail had the imprint of Hickok's knuckles on their chins or gun barrel on the top of their heads. Unlike Smith, Hickok did not hesitate to display his ivory-handled Colts, and his demeanor clearly indicated he would use them at any sign of serious trouble. Abilene, for a time, was relatively peaceful, with the cowboy rowdiness kept at a manageable level.

But there were those who continued to resist the rule of law—especially the Texans, who didn't like the former Yankee scout who was now a marshal, anyway. One night in a saloon, several cowboys began a brawl. Hickok came in and finished it, tossing the bruised Texans out into the street. Back at their camp outside of town, the reports of the marshal's rude behavior angered their fellow cowboys. They vowed to enter Abilene the next day, subdue and handcuff Hickok, and hang him from the tallest tree on the main street.

The marshal was tipped off that about two dozen Texans were riding in, and it was easy to guess their intentions. The cowboys were surprised to encounter Hickok waiting for them in the middle of the street, outside the Last Chance Saloon—the same establishment several of them had been evicted from the night before. His usual array of weapons included a Winchester, the repeating rifle first manufactured and distributed five years earlier.

Hickok aimed it at the men at the front and center of the group and said, "Hide out, you sons of bitches."

Clearly, the cowboys had the odds. Even if Hickok emptied the rifle and both his six-shooters, there were more Texans than bullets that would find their mark in a chaotic gun battle. But the apparently fearless marshal had an almost hypnotic effect on them. And it was also clear that the men who led the hanging party would be the first to taste lead. There was a minute of tense silence as Hickok's cold-steel eyes gazed at the mounted men. Then, in twos and threes, they turned their horses and rode back out of Abilene to their camp. Time to return to Texas, where it was a lot safer.

The mayor and city council may not have considered that hiring Hickok, a legendary man-killer, could attract other shootists looking to gain a reputation. Every so often, there was a rumor of such a gunman coming to town, but no one seriously challenged Wild Bill. According to Henry Jameson, "At least eight gunners from the south were known to have come to Abilene on a specific assignment to get him. To bump him off would have added to the prestige of any man who would get away with it. Bill knew most of the eight gunmen and would greet them cockily. 'Sure am glad to see you, damn glad,' he would say. 'But hand me those guns.' They lost their courage and did."

The lawmakers also may not have considered that the marshal would enforce the law on them, too. His job description included attending city council meetings. If Hickok had to waste his time being there discussing his budget and the conduct of his deputies—one of whom was Tom Carson, a nephew of his old hero Kit Carson—the council members had damn well better be there, too. One day when the meeting time came and there was not a quorum, Hickok set out to find the missing lawmaker, S. A. Burroughs. The marshal returned with Burroughs, who promptly left again rather than remain for an important vote. Hickok set off once more. With delight, the local press reported on the outcome—the strong-shouldered marshal carrying Burroughs out of his place of business and to the council chamber, his head bouncing off Hickok's back and his feet flailing in protest.

There were any number of saloons to choose from, but for Hickok, the Alamo was his headquarters. There was an official marshal's office that Smith had inhabited, but Hickok stationed a deputy there.

He preferred to be more in the thick of things to keep his eyes on cowboys where they were most likely to congregate. He could also do a little gambling and enjoy the occasional shot of whiskey.

And the Alamo was the most elaborate of the city's saloons, which suited the more civilized tastes Hickok had acquired by this time in his life when he was spending less of it as a plainsman. The Alamo had forty feet of frontage on Cedar Street and faced west. The west entrance had three double glass doors. On the south side was the long bar with polished brass rails and fixtures. There was another bar at the rear, and above it was a large mirror. On the walls were paintings that imitated Renaissance nudes. Almost all of the floor space was covered by gaming tables. The saloon had its own orchestra, which performed from the afternoon until well into the night. Marshal Hickok usually sat at one of the tables playing poker, facing the nearest door.

More than a few residents objected—though only among themselves, certainly not to Hickok—about his use of the Alamo. It was not the appropriate place for the town's top peace officer, and the marshal might be spending more time there than he should while his deputies did more of the patrolling. That summer, during the peak cattle drive months, they included James Gainsford, who had helped to track down Tom Smith's killers; Brocky Jack Norton; and Mike Williams, in addition to Tom Carson. Hickok was probably aware of the gossip but didn't care. Plus, he believed he had fine deputies, especially Williams, who had quickly become a good friend.

No record was kept of the gunmen who visited Abilene with the notion of taking on Wild Bill Hickok, then thinking better of it and riding on. But on two occasions, the man who had become the most famous lawman on the frontier encountered young men who would go down as some of the most infamous outlaws of the American West.

O When John Wesley Hardin hit town, the precocious gunslinger was eighteen years old and on the run from an arrest warrant in Texas. Already, the son of a Methodist preacher was a veteran man-killer. His criminal career had begun four years earlier when he was expelled from school for knifing a classmate. The following year, he gunned down a former slave on an uncle's plantation in Moscow, Texas. Three army soldiers were dispatched to arrest him. Hardin ambushed and, depending on the account, killed one or all of them. The saying "I never killed a man who didn't need killing" has been attributed to Hardin, and he obviously lived in needy times because he is "credited" with sending as many as thirty men to the hereafter during his entire career.

When he arrived in Abilene, Hardin had no particular plans other than to see what all the fuss was about in this particular Kansas cow town. He knew who Wild Bill Hickok was, but it is possible that at least at first the marshal did not know Hardin. Or he didn't care all that much, if the only outstanding warrant on him was from Texas, and Hickok was not all that fond of the state. Hickok did inform the newcomer of the no-gun ordinance. In his autobiography, Hardin claims he surrendered his six-shooters using the "road agent's spin." His version of meeting the city marshal:

He pulled his pistol and said, "Take those pistols off. I arrest you."

I said all right and pulled them out of the scabbard, but while he was reaching for them, I reversed them and whirled them over on him with the muzzles in his face, springing back at the same time. I told him to put his pistols up, which he did. I cursed him for being a long-haired scoundrel that would shoot a boy with his back to him (as I had been told he intended to do to me). He said, "Little Arkansaw, you have been wrongly informed."

I shouted, "This is my fight and I'll kill the first man that fires a gun."

Bill said, "You are the gamest and quickest boy I ever saw. Let us compromise this matter and I will be your friend. Let us go in here and take a drink, as I want to talk to you and give you some advice."

Chances are, Hickok would not have fallen for this trick and allowed the teenager to get the drop on him. In any case, Hardin agreed to not wear his guns while out on the town and quickly came to admire the royally dressed, legendary lawman. Hickok made Hardin a deal—the marshal would pretend he had no knowledge of the Texas warrant if the teenager refrained from killing anyone while in Abilene.

The deal about not killing anyone did not last long. One night that summer while Hardin was asleep in the American Hotel, an intruder entered. Not waiting to learn of the man's intentions, Hardin grabbed a gun and fired, killing him. And also not waiting long enough to even pull on pants, Hardin jumped out a back window as Hickok hurried into the front lobby. Hardin landed in a small wagon, which he drove south, possibly preferring lawmen in Texas to Wild Bill's six-shooters. Along the way, he found a cowboy and took his pants and horse. Hardin told the cowboy to return the wagon and "give Wild Bill my love." He never set foot in Abilene again.

Hardin continued to evade capture for quite a while. He even went straight, marrying a Texas girl in Gonzales County, and they had three children. But domestic bliss didn't last. A killing spree in 1872 ended the lives of four men, and Hardin was arrested in Cherokee County by the sheriff. He escaped from jail and fled to Brown County, where he killed a deputy sheriff, Charles Webb, in Comanche, Texas, in May 1874. Furious Texas Rangers put John B. Armstrong on the trail of Hardin, who, after collecting his wife and kids, had gone east to Florida. It wasn't until 1877 that Hardin was located and arrested in Pensacola by Armstrong. He was found on a train, and when he grabbed his pistol, it got caught in his suspenders. His companion, nineteen-year-old James Mann, was less clumsy but also less of a marksman. His bullet went through the hat of Armstrong, who shot Mann in the chest, killing him.

After being convicted, it was hard time for Hardin, seventeen years of it in the Brown County prison, where among other occupations he studied law and headed the Sunday school. When released, he was admitted to the Texas bar and opened a law practice. During his incarceration, his wife had died, so he was free to marry, which he did to a fifteen-year-old, but the union was short-lived. So were the rest of his days.

In 1895, Hardin was practicing law in El Paso. One day, when he was standing at the bar shooting dice with a local merchant, John Selman, a man with a grievance—and who the year before had killed the appropriately named Bass Outlaw—came up behind him. Right after Hardin said, "Four sixes to beat, Henry," Selman shot him in the head. While Hardin was on the floor, Selman shot him three more times in the chest, just to be sure. Enough hometown jurors believed Selman's ridiculous claim of self-defense in the Hardin homicide that he was released. Selman was killed the following year by lawman George Scarborough, who in turn was killed in 1900 while pursuing outlaws in Arizona.

The other famous outlaw encounter Hickok had while marshal of Abilene? Well, "encounter" is an exaggeration. Sometime during the summer of 1871, Jesse and Frank James, accompanied by Cole Younger, came to Abilene. They may have believed that Abilene would be a good place to hide out, because that June, the trio, accompanied by Jim Cummins and Clell Miller, had robbed a bank in Iowa. The outlaws took a couple of rooms at Drovers Cottage. The James brothers were recognized by the desk clerk C. F. Gross, who probably kept it to himself. Only decades later, after Frank James had passed away, did Gross write several letters revealing the visit. It has been reported that Hickok knew of their arrival in Abilene, but the bank robbers packed up and left before being confronted by the marshal.

Overall, like in the other Kansas cow towns during the 1870s, the stiffest challenge came from drunken cowboys. Not all of them were from Texas, but enough of them were that residents in and around Abilene feared them. At times, the cowboys did not wait to get to a saloon in town to begin their mischief—they raided farmhouses for food and liquor. The farmers south of the city offered up a prayer for protection when they saw a big cloud of dust approaching from the south, signaling that a herd would soon pass by.

In his 1964 biography of Hickok, Joseph Rosa quotes from a letter sent to him that was written in 1936 by Lucile Stevens about an incident that had taken place when she was a child and her family saw that cloud of dust getting nearer. The family had been befriended by Hickok, who visited on Sunday afternoons and brought a sack of candy for the children. Stevens recalled:

> *The dust cloud frightened us terribly for we knew a herd was coming up the trail and the cowboys with these herds would kill any settlers they found. Usually riders were sent out from Abilene when a herd was coming, and the settlers taken to town for safety, but this time there had been no warning.*
>
> *We huddled around my father and then we saw a rider coming from the north.*

"Tis someone coming to meet them with whiskey," said my father. "That finishes it."

"What can we do?"

"Nothing. There's no way to get away or any place to hide on this prairie. We'll just have to take it."

He gathered us close and we waited. Then suddenly he cried, "Children, we're safe! I can see the rider's long yellow hair. Tis Marshal Hickok, and they'll not harm us now."

Even though that summer there were a lot of cowboys and just one marshal (with all of three deputies), Hickok and his Colt pistols and his reputation held the upper hand. He was quick to act, doing what he thought was right and damn the potential repercussions. "He often took justice in his own hands, contrary to all the conception of our courts," wrote Stewart Verckler in *Cowtown Abilene.* "As he was not trained as a peace officer, he saw no harm in running a man out of town, instead of locking him in the small jail. He had many enemies and many admitted they were out to get him in any possible way."

The toughest opposition Hickok faced in Abilene came from two men who would not strictly be considered outlaws . . . just entrepreneurs with dicey backgrounds. Their challenge, however, turned out to be more dangerous.

One of the more prominent saloons in town was the Bull's Head Tavern. It had been founded by Phil Coe and Ben Thompson, the latter still in the midst of establishing one of the more notorious reputations in the West.

Thompson was not a man destined to see old age, and there was some doubt he would survive the summer of 1871 because of his dislike of the marshal. He had been born in West Yorkshire, England, on November 2, 1843. While he was a child, the Thompson family immigrated to America, settling in Austin, Texas. As a teenager, Ben learned how to set type, and he was bent on becoming a printer. The Civil War changed those plans—two months after the attack on Fort Sumter, he enlisted in the Second Regiment, Texas Mounted Rifles, H Company, and somehow his brother, Billy, barely sixteen, managed to join the Confederate army, too. Ben was wounded during the Battle of Galveston in 1863, but he returned to his regiment, and he and Billy saw further action.

When the war ended, Ben became a mercenary, finding work fighting for Emperor Maximilian in the Mexican revolution. Along the way, he acquired a wife, whom he shipped north to Texas. When word reached him in Mexico that his wife had been attacked by her own brother, Ben returned to Texas and beat up the abuser. The injuries were so bad that Thompson was tried and convicted of attempted murder and sent to the prison known as the Huntsville Unit. His stay was a short one, though, as he received a full pardon.

Ben Thompson hit the road as a gambler, working his way up into Kansas, and was recognized for his fine clothes, mustache, and top hat. Many years later, Bat Masterson would write that Thompson "was a remarkable man in many ways and it is very doubtful if in his time there was another man living who equaled him with the pistol in a life and death struggle. The very name of Ben Thompson was enough to cause the general run of 'man killers,' even those who had never seen him, to seek safety in instant flight."

Along the way, Thompson had teamed up with Philip Haddox Coe, who was, according to Theophilus Little, a citizen who would go on to be a mayor of Abilene, "as vile a character as I ever met." The Bull's Head Tavern & Gambling Saloon—its more elaborate full name—was their pride and joy . . . and a reservoir of gambling profits. Set at the outskirts of town, it was the first drinking and gaming house the trail hands encountered as they entered Abilene. Whatever business it achieved was apparently not enough for the owners, because one day, they painted a huge bull on one of the outside walls . . . with the bull's anatomy depicted in graphic detail. Shocked citizens complained. Marshal Hickok ordered it removed, and Thompson refused. Instead of going for his gun, Hickok went for a can of paint and a brush and covered the bull.

As tough as he reportedly was, Thompson was not about to go up against the legendary man-killer himself. (He later told a friend about Hickok that he "had two hells in his eyes.") Instead, Thompson tried to convince John Wesley Hardin to do it, by telling him tall tales about Hickok's hatred of Texans. The teenager really didn't care and by now considered the marshal something of an idol. Finally, Hardin had enough of Thompson's talk.

"I am not doing anybody's fighting just now except my own, but I know how to stick to a friend," he said. "If Bill needs killing, why don't you kill him yourself?" Thompson demurred, increasing his life expectancy.

Neither was Coe about to try to outdraw Hickok, even though by the time of his residing in Abilene, Coe had acquired a reputation as a gunfighter. Born in July 1839 in Gonzales, Texas, he joined the Confederate army the first year of the war, and when he left in April 1863, he was a member of the Thirty-Sixth Texas Cavalry. He wandered south into Mexico, and it is believed it was there he hooked up with Ben Thompson, with both men being mercenaries for the embattled emperor, who was executed in June 1867.

Over time, Coe worked his way back north, through Texas and then up into Kansas, living and gambling in Salina in 1870. He arrived in Abilene a month after Hickok did, reuniting with Thompson. He had gotten to be friends with John Wesley Hardin, so Coe also suggested that Hardin show in the most emphatic way that the teenager could whip the thirty-four-year-old marshal in a fair gunfight. Again, Hardin was not so inclined.

When the two owners of the Bull's Head did not paint another bull, or any other animal, on the side of their saloon, word spread that Hickok had intimidated them into submission. Hearing the gossip, an enraged Coe confronted the marshal and declared that he, too, was a stone-cold shootist and "I could kill a crow on the wing." Hickok coolly gazed at him, then queried, "Did the crow have a pistol? Was he shooting back? I will be."

Several accounts suggest that what escalated the tension between Coe and Hickok beyond Wild Bill's having emasculated the Bull's Head wall was that they were seeing the same girl. In a typical Kansas cow town like Abilene where the men far outnumbered the women, rivalries were common. Jameson even identified her as "a dance hall girl named Jessie Hasel."

This was not uncommon for Hickok. Domestic bliss for any length of time was not his style. Henry Jameson reported that he "always had a mistress in every town. One of his favorites in Abilene was supposed to have been an Indian girl whom he kept in a nice little cottage on the outskirts of town."

Whether or not this was true—she could have been another one of his "Indian Annies"—Hickok enjoyed consorting with several women while in Abilene. However, it was at this time in Abilene that his love life took a dramatic turn—when the circus came to town.

Sep the 28 . 1856

Dear mother you day wright
often how have I when it
has be more than three months
since I left home and only
received to letters from
home you want to know
what I am doing you dont
know what I com to Cansas
for os you would not ask
me that I will tell you
before long what I am doing
and what I have been doing
the excitement is purty much
over · have seen since ive been
hary sites that would make
the wickidest harts sick believe
me mother for what I say is
true I cant com home home
tis fall It would not look
will tell the boys all to write
Miss ish I hope is well and isibell
tis is from yours J B Hickok

A letter written by Jim Hickok to his mother, Polly, on September 28, 1856,
describes his teenage adventures in Missouri and Kansas. (*Courtesy of the Kansas
State Historical Society*)

In Santa Fe, Kit Carson befriended Jim Hickok, who as a boy had read pulp stories about Carson's adventures . . . only a few of them being true. (*Courtesy of the Library of Congress*)

Titled "The Struggle for Life," this illustration published in *Harper's New Monthly Magazine* offers a much-exaggerated depiction of Hickok taking on the McCanles "gang." (*Courtesy of the Nebraska State Historical Society*)

The abolitionist John Brown and his sons were responsible for the Pottawatomie Massacre during the "Bleeding Kansas" years. (*Courtesy of the Library of Congress*)

The fiery James H. Lane rose through the ranks of the Free State movement to represent Kansas in the U.S. Senate. (*Courtesy of the Library of Congress*)

William Quantrill was the most notorious of the leaders of guerilla groups who brutally murdered and plundered settlements in Kansas. (*Courtesy of the Kansas State Historical Society*)

A raid by an army led by William Quantrill in 1863 killed close to 150 people and left Lawrence, Kansas, in ruins. (*Courtesy of the Library of Congress*)

"For Life or Death," also published in *Harper's New Monthly Magazine*, purportedly illustrates one of Hickok's many daring escapes during the Civil War. (*Courtesy of Nebraska State Historical Society*)

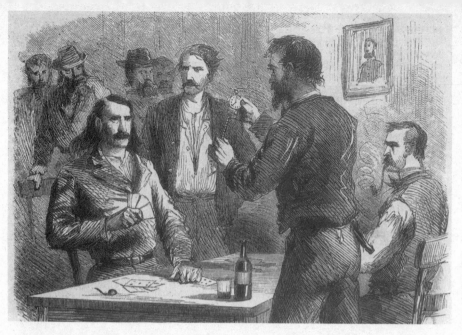

Another *Harper's New Monthly Magazine* illustration shows the poker confrontation between Hickok and Davis Tutt that led to their gunfight in Springfield, Missouri. (*Courtesy of the Nebraska State Historical Society*)

Stanley met Livingstone several years after Henry Stanley met Wild Bill Hickok. (*Courtesy of the Library of Congress*)

Both George and Elizabeth Custer were mightily impressed by the fine features of frontiersman Bill Hickok. (*Courtesy of the Library of Congress*)

During his Army scout days, Wild Bill (*at left, in white hat*) was a frequent visitor to Fort Harker, as shown in 1867. (*Courtesy of the Kansas State Historical Society*)

An idealized portrait of Buffalo Bill in 1872. He and Wild Bill shared a long friendship and many adventures on the frontier and the stage. (*Courtesy of the Library of Congress*)

The stockyards built by the McCoy brothers in Abilene became a centerpiece of a town growing faster than law enforcement. (*Courtesy of the Library of Congress*)

Drovers Cottage was not only a symbol of Abilene's prosperity but a favorite meeting place for local and visiting businessmen. (*Courtesy of the Library of Congress*)

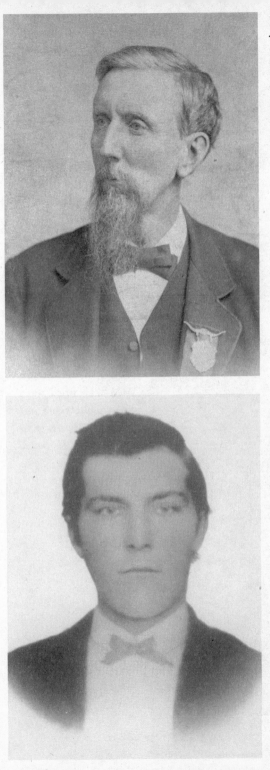

Joseph McCoy and his two brothers brought prosperity to Abilene by making it the intersection of the railroad and cattle drives up from Texas. (*Courtesy of the Kansas State Historical Society*)

John Wesley Hardin and Wild Bill worked out an uneasy truce during the young gunman's short visit to Abilene. (*Courtesy of the Library of Congress*)

Ben Thompson, shown here as a peace officer in Austin, ran afoul of Marshal Hickok in Abilene. (*Courtesy of the Kansas State Historical Society*)

Agnes Lake Thatcher Hickok, the only woman Wild Bill married, was a circus pioneer and impresario. (*Courtesy of the Kansas State Historical Society*)

California Joe Milner, one of Hickok's best friends, shown here in the Black Hills in 1875. (*Courtesy of the South Dakota State Historical Society*)

It is believed that this photograph of "five plainsmen" was taken in 1875 and includes, in addition to Hickok (*second from left*), Colorado Charley Utter, and Texas Jack Omohundro. (*Courtesy of the South Dakota State Historical Society*)

Calamity Jane during the time she claimed to be serving as a scout for Gen. George Crook on his Indian-fighting expeditions. (*Courtesy of the Library of Congress*)

The rough-and-tumble Deadwood, South Dakota, in 1876, when Wild Bill came to town. (*Courtesy of the Library of Congress*)

"The Trial of Jack McCall" became a popular production on the frontier, depicting the conviction of the cowardly assassin. (*Courtesy of the South Dakota State Historical Society*)

Calamity Jane at Wild Bill Hickok's grave in Deadwood in 1903, not long before she died and was buried next to him. (*Courtesy of the Library of Congress*)

Chapter Fourteen

A THREE-RING ROMANCE

The Hippo-Olympiad and Mammoth Circus was the grand name of the production that arrived in Abilene during the summer of 1871. It was owned and operated by a pioneer in the male-dominated industry, Agnes Thatcher Lake. She had one of the most remarkable lives of any nineteenth-century American woman—which included being the love of Wild Bill Hickok's life. This fact has been overshadowed by the notoriety of Calamity Jane and the fabrications about her "romance" with Hickok, robbing Mrs. Lake of some of the spotlight she deserves in American history.

Maria Agnes Pohlschneider was born on August 24, 1826, in what is now northwestern Germany. She was the ninth child of her parents, Friedrich and Catharina, who were farmers. When Agnes was six, she and her father, by then a widower, and three of his sons sailed to the United States. They were at the forefront of a robust German migration, which saw close to two hundred thousand citizens of that country look for a new life in America between 1833 and 1843. They landed in Baltimore and traveled west to settle near Cincinnati because that city had become a haven for German immigrants. The father would soon be known as Frederick Mersman, having Americanized his first name and adopted a version of his original last name.

Agnes actually lived out the fantasy some children have of running away to join the circus. This was not what Frederick Mersman had in mind for the only daughter under his care. The expectation, when she was turning sixteen, was that Agnes would settle down with a German-born merchant and raise children in some comfort in Cincinnati. In fact, a grocer had already been selected for her. But then the circus came to town, and with it was a performer billed as Bill Lake.

William Lake Thatcher had joined the Mammoth Circus & Gymnastic Arena Company when he was seventeen. Listed as "Master Thatcher," he performed horse-riding tricks. He also worked as a juggler and a clown, and he had a dog act. He was adept at putting up and taking down the huge white tents and driving wagons. Whatever it took to make a living in the circus business, Master Thatcher could do it, and any production was glad to have him. By the spring of 1846, when Agnes was nineteen and the Great Western Circus arrived, it was the thirty-year-old Bill Lake she saw perform.

Agnes was so smitten that she immediately ran off with Bill, which both appalled and frightened the Mersman family. A clown was perhaps the last person her father and brothers thought she would marry, and they knew something of what a rough, itinerant existence circus life was. Undeterred, Agnes and Bill were married in Louisiana, and she began her career as a performer, one that would include becoming a circus legend and pioneer and having a daughter who became an international star.

For the first year after their marriage, Bill taught Agnes the circus life, which entailed not only performing a variety of acts but doing everything involved with setting up and breaking down and moving such a complicated operation. Then in 1847, she made her debut as an equestrian and singer with the Rockwell & Company's New York Circus. The following year, the couple were in Cincinnati, where Agnes was reunited with her family and she performed a slack-wire routine, though she was pregnant. She gave birth to a stillborn baby, but this did not stop her return to the rings. In January 1849, in New Orleans, Agnes gave birth to a boy. Alas, the city was deep into a cholera epidemic—the baby contracted it and died at only twelve days old. The couple continued to thrive professionally, at least, with Bill gaining fame as a clown and Agnes as an equestrian. And finally, they had children.

In 1858, the couple adopted a seven-year-old, Alice, and around the same time another young girl, Emma, joined the family. Both were already or soon to become performers, Alice as an equestrian and Emma as a dancer playing the hornpipe. Several years later, Agnes and Bill adopted William Dale, the seven-year-old son of another circus performer who had passed away. Billed as Little Willie, he became a rider with the circus, too. And during these years, the Lakes had become popular enough performers and had saved sufficient funds that they could own their own circus company.

Actually, with various partners—including for a time James Anthony Bailey, who would later team up with P. T. Barnum to form the world's most famous circus—the Lakes owned several companies, with a few simply going out of business during the difficult Civil War years when large swaths of the South and Mid-Atlantic states were off-limits. They persevered, however, with Bill Lake being both a clown and an animal trainer and Agnes doing just about everything else. During one stop in December 1864, troops under General George Thomas arrived at the circus and confiscated all its horses to

182 · TOM CLAVIN

be used in an attack on the Confederate forces of General John Bell Hood—thus, the pampered four-legged performers overnight became cannon fodder.

With paying customers still scarce when the war ended, Agnes Lake left the American circuit for the arenas of Europe. There, heading a production titled *Mazeppa*, a show featuring amazing feats of horse-riding skill, Agnes became a star. She performed in Prussia and Germany and elsewhere, and when she returned to the States, *Mazeppa* was in great demand. At forty, married for over two decades, and more or less having raised three children, Agnes Lake was one of America's most popular performers.

She also suffered a series of tragedies. Two younger brothers died, one from alcoholism and the other from tuberculosis. Late in 1867, her oldest daughter, Alice, who was emerging on her own as an equestrian, was married to John Wilson, who had once worked for her parents' circus. The honeymoon trip included taking a steamer from Mobile to New Orleans. During the trip, Alice fell overboard and drowned. An especially devastating event took place in 1869: Bill Lake was killed. Such was the couple's stature by then that the news was carried by publications around the country.

It happened in Granby, Missouri, on August 21. The Lakes' Hippo-Olympiad was in the midst of a successful summer tour, with newspapers proclaiming Bill Lake the "Napoleon of Showmen." After that evening's performance, a man named Jacob Killian was found hiding inside a tent, apparently hoping to not pay to see a minstrel show. He argued with ushers, and Lake was summoned. When he arrived, he grabbed Killian and went to throw him out of the tent. The man pulled out a revolver, which Lake wrenched from him. A cursing and threatening Killian was deposited outside.

A few minutes later, Killian reappeared. Having possessed or ob-

WILD BILL · 183

tained another revolver, he approached Lake and fired. The bullet struck Lake in the upper right chest. "My God, boys, I am killed!" he exclaimed. "Carry me home." Lake was brought to his room at a nearby hotel, where, a few minutes after a distraught Agnes arrived, he died.

The killer, described in newspaper articles as a "drunken ruffian," escaped. A reward, which included a contribution from the governor of Missouri, was raised, and a manhunt ensued. He was captured several weeks later, outside St. Louis. However, it would not be until five years after that Killian would go on trial. By then, some witnesses had drifted away, and Agnes herself did not attend the proceedings. Still, the prosecution's presentation and a handful of remaining witnesses were enough to produce a guilty verdict. Agnes and her family were shocked when the sentence was less than four years in prison.

Killian served his time and was released. Soon after, while in Short Creek, Kansas, Killian was murdered. In the subsequent trial the defendant, A. S. Norton, was acquitted by the jury.

Though left a grieving widow at forty-three in 1869 with two children still under her care, Agnes Lake determined to carry on. She had no choice—the circus was her entire life, and it was an all-consuming one.

"Following the White Tops" was the phrase describing people who were with the circus. The first equestrian display dubbed a "circus" in the United States was held in 1793 in Philadelphia, and one of the impressed patrons was President George Washington. By the 1860s, there were as many as two dozen or more large companies crisscrossing the United States and the western territories. Most of them set off in the spring, worked their way north and west through the summer, retreated south in the fall, and spent the winter resting up and preparing for the next season. The circus was also known as a "wagon show" because the nomadic troupes traveled in wooden wagons, and some of them were transformed into stages featuring performers who did not require much space. With the so-called freak shows, for example, the "acts" simply had to sit or stand on a platform and be ogled by amused or horrified patrons.

In 1871, there were twenty-six such traveling shows active in America. They included John Robinson's Circus, Menagerie, and Museum; Frederic H. Bailey's Circus and Menagerie; P. T. Barnum's Circus, Menagerie, and Museum; Mrs. Agnes Lake's Hippo-Olympiad and Mammoth Circus; and Adam Forepaugh's Circus and Menagerie. Many of the owners and managers and performers had worked for or with one another in previous circus incarnations. While inevitably there were rivalries and competitive conflicts, circus people were something of a society unto themselves.

Gil Robinson, a third-generation circus proprietor, remarked in his memoir *Old Wagon Show Days* that "circus people fairly earned the association of roughness which has always clung to them. But they were not a rude lot; under the skin they were, and have always remained, gentle and tender-hearted." One example he pointed to was that when a traveling show came to a town "where a circus man of any prominence is buried, memorial services are held at his grave between the matinee and the night show. Every trouper with the show attends, as well as a large number of the citizens of the town, who are attracted by the rather [strong] display of sentiment."

Many of the circuses were alike in having riding exhibitions, trampoline and trapeze acrobats, lion and tiger tamers, freak shows, elephants and hippos, fire-eaters, and of course clowns. The most prominent clown of the nineteenth century was Dan Rice. He joined the Robinson family's show in 1840 and traveled with its extended branches for fifty-three years. At the peak of his career, he earned one thousand dollars a week and thus was one of the highest-paid entertainers in the country.

The occupation the Robinsons, the Lakes, and vigorous entrepreneurs like Barnum and Bailey chose was often not a comfortable one, especially for the everyday performers who often doubled as the road crew. They did not eat in restaurants or sleep in hotels. They made camp on the outskirts of towns, ate what was cooked over open fires, and slept in or under their wagons. Only the worst weather stopped them, because if there was no show, there was no income. Treacherous and just plain poor traveling conditions had to be overcome. In the South, for example, for years after the Civil War, Gil Robinson recalled, "it was necessary to send out a brigade of workmen with pickaxes and shovels to repair the highways before it was possible for the show to move." Where bridges had been destroyed and not replaced, the traveling shows had to figure out ways to ford streams and rivers, which could involve "the use of block and tackle."

The expansion of the railroads west meant fewer long wagon trains and new opportunities. As settlements grew, so, too, did the potential audiences, especially in areas that had few if any forms of entertainment other than singing and dancing girls in saloons, places not frequented by women and children. The wagon shows working their way west could cover thousands of miles in long, circuitous routes in a single season. They usually found grateful audiences. According to Linda A. Fisher and Carrie Bowers, in their biography of Agnes Lake, "The performances, however brief, gave isolated communities a break from the monotony of pioneer life and fueled the imaginations of individuals far from America's bustling cities."

When Mrs. Agnes Lake's Hippo-Olympiad arrived in Abilene on July 31, 1871, its pioneering proprietor—she was the first woman in America to own a circus—was still mourning the shocking loss of her husband. And about to turn forty-five, with a family to raise and a cumbersome business to run, Agnes may not even have been thinking of a romantic involvement. Then she met the eleven-years-younger Wild Bill Hickok.

Her circus troupe and animals had notched thousands of miles on the rails that season, going as far west as Salt Lake City. The local press had been trumpeting the impending arrival of the circus, and people couldn't wait to pay for tickets. Watching clowns, horses, hippos, and such disembark at the train station was a show unto itself, as was the parade down the main street. As work crews set up just to the west of the city, Agnes went to the marshal's office to secure the necessary performance permits. Without going into any detail, Fisher and Bowers report that when Agnes encountered Hickok "their meeting left a marked impression on them both."

It was probably more than that, because what began in Abilene would continue for the next five years.

Most likely, Hickok attended at least one of the two or three circus performances to provide the required security as well as to see what kind of operation Mrs. Lake was taking all over the country. He had a lot of company. According to *The Abilene Chronicle* of August 3, "The attendance was large at each performance." There would be no lingering to get better acquainted, though. Agnes was a very self-disciplined businesswoman, and she had a lot of mouths to feed. The show must go on. After the final performance, the Hippo-Olympiad packed onto an eastbound train for a weeklong gig in St. Louis.

The Lake circus season ended in late October in her former hometown of Cincinnati. From there, Agnes traveled to a farm in Kentucky she had purchased after her husband's death. There, waiting out the winter, she tried to reconcile the lurid tales readily available in the dime-store novels and pulp publications about or featuring Wild Bill Hickok with the charming, soft-spoken lawman who had taken at least a piece of her heart.

The appearance of the circus in Abilene and of Agnes Lake in Hickok's heart did not do anything to improve the situation with Ben Thompson and Phil Coe. Thompson left town to bring his family back to Texas, and injuries from a buggy accident there prevented him from returning to Abilene. Coe would have to harbor the resentment against Hickok all by himself in the coming weeks. Finally, on October 5, that resentment boiled over.

The first week of that month was something of a climax to another profitable cattle drive season, and many of the Texans in town wanted to have one last hurrah before returning south. The festivities began at the Applejack Saloon, and then the expanding group of cowboys worked their way to other saloons, plucking local people off the street to buy them drinks. Hickok was in a nearby boardinghouse eating supper, and when the crowd approached, he stepped outside. However, he saw no guns were involved, just some mischief, so he gave them enough money for drinks at their next stop, the Novelty Theatre.

Sometime later, around 9 P.M., Hickok and his friend Deputy Mike Williams were outside the theater, but the crowd of cowboys had already moved on. The lawmen heard a shot coming from Cedar Street. "Be right back," Hickok said, and he walked away. He found the crowd outside the Alamo, and the only one displaying a gun was Phil Coe, who contended he had just shot at a dog. The marshal was about to turn away when Coe turned the gun on him.

The Bull's Head co-owner was not fast enough. In an instant, Hickok drew and fired both of his Colts, with one witness reporting that "he fired with marvelous rapidity and characteristic accuracy."

Simultaneously, Coe got off a couple of shots, which went astray. He was hit twice in the stomach. After being in agony for four days, he died.

There was another death seconds later. Hearing the flurry of gunshots, Williams had rushed to help Hickok. When, with gun drawn, he abruptly appeared at the corner of Hickok's vision, the marshal wheeled and fired each pistol. Both bullets hit their mark, and Williams was dead by the time he met the street.

"If any of you want the rest of these pills, come and get them," Hickok told the crowd, which began to back away. To the cowboys: "Now, every one of you mount your horses and ride for camp damn quick."

As they were complying, Hickok fully realized he had shot and killed Williams, not a Coe accomplice. At that moment, Wild Bill began to change inside. For much of his adult life, he had adhered to the philosophy that he'd killed only those worth killing, meaning Confederates and related enemies during the Civil War, people who intended to do him harm after the war, and Indians anytime. Coe, obviously, would have mercilessly gunned him down if he hadn't reacted fast enough. But Mike Williams was a different matter. He was a good man, a good deputy, and a good friend, and he sure didn't deserve killing. Certainly, not at Hickok's hands.

This was not an event that Hickok spoke or wrote letters to family back in Illinois about, so it can only be surmised what he was thinking. Wild Bill, probably for the first time, felt regret. He had reacted too quickly and with deadly force. Hickok, the most famous and feared lawman on the frontier, began to doubt himself.

But the night's events were not over. Hickok managed to disperse the cowboys and others in the crowd. Noting that Coe was still alive, he sent for a preacher to attend to him. He picked up Williams's body and carried him into the saloon, laying him out on the largest poker table. Then, making sure he replaced the bullets in his pistols, and with a fully loaded shotgun, Hickok went back out into the cool autumn night.

He went from one saloon to another, telling the Texans to get out of Abilene or die right there. Word spread faster than Wild Bill could walk, and the last saloons he visited were pretty much deserted. Every cowboy was cleared out. It would be several days before thirsty men left their camps and ventured back into town, hoping the hotheaded Hickok had cooled off.

The day after the shootings, Hickok wired Williams's mother in Kansas City with the tragic news and also sent money for her travel to Abilene. He purchased a fine casket, and after Mrs. Williams arrived, Hickok arranged for a service. He paid all the bills for mother and son to be sent back to Kansas City.

When Ben Thompson got word of Coe's death at the hands of the frontier's most famous gunfighter, he realized chance had allowed him to escape the same fate. This changed him, too. Though he continued to have the reputation as a quick-on-the-draw gunman, Thompson mostly acted on the right side of the law. He encountered Wyatt Earp, who was then a young deputy, in Ellsworth, where Ben and his brother, Billy, accidentally killed a marshal. (Ben was not charged, and Billy was later acquitted.) Ben sort of redeemed himself by saving Bat Masterson's life in a shoot-out in Mobeetie, Texas, and went on to live a reasonably lawful life as a gambler, killing just a couple of men in what were ruled self-defense actions, and he even spent some time as a peace officer in Austin. He was forty-one when he was killed in a gunfight in a vaudeville theater in San Antonio. Ben Thompson's body was returned to Austin, and his grave can be found in the Oakwood Cemetery there.

Hickok may have hoped that the killings of Coe and Williams would have been even more of a deterrent to would-be assassins. A few weeks later, that hope was dashed. Three men arrived in Abilene and let it be known their purpose was to kill Wild Bill. They claimed to have been hired by the mother of a man whom Hickok had killed— some accounts having her being Phil Coe's mother in Texas—and the price on Hickok's head was ten thousand dollars.

When the marshal heard this, he had a decision to make. It was quite possible that in a shoot-out in the middle of the street, Hickok could have prevailed over all three. And issuing such a challenge to the trio would be smarter than risking an ambush. But he was the law, and it wouldn't do right by Abilene to have its peace officer provoking a shoot-out. Innocent people could be killed, and when word spread of such a dramatic event, even more men with ambitions or dollar signs in their eyes might want to take a turn. Hickok said he was leaving town on the next train to Topeka.

The three men had not come to Abilene to rid it of its marshal. They couldn't have cared less about the city. They wanted to kill Hickok and collect the ten grand. If he got away, they got nothing, so when that train to Topeka left, they were on it. They sat in one of the coaches, waiting to make their move. They waited too long. Hickok and his sawed-off shotgun surprised them. He forced them between cars and, with the train going at a good clip, convinced them to jump. They never reappeared.

Hickok had made the right move, but he couldn't shake the feeling of being a marked man, not just in the streets of Abilene but throughout the frontier. At just thirty-four, he was already beginning to feel tired of being a legend. There was no hiding out for such a man. Outlaws and assassins and bogus bounty hunters like the three men he had just outwitted would find him easily enough, especially if he stayed in Abilene. Maybe being a roaming plainsman again was a good idea . . . though no amount of travel would distance him from his sorrow over killing Mike Williams.

Hickok may have sensed his lawman days were coming to a close only weeks before they actually ended. This coincided with the beginning of the end of Abilene as a thriving cow town. More of the city's population, tired of the Texans and the havoc they caused, wanted Abilene to pursue other businesses. Farmers and their farmland took up more space than grazing lands. A group called the Farmers' Protective Association objected to cattle tromping on agricultural tracts. The railroad had moved on, and towns farther west were closer destinations for the herds shuffling north from Texas. The city council considered a proposal to ban Texas cattle altogether. And there were objections to the high taxes caused by the law-enforcement budget.

In Abilene, anyway, Hickok had become obsolete. On December 13, 1871, after only eight months in office, the marshal was let go. "Where Abilene's star went into a decline, its Cowtown era a memory, Wild Bill's was on the ascent," comments Joseph Rosa. "Abilene did much for Hickok. His brief period as the city's marshal had spread his legend down the trail to Texas and to other places. Come what may, his fame was now assured."

There was no need for Abilene lawmakers to hand Hickok a pink slip—he had already gone, on his way to the final act of Wild Bill's life.

ACT III

*An older Wild Bill, in 1875, the year before
his fateful journey to Deadwood.*

(COURTESY OF THE KANSAS STATE
HISTORICAL SOCIETY)

➤➤

A reputation always changed slower than a man.

—PETE DEXTER, *DEADWOOD*

Chapter Fifteen

THE RUNNING OF THE BULLS

With the town fathers concluding that Abilene was safe enough that it did not need a marshal, Wild Bill Hickok was suddenly out of a job. With his experiences in Hays City and Abilene as well as being a frontier federal marshal, lawman had become his primary occupation. By the end of 1871, his fame was as much as a lawman as a gunfighter. With Wild Bill, the two occupations were intertwined. Smith may have been the more peace-loving peace officer by keeping his guns concealed and relying more on his fists, but Hickok was more the prototype for an effective sheriff or marshal—be the toughest and the quickest, and kill those who need killing.

Ironically, during the 1870s and into the '80s, this was the kind of lawman more towns and counties began to shun as they became more "civilized" and a law-and-order system became further entrenched. Hickok was both the prototype and the first victim of progress on the American frontier. He would stay the same, true to himself, while the West changed around him.

The firing was also bad news because Abilene had become something of a safe haven for Hickok. True, there were citizens who did not like him, and as those bounty hunters on the Topeka train had demonstrated, there could be the occasional visitor looking for trouble or a reputation. But Hickok was on his own turf, and Abilene gave him a home-field advantage, especially because there were also many residents who did like or at least respected him. He had become one of theirs.

Essentially homeless, as 1871 turned into 1872, Hickok returned to his wandering ways, at first staying in Kansas. He was gambling a lot and possibly drinking even more than before, even though he had to recognize that being a gunfighter without a badge meant he was more exposed as a marked man and could not afford a weakness. As he moved about, he was like a turtle without its shell, very vulnerable out in the open. In any town at any time, a man-killer could want to prove he was *the* fastest, and the most direct and visible way to do that was to outdraw and kill Wild Bill. There was nowhere to hide; everyone everywhere on the frontier knew Hickok. And he wasn't about to change his distinctive and immediately recognizable appearance. By this time in his life, he would not be one to blend in, even if that attitude cost him his life.

Hickok was a celebrity. He was famous. He was feared. He was already a legend. It is estimated that over fifteen hundred dime novels were written just about Buffalo Bill Cody, beginning in 1869, when he was only twenty-three, into the 1930s, and during the early years Wild Bill was in that same category of iconic western hero. He had risen to the heights of both reputation and fabrication . . . and now the slow, inexorable descent began. Like a Hamlet or Macbeth or another of Shakespeare's tragic heroes, there would be no escaping his fate.

But Hickok tried. He decided to move on from Kansas, hoping to find shelter where he was less well known. He worked his way west and wound up in Colorado, where he found a man who would become one of his best friends.

In Charles H. Utter,* as he was known at the time, Hickok might have thought he was consorting with a shorter version of himself. Utter was about average height for a man in the 1870s, five foot six, but he wore fringed and beaded buckskins, his curly light-brown hair hung to his shoulders, he, too, took a bath daily (though it was more often outdoors), he was fastidious about his dress, he wore a revolver on each hip, and he derived much of his income from gambling. A huge difference was there were no reports of Utter being a man-killer. It probably helped the friendship of the two men that Utter was not a magnet for violence, and perhaps Hickok felt a bit safer. As with Buffalo Bill Cody and California Joe Milner, Hickok's friendship with Utter was among his most enduring.

Utter had been born near Niagara Falls, the New York side, in 1838, but he grew up on a farm in Illinois his parents owned next to the property of William Bross, who was for a time the state's lieutenant governor. Young Charley was a frequent visitor to the Bross home, and he would later accompany the former state official on hunting and exploring trips to Colorado.

Utter's life of roaming adventure began when he was nineteen. The United States was in the midst of an economic depression, and he left the family farm to find work elsewhere, heading west. Like Hickok, who was only one year older, Utter wound up in Kansas. However, unlike Hickok, he didn't stay long. An area soaked with blood from

*As will be seen in various accounts, Charley and Charlie were used interchangeably to refer to him.

Bushwhackers and Border Ruffians and Red Legs and Jayhawkers was not for him. Utter heard about gold being found near Pikes Peak. Sometime in 1858, he arrived in Middle Park, an area in Utah Territory at the time (it later became part of Colorado), west of the Snowy Range. He was the only white man there, and no one bothered him while he was busy trapping game and prospecting for gold. He built a cabin there and was befriended by Ute Indians who passed through on hunting expeditions.

Over the years, Utter gained the reputation of being a first-rate trapper and hunter. Prospectors began to show up, mines were dug into hillsides, and towns sprang up around them. Utter continued his own way through the Civil War, which had little impact on Middle Park and its immediate surroundings. He had a couple of sidelines, one being as a territorial clerk who recorded land claims, the other as an interpreter between Indians and government agents. Otherwise, though, he spent months on his own. An article in the June 28, 1865, edition of *The Daily Miners' Register* began, "Charley Utter, our agreeable young mountaineer friend, came over from his far off haunts yesterday. For many months Charley has lived alone in the unexplored regions of the Parks, upwards of two hundred miles from the habitations of white men, with no companion save a trusty dog, and an occasional cinnamon or grizzly visitor."

Apparently, his appreciation of solitude had its limits. The following year, he relocated to Empire, Colorado, building a ranch on Bard Creek. In September 1866, Charley Utter married Matilda Nash, who was all of fifteen. An item in *The Denver Tribune* two years later remarked that since "he got married [he] has lived a civilized life." Utter was residing in Georgetown, Colorado, then, and he and his wife had at least one child. In June 1871, Utter could not have been aware of the coincidence of Agnes Lake's circus troupe performing in Georgetown several weeks before it reached Abilene, but he and his family probably attended.

Though a family man, Utter was still a keen gambler, and most likely, he was at a gaming table in a hotel or saloon in Georgetown in early spring 1872 when Wild Bill Hickok strolled in. As the careful former marshal scanned the occupants, his blue eyes may have settled on Charley Utter because of their similarities of dress. They became friends immediately. "He was out of work and put in most of his time playing poker," wrote A. D. McCandless in a letter to the Kansas State Historical Society about Hickok when McCandless, who would become a lawyer, worked at a mine outside Georgetown. "He was very pleasant and agreeable, and never had any trouble while there."

But Hickok stayed, at most, only two months. Then he moseyed on east, winding up back in Kansas City. It was there that he received what could reasonably be said to be the most disturbing news of his life.

For some time, Hickok had been experiencing some difficulties with his eyes. There was occasional blurred vision and some irritation. For a clerk in a dry goods store, this would not have been cause for concern, but for a famous gunslinger . . .

He sought out a physician in Kansas City who was known to be an expert on eye ailments. The diagnosis given to Hickok was potentially devastating—he could eventually go blind. To this day, there are several theories as to what the exact condition was. The eminent researcher Joseph Rosa goes on for pages with different possible explanations, then concludes "that what Wild Bill really suffered with will remain a mystery, owing to the absence of medical records."

One plausible cause was secondary syphilis. Hickok was no stranger to "soiled doves," and many of the prostitutes on the frontier had venereal diseases. A possible consequence of that disease is iritis, resulting in cloudy vision, some pain in the eyes, and a sensitivity to light. Glaucoma was another possibility, as were trachoma and chronic conjunctivitis. Whatever the cause of his troubles, Hickok was not given much hope of reversing their course, and at the time, few remedies were available. Thus, a famous gunfighter whose accurate eyesight and quick reflexes had saved his life more than a few times was faced with becoming an invalid dependent on others . . . if he lived that long.

That could have been one reason why Hickok was open to a change of careers. Many people believe that it was Buffalo Bill Cody who created the concept of a Wild West show. This is understandable, as he spent decades organizing and presenting such productions, some of them featuring famous frontier figures like Annie Oakley and Sitting Bull, and others who purported to be. And Cody made a fortune doing it. But before Buffalo Bill ever trod the floorboards of a stage, Wild Bill tried his hand at being a producer and performer.

This would seem uncharacteristic, because Hickok was not an orator or actor and would seem more comfortable telling tales around a campfire under a starry prairie sky. But he couldn't have helped noticing how crowds gathered when he put on shooting exhibitions and how much people enjoyed the free entertainment. And thanks to Agnes Lake and her circus, Hickok had witnessed the joy of people as they sat watching acts involving horses and other animals perform. All this combined with two other factors in the spring of 1872 to provide the inspiration to produce a show: Wild Bill was bored, and he had accumulated several thousand dollars in gambling winnings.

Most likely, he had listened to talk in saloons by visitors from the east of circus troupes in addition to Agnes Lake's that crisscrossed the more populated areas, some of them including Wild West segments featuring men dressed as cowboys and Indians. Hickok had the idea of a show that would focus only on the West. Such an exotic exhibition would fascinate audiences, many of whom would not otherwise experience anything about the American frontier. Mostly, though, Hickok listened to the siren song of Colonel Sidney Barnett.

Barnett, who would live to the impressive age of eighty-nine, was thirty-six in 1872, a year older than Wild Bill when they met in Kansas City. The son of a museum owner on the Canadian side of Niagara Falls, Barnett had been sent west to recruit performers. To boost tourism, the Barnetts had originally tried to put together a production that would feature Indians from the American frontier, a couple of cowboys doing horse tricks, and supposedly authentic Mexican vaqueros. The younger Barnett rounded up several men willing to dress up and perform these roles. During a stop at Fort McPherson in Nebraska, Barnett met Texas Jack Omohundro and a group of Pawnee, and they were invited to Canada. However, when informed that the Indians would not be allowed by the Grant administration to cross the border, Texas Jack decided to pass on the production and remain in the States.

Barnett was persistent. He hired Indians from the Sac and Fox tribes who, unlike the Pawnee, were not subjected to the same travel restrictions. And then he met Hickok. Intrigued, Wild Bill agreed to invest in the project, whatever it was going to be, and serve as master of ceremonies, plus he would have an opportunity to see Canada, even if just a small corner of it. The two men conceived of a production titled *The Daring Buffalo Chase of the Plains*.

This idea should have been allowed to fade away like the next morning's hangover, but Hickok became truly enamored with it. He was told that Niagara Falls had already become a popular tourist attraction in the summer and a new, somewhat exotic show about the

American West would be a raging success. The cast of the show would include the new Indians signed up, cowboys who wanted a break from long, exhausting cattle drives, and, of course, buffalo.

In May, Hickok began to pull the production together. Three cowboys were found who probably thought a lark with Wild Bill to Canada could be more fun and profitable than returning to Texas. The nascent troupe traveled to Nebraska and found plenty of buffalo there. The challenge, however, was capturing them. As Cody and others had demonstrated, killing American bison was not a difficult task. And they could be herded into pens without too much trouble. But capturing and transporting a relatively small number, even with the promise of stage fame, was another matter. Hickok had done a lot of jobs in his thirty-five years, but this was not one of them.

The animals did not cooperate with being lassoed, and getting a rope on them anyway was especially frustrating because of their large heads and prominent horns. Hickok and the cowboys finally figured to cut a buffalo out of the herd one at a time, spook him, chase him across the prairie, and when he finally could not move another step, walk up and tie a rope around him. When they had apprehended six animals this way, Hickok and the cowboys made the ride to Ogallala, Nebraska, the trek slowed by having the buffalo behind them at the end of their ropes. Along the way on this poor imitation of a cattle drive, Hickok may have reflected that less than a year ago he was the most feared man in Abilene and his word was law . . . now this was his life.

It was another effort in Ogallala to push the buffalo up planks into a railroad car. An easier task was finding four Comanche who were happy to join Hickok's enterprise in exchange for food. It was viewed as a stroke of luck that one of the Indians was followed around faithfully by a small, tame cinnamon bear, and a second Comanche had a monkey as a pet. This could only make the *Buffalo Chase* show more exotic to the eastern audiences.

Toward the end of June, Barnett and Hickok and their motley entourage disembarked at the Niagara Falls train station. Word spread quickly that not only was Wild Bill Hickok, the legendary man-killer of the American frontier, in town but that he planned to put on an exciting production there that would portray the Wild West with real Indians and cowboys and even buffalo. The first performance of *The Daring Buffalo Chase of the Plains* was set for July 20, giving Barnett and Hickok time to create an arena, do advertising, sell tickets, and fine-tune the production.

Only the latter was done, and not very well, because there was no script, and none of the cast, especially the buffalo and the bear and the monkey, had acted before. By this time, Hickok was broke, with the cast eating up his stage stake. He couldn't advertise or even build an adequate enclosure. However, there was a lot of pent-up anticipation for the production, and it was believed several thousand would attend opening night at an arena ringed by wire, the best venue Hickok could create with moths in his pockets, and Barnett's finances by this point not much better. That would change, though, if all those people did show up and they dropped coins into the buckets that would be passed around.

According to newspaper accounts, the performance of *The Daring Buffalo Chase of the Plains* on opening night—and, it turned out, closing night—was indeed dramatic and eventful, and thousands of people did show up. The only scenario the "director," Hickok, had concocted was literally the title—have the buffalo run around the arena with the cowboys and Indians in pursuit. The problem was that after the six buffalo were pushed and otherwise persuaded to enter the enclosure, they simply stood still. They may have been mesmerized by the thousands of human faces staring back at them. That changed quickly, though, when Hickok fired one of his Colt pistols.

That got them going. The petrified buffalo rumbled around the makeshift arena. The four Comanche joined in, as did the three cowboys. They all were joined by a pack of dogs that ran through the porous wire-rimmed perimeter. And then, foreshadowing the running of the bulls at Pamplona, some daredevil spectators joined the chase and were in turn chased. The buffalo, thoroughly panicked by now, burst out of the enclosure. At about the same time, a spectator thought it would increase the excitement level to open the cages holding the bear and the monkey. The former ambled over to a sausage vendor and eagerly sampled his wares. The monkey sought high ground—it clambered up onto a wagon and began throwing whatever was in it at the crowd.

Hickok and the cowboys rode in the direction the buffalo had gone, which was into a residential neighborhood, where frightened occupants had barred their doors. (The Indians, seizing the opportunity, had remained behind with the bear at the sausage stand.) The exhausted beasts were found and were content enough to be escorted back to their corral. By this time, most of the spectators were heading home. The buckets yielded a take of $124.

That amount plus selling the buffalo to local butchers totaled enough to buy Hickok and his cast tickets on the train to Kansas City. Hickok bid farewell to Colonel Barnett and believed he was done with show business. He would, however, have other stage show experiences, the next being a dangerous one, involving Frank and Jesse James and angry Texans.

For a few weeks after his return to the less tumultuous entertainments of Kansas City, Wild Bill Hickok spent his afternoons and nights at the horse races and gambling in the saloons. During the fourth week in September, the Kansas City Industrial Exhibition was held. This was an elaborate event that offered people near the center of the country a glimpse of the future. For four days, spectators could examine industrial machines that would transform American manufacturing and enjoy sophisticated floral displays and performing horses. Given that sixty thousand people attended the exhibition—twice the number of people who lived in Kansas City—it is very likely that Hickok went to see it, too. That provided the potential for the frontier's most famous gunfighter to again encounter two of its most famous outlaws.

On September 26, the final day of the exhibition, workers were beginning to close it up when three men approached the ticket office. It was near sunset, so the thousands of patrons filing out may not have immediately noticed that the men were wearing masks. Apparently, no policeman or someone acting as a security guard did, and upon learning these were Frank and Jesse James and a compatriot, he might well have fled, anyway. All three drew their guns. The horrified patrons stopped in their tracks. Two of the masked men set about taking money and jewelry from them while the third helped himself to the ticket office cash box. As a bit of punctuation to the robbery, one of the outlaws fired a shot into the ground. The bullet ricocheted and struck a girl in the lower leg. The men backed away, jumped on horses, and took off.

Their timing was good and bad. It was good in that Hickok either was not there that day or had already left. Though not a lawman, it is not far-fetched to think that he might have felt some responsibility to protect the people being victimized and bullied, especially with a girl being wounded. And with rumors having circulated that the

James gang had passed through Abilene the previous year with no interference from the marshal, Hickok may have felt compelled to restore his honor—how nice that an opportunity to do so had landed in his lap. The thieves' timing was bad in that their entire haul was $978 . . . when a half hour earlier, the treasurer of the industrial exhibition had transferred $12,000 to a vault.

But there was a consequence that was certainly unintended. To this point, Jesse James and his brother were not much more than Missouri-born Civil War guerrillas who had chosen a life of crime and debauchery. John Newman Edwards, owner of *The Kansas City Times,* saw the exhibition robbery as an opportunity to create a legend, and of course sell more newspapers. *The Times* published dozens of articles, many written by Edwards himself, that revealed the "real" story about the James brothers. They were heroes of the South forced to commit crimes to fund resistance efforts against the oppressive northern occupiers, and on top of that, they were modern-day Robin Hoods taking from the rich to give to the poor. Many readers bought this image.

So did Frank and Jesse James. During the ensuing years, they employed different tactics, eschewing robberies like that of the industrial exhibition, and shooting girls, albeit accidentally, and instead taking money belonging to big banks and their fat-cat executives who traveled on trains. For many people, this heroic image persisted until the murder of Jesse in April 1882. (Stories also persisted for years that Hickok did indeed challenge the James gang that day and sent them away empty-handed . . . but, alas, not true.)

What were the odds that if Hickok had known about a James gang robbery (and shooting) in progress, he would have gotten involved? Pretty good, actually, because of an incident *The Topeka Daily Commonwealth* reported in its September 28 issue. During one of the days of the industrial exhibition, a large group of Texans demanded that the house band play "Dixie." The intimidated musicians began to play the tune very much associated with the Confederacy, but many of the spectators objected. The Texans urged the band to continue. Suddenly, Wild Bill Hickok stepped out of the crowd "and stopped the music," according to the newspaper account. The Texans' pistols "were presented at William's head, but he came away unscathed."

At some point that fall, Hickok relocated to familiar Springfield, Missouri. An unfortunate and inaccurate story had him in Nebraska that November—another example of Hickok, especially as he got older, having no control over his reputation.

That month, three members of the Oglala Sioux were murdered near the Republican River. It was initially believed that Pawnee had killed Whistler, Badger, and Handsmeller because of a conflict over hunting grounds. The U.S. Army was asked to investigate. Its point man in the effort was Lieutenant Frederick Schwatka, one of the more fascinating yet virtually unknown men of his time. Among his exploits was helping to exonerate Hickok of murder.

Schwatka, who was only twenty-three in the autumn of 1872, was born in Illinois but came of age in Salem, Oregon. He attended Willamette University, then West Point, graduating in 1871. He was assigned to the Third Cavalry in the Dakota Territory. At the time of the investigation into the deaths of Whistler and the two other Sioux, he had added to his responsibilities studying both medicine and law. In 1875, he would be admitted to the Nebraska bar association and receive a degree from Bellevue Hospital Medical College in New York.

But first Lieutenant Schwatka had a murder mystery to solve. By questioning farmers and other settlers, he learned that one of the men probably involved, Jack Ralston, was known to be a member of "Wild Bill's outfit." The army did not try to keep this revelation hidden, and suddenly, it was being trumpeted that the man-killer Wild Bill Hickok had claimed three more victims. As Schwatka's investigation continued, however, the prime suspect became William Kress, known as "Wild Bill of the Blue River," not Wild Bill of everywhere else on the Plains. Ralston confessed that he and Kress had lured the three Indians to their campsite with promises of coffee and food, then killed them to steal their ponies.

Having exonerated Hickok, Lieutenant Schwatka went on to other duties. Though a Renaissance man of the Plains, he was a warrior when the occasion called for it. At the Battle of Slim Buttes, the first significant action against warring Indians after the demise of Custer and his men at Little Bighorn in 1876, Lieutenant Schwatka led the charge that resulted in a resounding victory. But he wasn't about to confine his talents to the Plains indefinitely. In 1878, he was on the schooner *Eothen* to the Canadian Arctic, leading an expedition for the American Geographical Society. The adventure included the longest sledge journey ever made by time and distance, encompassing 2,709 miles in eleven months. In 1883, Schwatka led the longest raft journey ever made, 1,300 miles down the Yukon River to the Bering Sea. For these and subsequent feats of exploration, he was honored with medals from an array of countries and scientific societies, and he was accepted as a member of the geographical societies of Bremen, Geneva, and Rome.

Alas, the trips had taken their toll, including making everyday real life seem dull by comparison. The celebrated Schwatka was forty-three when he died in Portland, Oregon, from an overdose of laudanum.

Hickok spent much of the winter of 1872–73 in Independence, confined there by both harsh weather and a lack of motivation to go anywhere else. Then as the winter waned, he was murdered. As *The Topeka Daily Commonwealth* reported, Hickok was "Riddled with Bullets at Fort Dodge."

Chapter Sixteen

THE RELUCTANT THESPIAN

In early March 1873, it was reported that Wild Bill had been shot six times by two men in Fort Dodge. Hickok had been drinking with them in a saloon when the lights abruptly went out and gunfire began. The fatal shot was the bullet that struck him in the center of the forehead and was embedded in his brain. A Kansas City newspaper reported the assassins had been friends of Phil Coe, and other newspapers followed suit in printing accounts of the revenge killing.

It was with much surprise that readers of *The St. Louis Weekly Missouri Democrat*, who along with followers of many other news outlets were mourning the demise of a true frontier legend, read the following, dated March 13: "Wishing to correct an error in your paper of the 12th, I will state that no Texan has, or *ever will*, 'corral William.' I wish you to correct your statement, on account of my people." The letter was sent from Independence and signed "J. B. Hickok or 'Wild Bill.'" And he added a PS: "I have bought your paper in preference to all others, since 1857."

The letter was reprinted in other publications, including the PS. As Wild Bill stated, it would take more than a fake report to kill him off.

Hickok apparently was not scarred enough from his first foray as a stage performer, because less than a year after the Niagara Falls disaster, he signed up for another production. This one would involve his good friend Buffalo Bill Cody and the enterprising novelist and huckster Ned Buntline.

Buffalo Bill had achieved recognition as the best scout on the frontier, and his skills as a tracker and fighter were in much demand. His reputation was further enhanced in 1872 when he became one of only four civilian scouts to be awarded the Medal of Honor for valor in action during battles with Plains Indians. Cody was also sought after by high-level American politicians and visiting foreign dignitaries who wanted him to lead hunting expeditions and regale them with tall tales along the way. Dime novels were being churned out depicting adventures it would have taken Cody at least three lifetimes to undertake.

By this time, he and Louisa had three children—Arta Lucille, Kit Carson, and Orra Maude—so he apparently managed to get home from time to time.* He recognized, however, that he did have a dangerous occupation, which might not be wise for a man with a growing family. His fame came from being run ragged on the frontier as a scout and campfire entertainer and occasional Indian fighter. Perhaps there was a much safer way to exploit that fame.

A lot of what J. W. Buel wrote in his books, including *Heroes of*

---

* Sadly, Cody and his wife would outlive three of their children—Arta, who died at thirty-eight; Kit, who died at six; and Orra, who died at eleven. Their fourth child, Irma Louise, died at thirty-five, in 1918, a year after Cody died and three years before a heartbroken Louisa passed away.

the Plains, has to be taken with a box of salt. However, more cre-
dence can be given to the reporting he did in the 1870s when he was
a young staffer with *The Kansas City Journal.* Hickok told him that
he was "severely money-bound" because his primary occupation at
that time (in addition to assuring people he was still alive) was gambling, and that wasn't going well. Worse than a streak of bad luck
was a new administration in Kansas City that had a dim view of the
gaming tables and the men who sat at them. There were police raids
on saloons, some gamblers were picked up and shown the inside of
jail cells, and even Hickok was arrested for "vagrancy." This charge
usually meant a man was hanging around with no visible means of
support, and with gambling being severely curbed by the cops, that
was a pretty accurate description of him.

With his eyesight declining, Hickok could not return to being a
peace officer, certainly not an effective one. He had to consider that
gunfights he would have easily won before might not turn out so well
now. The same went for another former occupation, scouting. The legendary frontiersman was in a bad way with few, if any, prospects.

So when Cody showed up wearing a long fur coat and reeking of
newfound success as an entertainer, Hickok paid attention to his pitch.
Scouts of the Prairie was the production. Buntline had written it, and
he claimed to anyone who would listen that in a fit of inspiration it
had taken him just four hours to compose. (After seeing the play in
a tryout, some critics wondered why it had taken that long.) Cody explained he had lined up the financing to produce the play and take it
on the road. Wild Bill had only to play the part written for him and
collect his pay.

It was tempting, but at first, Hickok responded, "No more theatrical business for me."

Though he was tactful about it, Cody could see that his old friend and mentor was frayed around the edges. His city clothes were not as fine and tidy as before, and he was drinking more than was smart for a man one ambitious gunslinger away from the grave. He pitched the plot again, which was nothing more than Buffalo Bill, Wild Bill, and Texas Jack Omohundro around a campfire telling stories about their experiences as plainsmen, occasionally interrupted by gunfire and chasing off intrusive Indians. Buntline himself would play the leader of a group of white settlers passing through. During a tryout of the evolving production in Chicago, the playwright, who had clearly been drinking, offered one of his well-worn temperance lectures; it was ended when a few stage Indians tied him to a tree to burn him alive, and the audience reacted with wild applause and cheers.

From Cody's point of view, *Scouts of the Prairie* had been conceived as a melodrama. But in the Chicago tryout, the play was received as a comedy. Most important: people had paid to see it, and even more of them would do so if the most famous gunfighter in the American West was in it, too.

This was not to overlook Texas Jack's contributions. By 1872, he, too, was one of the more well-known scouts and Indian fighters on the Great Plains. He and Buffalo Bill had become regular traveling companions, such as when they guided a hunting excursion led by Lieutenant Colonel George Custer that included Grand Duke Alexis of Russia, and they were side by side during the engagement that earned Cody his Medal of Honor. That same summer of 1872, Texas Jack was chosen to lead the Pawnee off their reservation for a big buffalo hunt—which is why Barnett found them together in Kansas City—and Omohundro earned from the natives the name "Whirling Rope."

It did not take Hickok too long to be seduced by Cody's invitation and to agree to be a member of the cast. The closer was Cody's offer of a hundred dollars a week. Not only would that be more than twice what he earned as the marshal in Abilene, but a steady and very good salary would make all the difference in the world right about now for Hickok. And about to turn thirty-six, middle-aged by frontier standards at the time, he had no other prospects.

In addition to withholding that much of the popularity of *Scouts of the Prairie* was the unintended laughter it created, Cody may not have volunteered that there had been more previous performances of the play than the Chicago tryout. It had lumbered through St. Louis, Cincinnati, Buffalo, and Albany. Then the production plodded on to New York City, playing at a theater known as Niblo's Garden. A typical review was published in *The New York Herald,* which opined that "everything was so wonderfully bad it was almost good." The cast was treated with some gentleness, except Buntline, who displayed "simply maundering imbecility." *The New York World* sniffed that the production was "very poor slop."

This would be Wild Bill's new adventure. Given that Hickok was soft-spoken and usually not keen on calling attention to himself, Cody could not have expected that his naive friend would improve the quality of *Scouts of the Prairie.* However, his name and presence should be just what the box office needed.

The play, slightly revised and with Hickok replacing Buntline in the cast, and retitled *Scouts of the Plains,* was to try again at Niblo's Garden in New York. Another cast member was not as famous as Hickok and Cody but was a much more accomplished actor. The twenty-six-year-old Giuseppina Morlacchi was born in Milan and attended the La Scala dance school. Her stage debut as a ballerina came in Genoa in 1856, and, known for her skill and beauty, she became a popular attraction on stages on the Continent and in England. She crossed the Atlantic in 1867 to perform in musicals and is credited with being one of the first dancers to introduce the cancan to America. Her popularity increased in the United States, and her manager insured her legs for $100,000, which prompted one newspaper wag to write that the dancer and actress was now "more valuable than Kentucky."

That Morlacchi was by 1873 a member of the *Scouts of the Plains* cast could imply that her stage career had not thrived in recent years. The truth was, that August, she had become Mrs. Omohundro, and she preferred to be on the road with her husband, especially one who was so attractive to the ladies. And she was probably paid well for the time, which may have been her top priority. And Cody could be very persuasive, as Hickok learned.

To give the play even more audience appeal, several attractive women were added to the cast, mostly to enter and exit the stage looking attractive. And to supervise the overall production was Arizona John Burke. Also known as Major, Burke never set foot in Arizona, nor did he serve in the military. He was born in New York City, but in 1866, when he was twenty-four, he was in Montana Territory and met Cody, who was then scouting for the Third Cavalry. They became fast friends, and as Buffalo Bill moved more into show business, Burke became his publicist, press agent, manager, and anything else that needed doing. Theatrical folk awarded him the title "Prince of Press Agents."

Burke remained in those capacities for Buffalo Bill through the Wild West show's decades of performances, until Cody's death in January 1917. Burke died penniless and alone three months later. He was buried in an unmarked grave in Mount Olivet cemetery in

Washington, D.C., and did not receive a proper headstone until a century later.*

Making his acting debut on a New York stage would be daunting for an experienced thespian, but for a prairie gunslinger, it could be a disaster. Hickok, however, did not skulk into town. According to a reminiscence written by Burke, the famous plainsman arrived at the Forty-Second Street Depot in New York wearing a cutaway coat, flowered vest, ruffled white shirt, salt-and-pepper trousers, string tie, high-heeled boots, and a broad-brimmed hat. He had booked a room at the Brevoort Hotel on lower Fifth Avenue, one of New York's well-known establishments, where Cody was staying.

Outside the train station, Hickok got into a horse-drawn cab and was taken to the hotel. Cody had told him to pay two dollars, and upon arrival, that is what he did. The driver demanded five dollars. Hickok informed him that all he would receive was the two dollars. Climbing down, the driver growled, "You long-haired rube, I'll take the rest out of your hide." A minute later, Hickok was strolling into the hotel lobby, carrying his own suitcase because the bruised and dazed driver was not able to be of further service.

That the legendary shootist Wild Bill Hickok was in New York City was indeed a boost to the box office. He was hailed as something of a celebrity as the well-dressed gunfighter strode to and from the theater on Broadway near Prince Street. Inside Niblo's Garden, during performances, the audience was witnessing up close not one

---

*The Whole Foods and Sprouts marketing executive Joe Dobrow paid $3,100 for the headstone. The April 12, 2017, ceremony, the one hundredth anniversary of Burke's death, was live-streamed on Facebook and included mountain stones placed on the grave and the headstone dedication. The epithet carved on it was HOT AIR AND KIND WORDS DISPENSER.

but two heroes of the American West, detailing their most dangerous and thrilling adventures. A few of them were actually true.

The excitement was not rubbing off on Hickok, though. The opportunity to become the next Edwin Booth did not inspire a personality change. It all seemed kind of silly to be an actor pretending to be someone else and sillier still to be Wild Bill Hickok pretending to be Wild Bill Hickok. And it was annoying that people laughed at his lines. Back in the West, if someone had laughed at him, Wild Bill might have gone for his gun. Now he had hundreds of people laughing—what was so funny about this dumb dialogue, anyway?—and he had to stand up there and take it.

Mostly, the theater brought out the puckish part of Hickok's personality. To tolerate the swings between boredom and embarrassment, he played practical jokes. In a scene when the "Indians" were supposed to be killed by Hickok, he instead fired blanks from the guns near their legs to make them dance for the audience. There were times he appeared to forget a line, and he watched the other actors squirm as the silence lengthened and the audience began to titter.

Making it worse was that much of Buntline's hackneyed dialogue remained in *Scouts of the Plains*. By this point, Cody, Omohundro, and Morlacchi were veteran troupers (and getting paid well enough) that they could figuratively hold their noses and get through each performance. Hickok, troubled by bouts of stage fright, had to bellow each soliloquy, such as the one after a rescue of Pale Dove, played by Morlacchi: "Fear not, fair maid! By heavens, you are safe at last with Wild Bill, who is ever ready to risk his life and die, if need be, in defense of weak and defenseless womanhood!" (He may have recalled that former girlfriend Susannah Moore had proved anything but weak and defenseless during their Civil War exploits.)

The crowds were not put off by the sketchy acting and poor

dialogue. "The money was flowing in," Louisa Cody recalled. "Bad as the 'stars' knew their play to be, it was what the public wanted, and that was all that counted. Week after week they played to houses that were packed to the roofs, while often the receipts would run close to $20,000 for the seven days. It was more money than any of us ever had dreamed of before."

Hickok felt like he was risking his integrity and dying a bit with every performance because he became further convinced that acting was a foolish occupation. One night, hoping to escape attention, he took one of his real pistols and shot out the spotlight that had been fixed on him. The audience applauded the dramatic reality of the production as well as Hickok's famous marksmanship.

There may have been another, much more serious reason for this incident. Hickok's vision continued to deteriorate. Sensitivity to light was one symptom of whatever the true ailment was. When he was out and about during daylight hours (which was not often), Hickok sported a pair of dark-hued spectacles. Supposedly, during performances, when he could not protect his eyes with glasses, the theater's lights were bothersome, especially a spotlight trained on him. It could be that on the night of the shooting, his frustration boiled over.

Cody was not pleased with such unpredictable and destructive behavior, especially when payment for damage came out of his pocket. He and Texas Jack ad-libbed when Hickok went blank onstage or gagged on Buntline's dialogue. When they realized that Hickok gave a more natural and compliant performance after a few shots of whiskey, they encouraged imbibing before the curtain went up—until one night. One scene had Wild Bill, Texas Jack, and Buffalo Bill passing around a bottle as they sat at a campfire offering stories about adventures on the Great Plains. Fed up with the iced tea the bottle contained, Hickok suddenly spit it out and shouted, "You must think I'm the worst fool east of the Rockies that I can't tell whiskey from cold tea!" He then called offstage for someone to bring him a bottle of real whiskey.

The audience cheered in agreement. A bottle was produced, and Wild Bill took a long pull and then told a story as casually as if he'd been sitting at a gaming table in an Abilene saloon. That was the good news. The bad news was from that night on, Hickok wanted whiskey before and during each performance. His acting became even more unpredictable, and during his scenes with Pale Dove, according to Cody, Hickok "grew fonder of the heroine onstage than the script stipulated." This added to the tension already percolating offstage between Texas Jack and Arizona John Burke caused by the latter trying to steal away the affections of the beautiful Miss Morlacchi.

Critics finally gave up on panning *Scouts of the Plains,* and audiences kept flocking to it through the fall of 1873 and the winter. As spring approached, Cody and Burke decided to get out of New York while the getting was good and to take the show on the road. By this time, Hickok had settled into the city life well enough, especially the saloons and high-quality liquor—which, thanks to the handsome and steady paychecks, he could afford. While still having a reserved personality, he enjoyed the attention and deference given to a celebrity. So Hickok was not keen on going on tour. He was overruled. The demand for the production was out there, and he couldn't welsh on a contract.

The troupe's first stop that spring would be Titusville, Pennsylvania, known for hosting the nation's first oil boom. This did not tempt Hickok from the city comforts, but he packed his bags and went along.

Beginning with Titusville, the players found even more appreciative audiences. In New York, there was no longer much excitement about Wild Bill Hickok and Buffalo Bill Cody being in town, especially in such a wheezing vehicle as *Scouts of the Plains*. In towns and smaller cities, however, the arrival of the two legends generated much excitement—and ticket sales.

The troupe got off the train in Titusville and checked into their hotel, which was adjacent to the theater. To kill the few hours before the first performance, Hickok, Cody, Texas Jack, and Burke went downstairs to play billiards in the parlor. But just outside the door, they were stopped by the hotel's manager, who explained that presently playing billiards were several oil-field roughnecks who had made noises about challenging the Cody company to a game or anything else competitive. The manager begged them to avoid a confrontation. Cody agreed and persuaded the others to return to their rooms.

Though they had been friends since before the Civil War, somehow Cody had underestimated Hickok's competitive nature. Later, while Burke and Buffalo Bill were at the theater making sure all was ready for the local debut of *Scouts of the Plains,* Hickok stepped into the billiard room. He didn't know what to expect and was prepared for anything . . . except for what happened. One of the hulking oil men clapped a hand on his shoulder and said, "Hello, Buffalo Bill. We've been waiting for you all day."

Hickok had been greeted with a lot worse than being confused with Cody, so with a grin he removed the man's hand and said he was not Buffalo Bill. He was informed that he was a liar. Bristling, Hickok replied, "You're another."

The hotel manager had rushed next door to alert Cody about a possible confrontation. He and Burke arrived to find Hickok in the midst of fighting five large men. Actually, they did not witness the brawl, just heard the commotion within, then quiet; then a barely ruffled Hickok emerged from the parlor. He reported that he had subdued the "hostiles" by knocking the apparent leader out with one punch and disposing of the others with a solid wooden chair. "They won't bother us anymore," Hickok declared. Then, whistling, he went up to his room to ready for that evening's performance. Cody and Burke had to applaud the one he had already given.

During the spring and into the summer of 1874, the *Scouts of the Plains* tour was successful. There were no further confrontations reported. A close call was in Portland, Maine, when the troupe was staying at the United States Hotel. After one night's show, a tired Hickok voted against hitting a saloon and instead repaired to his room before midnight. Soon after he drifted off, there was a burst of shouting from the next room. Irritated, and clad only in a nightshirt, he went out in the hallway and knocked on the door. It was opened to reveal several of the city's prominent business leaders using the room as a gambling den. Hickok's irritation faded as the men offered him a seat at their poker table and access to their bottle of whiskey.

By dawn, he was up seven hundred dollars and feeling more refreshed than if he had enjoyed uninterrupted slumber. Grinning, Hickok said, "Let that be a lesson to you gentlemen about destroying a man's sleep," and he pushed the cash into a pocket. True, the men were out the money, but no doubt it was worth it to for years tell the story about an all-night poker session with Wild Bill Hickok in a nightshirt.

But being on the road, with no end in sight and with audiences continuing to lap up the "slop," was wearying. And if indeed there was a light-sensitivity issue, it was probably painful for Hickok, too. One stop had the production in Rochester, and during a show, a footlight lamp exploded as he sat near it. The sudden searing light was like knives in his eyes. A doctor was called and treated them with some drops and later fitted him with glasses with thick blue lenses. Hickok was not only embarrassed—even more than by having to still be reciting Buntline's dialogue—about wearing the odd contraption but concerned that others might come to realize his eye issues were not temporary.

Either he decided it was time to go or the barely suppressed frustration did it for him. One night, standing in the wings with Louisa Cody, Hickok exclaimed, "Ain't this foolish? Ain't it now? What's the use of getting out there and making a show of yourself? I ain't going to do it!"

A couple of nights later, Hickok simply left the production. He had played another practical joke on a few "Indians" with the pistol of blanks, and Cody asked him again to behave himself. Without a word, Hickok took off his buckskin outfit, put on his usual clothes, and left the theater. He had the stage carpenter deliver a message to Cody: "That long-haired gentleman, who walked out a few minutes ago, requested me to tell you that you could go to thunder with your old show." He was done with show business this time for certain . . . or so he thought.

Though the production had often played to full theaters for close to a year, Hickok had not saved much of his salary, having spent it on top-shelf liquor and gambling. So, before he left Rochester, Cody and Texas Jack—who despite everything else remained his devoted friends—ponied up a thousand dollars as a gift for their departing cast member. Then Hickok and *Scouts of the Plains* went their separate ways.*

---

*By the end of the tour of *Scouts of the Plains*, for Arizona John Burke, there was a loss in addition to Hickok's departure. His amorous attentions were spurned by Mlle Morlacchi. She decided to stick with Texas Jack, and the couple rode off into the sunset together. Texas Jack alternated between being a correspondent for *The New York Herald*, writing about frontier events, and accompanying his wife on tours with other stage productions. It was during one of their tour stops, in Leadville,

There was another reason for Hickok's distress: Agnes Lake was in Rochester. Once more, she was on tour, this time with the 1874 edition of her circus. She may have noticed an advertisement for *Scouts of the Plains* or he saw one for the circus, but in any case, they were reunited, albeit briefly. Whatever feelings had been kindled in Abilene were still there between them.

Several accounts offer what was said between them during apparently their only meeting in Rochester (some suggest the meeting was in New York) . . . and they can be considered fiction, because there were no witnesses and no letters or journal entries. One version by Frank Wilstach even has Hickok saying, "Fact is, I'd be mighty glad to hitch up in harness with you, because I think we'd make a splendid team." Even Ned Buntline would be hard-pressed to dash off such dialogue. It is believed that the two did not try to hide their feelings—Wild Bill and Agnes were not adolescents but thirty-six and forty-seven, respectively—and may well have discussed marriage. If Hickok proposed, one hopes it was in a way that did not view Agnes as a mule.

The most likely scenario is that once again the two had crossed paths when both were unwilling or unable to give up what they were doing in their lives. Agnes had a circus to run and a payroll to meet and a daughter to support who was on her way to eclipsing her mother's achievements as a circus star. Perhaps if Hickok was willing to sign on to help her . . . But he wasn't so inclined. He was stuck in *Scouts of the Plains,* and as much as he liked Agnes, helping her run a circus was more than he could stomach at that particular time. Also, it was clear to him how much energy and effort Agnes put into the

---

Colorado, in June 1880 that Texas Jack contracted pneumonia and died, one month shy of his thirty-fourth birthday. A grieving Morlacchi quit the stage, went to live with a sister, and died in 1886 at thirty-nine.

circus, top to bottom. That wouldn't leave much left over for a new husband.

So the circus, with Agnes Lake, moved on, a full summer of engagements lying ahead. Soon after, Hickok had his meltdown and declared he was done with *Scouts of the Plains*. He pocketed the thousand-dollar gift, packed his bag, and took the train out of Rochester.

Unlike his last retreat after a failed production, Hickok did not head to Kansas City. He had mostly enjoyed his stay in New York, and he decided to pay the city another visit. While he could have suffered an unlucky streak in Kansas City, the unhappy fact was that gambling was not good to him in New York, either. He was already in a foul mood over this when he was informed that a production of *Scouts of the Plains* with even fewer theatrical standards and an actor billing himself as Wild Bill Hickok was playing in Binghamton. Incensed, Hickok took a train there.

Indeed, such an imitation was being performed in Binghamton. Hickok attended that night, sitting in the first row. He was appalled by what he saw—not just that it was a second-rate version of what had been a third-rate play to begin with, but seeing it from the perspective of the audience, Hickok was intensely embarrassed to have been in it.

During a scene when "Hickok" is fighting off several Comanche warriors, the real Wild Bill could not take it anymore. He jumped up onto the stage. A manager rushed from the wings to stop him, and Hickok tossed him into the orchestra pit. He then punched his impersonator, sending him through the cheap background scenery. As the curtain came down, Hickok stepped off the stage and went back to his seat, announcing to the audience that it was now okay for the show to go on.

The cast, however, was too frightened to reappear, and the curtain stayed down. A policeman came down the aisle and told Hickok he was under arrest. Insulted that there was just the one police officer, Hickok told him that he would need help with the arrest. The cop believed him and waited until another officer arrived. "Better get more help," Hickok told the uniformed duo. Finally, a sheriff showed up and asked politely, "Now, Mr. Hickok, will you accompany us to the jail?"

He did. He spent the night in the Binghamton brig. The next morning, a judge fined him three dollars, and then Wild Bill Hickok headed to the train station. *Now* he was done with show business.

Chapter Seventeen

THE CHEYENNE LOAFER

It would be George Armstrong Custer who gave Wild Bill Hickok fresh purpose. First, however, the aging gunfighter endured a period of wandering and wasting time and watching the American West begin to pass him by.

To recover from the experiences in show business, and finally done with New York, Hickok returned to where he was most comfortable, the saloons and gaming tables of Kansas City, Topeka, and Independence. He had no job waiting for him and no prospects. He had earned money from gambling before, and he expected to do so again. He had no interest in patrolling the streets as a lawman again or in enduring the rigors of the trail as an army scout, even though veteran scouts were in even greater demand because of renewed resistance among the Plains Indian tribes. From time to time, Hickok interrupted the daily gambling schedule to put on shooting exhibits. Though his eyes continued to bother him, no one seemed to notice that his feats were not as impressive as they had once been.

Even with the Washita Massacre in 1868 and the court-martial for abandoning his troops, by the summer of 1874, Lieutenant Colonel Custer was back in favor with his military superiors. He and his Seventh Cavalry were chosen to undertake a mission into the Black Hills of South Dakota.

It was not overlooked that the Treaty of Fort Laramie signed in November 1868 ending what was called Red Cloud's War prohibited the U.S. Army from making just such excursions into Paha Sapa, what the Lakota Sioux called the Black Hills: "No persons except those designated herein shall ever be permitted to pass over, settle upon, or reside in the territory described in this article." It was precisely for the protection of that area that the war had begun in the first place, in 1866. Despite requests, complaints, and then warnings about too many migrants along the Bozeman Trail and the construction of forts, the influx of whites only grew stronger, especially in the year after the Civil War when the Bluebellies could turn their eyes from the South to the West.

Red Cloud, seconded by his wartime protégé Crazy Horse, launched a series of attacks leading up to the most devastating one on December 21, 1866. Captain William Fetterman led his eighty men into an ambush, and all were killed by the coalition of Sioux, Cheyenne, and Arapaho who had rallied around Red Cloud. That the civilians and remaining soldiers at Fort Phil Kearny in northeast Wyoming were not also wiped out was due to a sudden and violent winter snowstorm that persuaded the tribes that they should make haste to their winter encampments.

Given the power and prestige of Red Cloud and the blood that had been spilled at the Fetterman Massacre* and other engagements,

---

*The Sioux name for the brutal engagement was the Battle of the Hundred-in-the-Hands, based on a dream a medicine man had in advance of the battle.

the administration of President Andrew Johnson tried to make the 1868 Fort Laramie Treaty work. Three forts along the Bozeman Trail were abandoned (and subsequently burned to the ground by Red Cloud), and army patrols turned away those who tried to explore or even just pass through the region. The Black Hills was not just a piece of territory the Sioux did not want violated but their most sacred place—a translation of Paha Sapa is "the Heart of Everything That Is." Intruding there, above anyplace else, would risk the resumption of war.

But six years later, the situation was different. Red Cloud, at fifty-three, had retired as a war chief. Crazy Horse was still two years away from joining up with Sitting Bull and their rendezvous with the Seventh Cavalry at Little Bighorn. The pent-up pressure of whites seeking to explore and exploit the Great Plains was greater, and bans on where they could go were being ignored. The army units on that frontier were in an unfamiliar position, having to transition from protection to crowd control.

And while the Grant administration officially adhered to the Fort Laramie Treaty, there were individuals within who were already plotting its demise. "I am inclined to think that the occupation of this region of the country is not necessary to the happiness and prosperity of the Indians," wrote Columbus Delano, the secretary of the interior, "and as it is supposed to be rich in minerals and lumber it is deemed important to have it freed as early as possible from Indian occupancy. I shall, therefore, not oppose any policy which looks first to a careful examination of the subject."

The treaty's fate was sealed when there were rumors of the richest mineral of all being present: gold.

Since the California gold rush of the late 1840s, gold strikes anywhere in the West had attracted prospectors, shopkeepers, entrepreneurs, and others looking to get rich. This was especially true in 1874, with the United States gripped by the Panic of 1873. Overspeculation in the railroad industry, inflation, and a large trade deficit had resulted in a depression that would last for six years, with unemployment peaking at 8.25 percent. What better time could there be for a gold strike to tantalize the thousands of workers idled by the economy and businessmen gone bust?

In July of 1874, frustrated by the rumor of gold, the army was doing its best to keep white people out of the Black Hills, which straddled the borders of South Dakota and Wyoming. It was determined that the rumor had to be confirmed or dispelled. Lieutenant Colonel Custer was ordered to lead a thousand soldiers and several geologists and miners from Fort Abraham Lincoln on the west bank of the Missouri River in North Dakota south into the Black Hills and do some exploring. Yes, this was a clear and deliberate violation of the treaty. But the Sioux were not equipped to do much about it but hope the Custer expedition would find nothing and return to where it came from.

At 8:10 on the morning of July 2, "Advance!" was called out, and Custer's caravan began to move out. "The companies wheeled by fours into line of march, guidons flying in the breeze, the band playing our battle quickstep, 'Garry Owen,' the officers dashing up and down the column with an air of importance, the men cheerful and full of chatter, and we cast our eyes for the last time on Fort A. Lincoln," recorded Private Theodore Ewert. "Up the valley, we saw the ladies of our command waving their scarfs and handkerchiefs in sad farewell, and just as we left the last ridge that overlooked the valley the men gave three hearty cheers."

Custer was certainly in his element on this expedition. "The idea of visiting new country and bestowing names on the land naturally appealed to Custer, but he viewed himself not as another Lewis and Clark so much as a plainsman, a restless soul who liked to see what was over the next hill," writes the western historian Brian Dippie. "He knew men like Wild Bill Hickok and Buffalo Bill Cody, and they were his ideal. They belonged to what has been described as a 'flamboyant fraternity,' with a dress code that ran to long hair, buckskins, and a broad-brimmed hat set at a rakish angle."

With such an intoxicating excursion, Custer may not have cared if he discovered gold at all. Unfortunately for the Sioux, in early August, one of the miners panning on French Creek found the coveted mineral. Initially, Custer tried to keep the discovery under wraps, but it did not help that he had allowed a wagon full of newspaper reporters to accompany his contingent and that the entire journey had been photographed by William Illingworth. (Also along for the trip was Lieutenant Colonel Frederick Dent Grant, son of the president.) Custer himself wrote in a letter that passed through many hands, "I referred in a former dispatch to the discovery of gold. Subsequent examinations at numerous points confirm and strengthen the fact of the existence of gold in the Black Hills."

By the third week in August, daily newspapers in the major cities back east were printing blaring headlines. The rush was on.

Though he was more dependent on the blue-lensed glasses, Hickok could still read newspapers. He saw the Black Hills gold discovery as an opportunity. At a well-weathered thirty-seven, he was not about to begin kneeling on the sides of creek beds panning for nuggets or clawing rocks for gold dust. In fact, kneeling anywhere had become a problem because of a touch of rheumatism. Adding to the sartorial impression Hickok made was that in addition to the blue-lensed glasses, he had taken to using a rosewood cane that had once been a billiard cue stick. This not only helped with walking when the rheumatism acted up but gave him another self-defense option.

Wild Bill was not ready for a rocking chair yet. He was a gambler and a very good one, and with the expected boom in the building of saloons in towns surrounding the Black Hills, and men suddenly with money in their pockets, he envisioned a way to make a lucrative living.

❧Hickok set off for Cheyenne, the town in Wyoming that had become the launching ramp for participants in the gold rush. However, just before he had left Kansas City, he received word that there were men in Hays City and Abilene who still bore grudges from his lawman days there and wanted a reckoning with him. They would be waiting when the Kansas Pacific train made stops in Hays City and Abilene on its way west.

In response, he telegraphed a message to the newspapers in those cities: "I shall pass through your prairie-dog villages on Tuesday. I wear my hair long as usual." When Hickok's train pulled into those stations, no adversaries awaited. Instead, when he appeared, his long hair flowing out of his black sombrero, crowds who had gathered in anticipation of a showdown saluted him with cheers.

There was another item in the press at that time that caught readers' attention. On July 21, as Hickok was on his train trip, *The Topeka Daily Commonwealth* reported that he "is suffering from an affection of the eyes, caused by the colored fire used during his theatrical tour." Probably, he could not avoid answering a question about his glasses, and the tour was the best explanation he could give. Telling the truth—that he had a degenerative disease—could have been a fatal mistake. While he might still draw a pistol faster than an opponent, by now, or soon enough, he might not see well enough to shoot him.

He arrived to find Cheyenne a hustling and bustling place. There had been rapid growth in just the seven years since General Grenville Dodge and a survey crew plotted the site in what was then Dakota Territory. He hoped the town that emerged would be named Dodge, but he had to be satisfied years later when Buffalo City in Kansas became Dodge City. Cheyenne was, predictably, named after the Indian tribe. There were already four thousand people living there in November 1867 when the Union Pacific Railroad arrived. From that point on, Cheyenne was an important railroad hub as well as a supply depot for prospectors, miners, and other explorers seeking and exploiting gold and silver finds in what became Wyoming Territory. It was nicknamed "Magic City of the Plains."

It could well have shared what Dodge City would be called: "Wickedest Town in the American West." As Joseph Rosa colorfully put it, "Cheyenne had the reputation of being the wildest, roughest place on the continent. It was filled to overflowing with a crowd of roughs, killers, gamblers, and prostitutes such as had never assembled at any one place in America, except perhaps at Abilene." This began to change in 1870 when T. Jeff Carr was elected sheriff of Laramie County.

Cut out of cloth similar to that of Tom Smith in Abilene, Carr took on a tough job without gunplay as his first option. Unlike Smith, Carr would have a long career in law enforcement. Hailing from Pittsburgh, he served in the Union army and then went west, finding his first peace officer position in Central City, Colorado. Carr had done a good amount of cleaning up in Cheyenne by the time Hickok got there, and he was about to add to his duties being superintendent of the Wyoming branch of the Rocky Mountain Detective Association, a post he would hold for thirty-three years. He would also hold posi-

tions as marshal of Cheyenne, U.S. marshal for Wyoming, and chief
deputy U.S. marshal, and he ran a detective agency in Cheyenne. He
would become a member of the "super posse" organized in 1900 that
went after Butch Cassidy and the Sundance Kid and the Wild Bunch.
He died in San Antonio at seventy-three, having bridged the time
periods of frontier and "modern" law and order.

It may seem indulgent to have just devoted a long paragraph to a
character who will appear again only twice in these pages. But there
is a direct relevance to Wild Bill Hickok. In Cheyenne in the fall of
1874 were both Thomas Jeff Carr and Hickok, representing the new
and old lawmen of the American West. Wild Bill had been a gunfighter with a badge, whose white-handled six-shooters compelled law
and order, always prepared to corral or kill those who strayed from
it. Carr represented the gradual civilizing of the frontier, when due
process and the judicial system made communities feel safe. He was
only five years younger than Hickok, but he represented the future,
while Hickok, though not yet forty and still on the sunny side of the
ground, was already being viewed as a relic of the "old" West.

Most likely, he recognized this. "Hickok was intelligent enough
to be aware that things were changing fast in the West," writes Richard O'Connor in his 1959 biography. "Soon there would no longer
be a place for his kind, the adventurer, the gunman. It was only a
matter of time before the whole cast of characters—gunfighters, badmen, road agents, professional gamblers, dance-hall queens—would
no longer be tolerated, let alone admired. He had retreated before the
steady march of respectability in Kansas, had seen the lace curtains
and bay windows replace the swinging doors and red lamps of the
parlor houses."

There are accounts that Hickok did not initially stay in Cheyenne because he was hired to guide an expedition of wealthy hunters. He had told a Kansas reporter that the party would consist of "about twelve English lords and noblemen." If this expedition did take place, it would be his last one because of his eye affliction. In September, he was back in Cheyenne and with his friend Colorado Charley Utter, who had come north from Colorado looking for new adventures and revenue.

The two friends may have enjoyed a good laugh over the story of Hickok's arrival in Cheyenne. He had hoped to ease his way into the town without being noticed, but this had not gone as planned.

His disguise consisted of the blue glasses and having tucked his hair up under the sombrero. After getting off the train, he made his way through the dusty streets, the tip of his cane digging into the dirt, to a complex of buildings containing a hotel, theater, and gambling hall called the Gold Room. Upon entering this room, Hickok spied a faro bank. Hickok put fifty dollars on the high card.*

He lost. Maybe a second fifty dollars would get the first one back, and more. This time he won. But the dealer handed him twenty-five dollars. Hickok wanted to know why so small an amount. He was told by the dealer that the limit was twenty-five dollars, and his lookout snickered.

"You took fifty when I lost," Hickok said.

"Fifty if you lose," the dealer pronounced, "and twenty-five if you win."

---

*One account of the Gold Room incident was written by Alfred E. Lewis and published in the Marsh 12, 1904, issue of *The Saturday Evening Post*. Lewis claimed it was reported to him by Bat Masterson, who was gambling in Cheyenne at the time. This is highly unlikely. In the summer of 1874, Masterson was only twenty and busy as both a buffalo hunter and a scout in Kansas and Texas, and was not the debonair gambler he would later become.

Hickok could have chalked this up to being new in Cheyenne and not knowing how the gambling house operated. He had learned, and it cost him seventy-five dollars. Instead, he bristled at being swindled and in such a discourteous way. He went with his anger and the arc of his cane, which came down on top of the heads of the dealer and his lookout. Two bouncers rushed to the scene and were also introduced to the former billiards cue stick. Now, there were four men on the Gold Room floor.

Others in the gambling hall closed in on the impertinent stranger. Hickok corkscrewed, showing his cane to all. In the process, his glasses and hat flew off. His hair had barely touched his shoulders when a patron cried out, "My God, that's Wild Bill Hickok—watch out or he'll blow us all to kingdom come!"

Finding this a more enjoyable bit of theater, Hickok made a motion toward his guns. That was all it took. It was later reported that patrons and remaining bouncers alike went out of the doors and windows "in blocks of five." Within seconds, the Gold Room was empty, save for the four groaning men on the floor and a petrified bartender who rose up from behind the bar . . . fortunately for him, without a weapon. Hickok retrieved his hat and glasses. He also took a stack of money out of the faro bank and headed for the door.

In a quavering voice, the bartender offered Hickok a drink on the house. He accepted, drank it back, placed the shot glass on the bar, and left.

Hickok rented a room in the hotel, and the next morning, he was visited by a man named Bowlby, the Gold Room proprietor, and the city marshal. They explained that seven hundred dollars had been taken, but of course, the matter could be resolved without any trouble. Hickok said, "I don't know as I ought to keep all the money."

Bowlby liked the idea that the money would indeed be returned.

But then Hickok added, "How about I split it with you instead, Mr. Bowlby."

That didn't sit nearly as well, but the marshal declared, "That settles that," and linked arms with the two men, suggesting they repair to the Gold Room for a morning drink. For Hickok, Cheyenne might be a lucky place after all.

He settled down there for an indefinite stay. Now that he would have a fixed address, he resumed writing letters to his mother and siblings in Illinois and to Agnes Lake. As rudimentary as the postal system was and despite the vast distances mail had to traverse in the 1870s, the letters did find her.

Return letters informed him that Agnes was struggling a bit. The expenses of the Hippo-Olympiad and Mammoth Circus had become overwhelming, and she had trimmed the production and merged it with other ones that were also having financial difficulties. The circus boom had at best plateaued as the Panic of '73 took hold. The twenty-two companies that went out on tour in the 1873–74 season represented a 30 percent decrease from the previous season. Only the smartest and strongest circus owners could expect to survive.

Agnes was also more focused on the career of her daughter Emma, who was emerging as one of the country's most popular equestrian performers. For Agnes, the 1874 tour was her last as a performer, preferring to present "Miss Emma Lake" to audiences.

Hickok spent his days and nights in Cheyenne quietly. He gambled and set aside some of his winnings. This far away from his familiar haunts in Kansas and Missouri, he apparently did not feel in danger. A woman named Annie Tallent, who would become known as the first white woman in the Black Hills and as a writer of pioneer life, includes in her book titled *The Black Hills* encountering Hickok for the first time, and he was not wearing pistols. He was dressed plainly and "might easily have been taken for a Quaker minister."

It was known that Tallent and her husband, along with twenty-six others, had tried to stake claims along French Creek but had been escorted out of the Black Hills by a U.S. Army cavalry patrol, making one of the few last feeble attempts to abide by the Fort Laramie Treaty. Encountering Tallent on the street one day, Hickok doffed his sombrero and, explaining that he expected to go there soon, asked her some questions about the Black Hills.

Tallent was at first put off: "I have often heard of Wild Bill and his reputation is not at all creditable to him. But, perhaps he is not so black as he is painted."

"Well, as to that, I suppose I am called a red-handed murderer, which I deny," Hickok said. "That I have killed men I admit, but never unless in absolute self-defense, or in the performance of an official duty. I have never in my life taken any mean advantage of an enemy. Yet understand, I never yet allowed a man to get the drop on me. But perhaps I may yet die with my boots on."

Impressed, Tallent answered his questions; then: "Wild Bill, with a gracious bow that would have done credit to a Chesterfield, passed on down the street and out of sight."

Colorado Charley was in Cheyenne because he knew the transportation business, and a rush to the Black Hills would mean a great demand for horses, wagons, mules, and supplies. In September 1874, he told a reporter from a Nebraska newspaper, "This rush is going to be a lallapaloozer." He arranged to buy horses and mules and equipment, which he expected to use, then resell at a good profit. And he and Hickok spent much time with their new friends in the Gold Room.

A man named Upton Lorentz was in Cheyenne at the time, seeking his own piece of the gold rush. In an article published in the May 1936 edition of *Frontier Times*, he recalled,

> *Wild Bill stood at the end of a long bar, opposite the entrance from the south or railroad side of the building. Never far from him, generally in front of the bar, could be seen Colorado Charley, a slight, well dressed man, with long fair curls to shoulder also, and perhaps but five feet six inches tall. It was said at that time that the position maintained at the bar by Hickok at the east end and Utter fronting him a short distance away, was a precaution against attack from enemies looking for a chance to get the drop on Bill.*

As 1874 ended, Hickok was not any closer to setting foot in the Black Hills themselves than when he had arrived, and while he had done plenty of gambling, he hadn't gotten rich from it. Perhaps a change of scenery would do him good, but he was stuck in place. "Wild Bill is still in the city," reported the December 3 edition of *The Cheyenne Daily News*, adding, "He is a noble specimen of Western manhood."

Maybe so, but hanging around was not gaining him anything. And Hickok was not the only one. The Magic City of the Plains was now bedeviled by an increasing number of loafers, men who had arrived and did not have the means or ambition to move on, joining those who had tried to venture into the Black Hills and were repulsed. That Hickok was lumped in with them was evident when the city marshal nailed notices around town stating that vagrants had twenty-four hours to leave, and if they did not go, they would be forced out of Cheyenne. One of the names listed was Wild Bill Hickok. When he saw one of the notices, he used his bowie knife to hack it to pieces.

One day soon after, Sheriff Carr was walking down the street when he spotted Hickok lounging outside a saloon. He called over, "Bill, I guess I'll have to run you out of town."

Hickok gazed at him for a few seconds, then responded, "Jeff Carr, when I go, you'll go with me."

Still, this seemed like a good time to leave Cheyenne. Hickok was soon to go on one last adventure that would involve not one but two women who loved him.

Chapter Eighteen

A WOMAN CALLED CALAMITY

The woman who would become known as Calamity Jane was born Martha Jane Canary in May 1856 near Princeton, Missouri.* Her father, Robert, had been born and raised on a farm in Ohio, and he and his wife, Charlotte, had moved to Missouri soon before the birth of their first child.

To say that Martha had a tough childhood would be a major understatement. Based even on frontier standards in the 1850s and '60s, it was a bad way to grow up. Robert Canary was not known as a hardworking farmer, and his wife liked to frequent local taverns and reportedly could swear as well as the most unruly patrons. "Time and again Charlotte bruised the social expectations of neighborhood wives," writes Richard W. Etulain in *The Life and Legends of Calamity Jane*. "Her brightly colored and eye-catching clothing, her

---

*There is not much doubt about where Calamity Jane was born, but there are varying accounts of when and what her last name was. "Canary" seems to be the twenty-first-century consensus among biographers.

cigar smoking, her public swearing, and her drinking (sometimes to drunkenness) negatively marked a woman when mothers were supposed to be more innocent."

A probable reason why the family had left Ohio was found in 1862 after Robert's father died. It was then discovered that the younger man had pilfered a significant portion of the family's inheritance. The executor sued Robert, but when the time came to serve the papers in Missouri, the Canarys had flown. They had gone gold-seeking in Montana.

When the family arrived in Virginia City, not all of the Canarys' six children had been born yet. Whatever money Robert had stolen must have run out, because by the end of 1864, the family was in desperate straits. Eight-year-old Martha and her two younger sisters, who offered a plausibly pathetic appearance wearing only calico slips, were sent out to beg in the muddy, sleet-showered streets. When they had filled a makeshift wagon with food and clothing donated by sympathetic—and appalled—residents, they trudged out of Virginia City to Nevada—not the state but the slovenly mining camp on the outskirts.

One day, a reporter for *The Montana Post* took note of the little beggars and, after talking to them, had his story. He determined that Charlotte Canary was a "woman of the lowest grade" and that she and her husband were "inhuman brutes who have deserted their poor, unfortunate children." Martha's parents did not have to suffer such criticism for very long. Charlotte died in another mining camp, this one called Blackfoot City, sometime in the spring of 1866. Robert loaded up his children and the family relocated to Salt Lake City, where he died the following year. At age eleven, Martha was the head of the family.

Incredibly, for the future Calamity Jane, life was about to get even

242 · TOM CLAVIN

rougher. The orphaned siblings were split up, taken in by families who either had kind hearts or could use extra hands with chores. Sometime later, Martha showed up at Fort Bridger in Wyoming, and an 1869 state census had her living in Piedmont. She had been taken in by an Alton family to be a babysitter to two young boys. According to Etulain, one of the boys, when he was an elderly man living in Nebraska, recalled that Martha "spent most evenings dancing with soldiers" and she was seen "dressed in a soldier's uniform at a party." His mother fired her.

Martha moved about quite a bit, mostly living in mining and railroad camps and near military forts. She worked at boardinghouses and hotels, cleaning and cooking and anything else that would keep a roof over her head.* With such a day-in and day-out hardscrabble existence, it is likely true that by her midteens, Martha was a prostitute. In a bare-bones autobiography she "wrote" over two decades later, however, she claims to have been busy as an army scout and Indian fighter.

By the early 1870s, she was living in Cheyenne. This was before the gold rush had begun, and Martha recalled that "there was not a respectable shelter in the place" and that "the proprietor of a tent was a lucky person indeed." She was by this time known as Calamity Jane. The reason why, she contends in her autobiography, was that during a fight against Indians, she had saved the life of an army captain, and the grateful officer declared she was "Calamity Jane, heroine of the Plains." There is no evidence to support this. (In addition, the captain apparently didn't know the definition of "calamity.") He also later said the story was an invention, but by then, no one wanted to spoil a good tale. More likely, the nickname reflected a dramatic person-

---

*Sadly, she would spend her last days doing the same thing.

ality, which those who knew her corroborated often and did not have to embellish.

What earned the former Martha Canary some measure of fame came when she was nineteen, in 1875. The year following the Custer expedition into the Black Hills saw a second one, this one commanded by Colonel Richard Irving Dodge. (Dodge City was not named after him, but coincidentally, he did command the fort there for several years.) At the request of William Ludlow and with four hundred men, Colonel Dodge escorted the geologists Walter Jenney and Henry Newton into the Black Hills. Ludlow was the chief engineer of the Dakota Territory, and after accompanying Custer the year before, he remained unconvinced that there were substantial deposits of gold in the region. If he were to prove this, the gold rush would ebb and, presumably, Paha Sapa would remain sacred land.

Embedded with the troops was Calamity Jane. (One of the teamsters driving a wagon was Harry Young, whom Hickok had helped out in Abilene.) By this time, it was common for her to dress like a man, as that made it easier to stay unmolested in the various camps, except when earning money for allowing herself to be molested was involved. That may have been her strategy on this particular expedition. However, she was not incognito for long. One day, she encountered an officer and saluted him. When he returned the salute, several other officers laughed. When the first officer wondered why, he was told the "soldier" he just saluted was Calamity Jane. Apparently, at least a few Bluebellies and officers knew who the soldier really was but saw no harm in it. The embarrassed officer did.

She would eventually be sent packing. But by this time, two Chicago reporters on the excursion who knew of her wrote stories about Calamity Jane, with a few basic facts sprinkled in among the many fictions. A photograph was taken of her at French Creek, and once the gold rush was in full swing—Ludlow's theory having failed to restrain anyone—a peak in the Black Hills was named for her.

One of the articles about Calamity Jane, published in *The Chicago Inter Ocean,* claimed that she "has the reputation of being a better horse-back rider, mule and bull-whacker (driver) and a more unctuous coiner of English, and not the Queen's pure either, than any other man in the command." It was also said about her that she could outdrink any man. Perhaps for the latter reason and the resulting behavior, several troopers were dispatched to escort Calamity Jane from the Black Hills back to Fort Laramie.

Interviewed in 1904 about Calamity Jane by *The Anaconda Standard,* a newspaper in Montana, Jack Crawford, who had served as a captain under General George Crook when Calamity Jane "served" under him, said, "She was simply a notorious character, dissolute and devilish, but possessed a generous streak which made her popular."

The next year, 1876, she was once again camp-following. Bowing to the pressure, the Grant administration essentially tore up the 1868 treaty and opened the Black Hills to settlers, prospectors, and whoever else wanted to stake a claim. Adding insult to injury, the remaining Sioux Indians, so as not to interfere with the influx of whites, were to refrain from hunting from the Powder River region to the Black Hills and to stay within the agencies, or reservations, that had been established for them. Some of the Sioux did not comply, so early that year, three separate army commands were ordered out to force the resisters to the agencies. Heading these commands were Generals Crook and Alfred Terry and Colonel John Gibbon.*

---

*Gibbon had an especially strong Civil War résumé. He commanded the "Iron Brigade" that fought with distinction at the Battles of Antietam, Fredericksburg, and Chancellorsville, and he commanded the defensive position that repelled Pickett's Charge during the Battle of Gettysburg.

If Calamity Jane had had her way, she might have died with others in the Seventh Cavalry at the Battle of Little Bighorn. She infiltrated Terry's command, which included Lieutenant Colonel Custer's troopers. Again disguised as a man, she drove one of the supply wagons. Again discovered, she was sent back, and in a way missed her chance for a different kind of immortality.

She was seen in Custer City and Rapid City, and then she was back in Cheyenne, where she was arrested for stealing clothes. On June 8, a jury found her not guilty, and she was let out of jail. To announce her release to the citizens of Cheyenne, she strolled through town wearing a gown the wife of one of the deputy sheriffs had provided so she had something decent to wear at her trial. Her next act was to rent a buggy. To prepare for whatever journey she had in mind, Calamity Jane celebrated her release "by getting speedily and comfortably drunk," according to a newspaper account.

She claimed she was about to ride the three miles to Fort Russell. Instead, she showed up at Fort Laramie, ninety miles away, and still quite drunk. When able, she pushed on to Fort Fetterman, and from there to Sheridan, Wyoming, this time infiltrating Crook's command. It barely survived a furious assault by Crazy Horse at the Battle of the Rosebud. Calamity Jane may have experienced some of the fighting side by side with the hard-pressed troopers, but that did not prevent her from being sent packing again, this time accompanying the wounded to Fort Fetterman.

In her version of events, which reporters eager for stories lapped up, at this time, Calamity Jane was not a persistent camp follower but a scout and messenger for General Crook. She claimed to be the "bearer of important dispatches" that had to get to Crook, and after swimming across the Platte River, she rode those ninety miles, the ordeal causing her to come down with a "severe illness." After fulfilling her mission, Calamity was taken back to Fort Fetterman in Crook's personal ambulance and spent two weeks lingering near death in a hospital before recovering. This puts her in a more favorable light than does a drunken buggy ride, but little of her account is true.

In any case, it was back to her calamitous ways, setting off to join up with General Crook again. This time, Calamity Jane posed as a teamster, and a wagon master, believing she was a man, hired her. She pulled her weight well enough that it was not until the command was near Fort Reno that she was discovered. She was arrested, and according to the recollection of one of the officers, she was "placed in improvised female attire." She may not have stayed in this costume long. Crook's chief of scouts, Frank Grouard, later maintained that after several scouts had to be dispatched elsewhere, Calamity Jane did indeed fill that role. Given her ability to ride and shoot and her by then plentiful knowledge of the territory—in an 1896 interview, she told a reporter, "I knew every creek an' holler from the Missouri to the Pacific"—this is not far-fetched.

When Crook's command was back at Fort Laramie, she got into a drunken row with several troopers and was offered accommodations in the guardhouse. When she was released, it was with encouragement to move on. A lot of people were heading to Deadwood, on the other side of the border in South Dakota, north of the Black Hills. The town seemed to have sprung up overnight. Calamity Jane just had to figure out getting there.

Thus, the timing was just right when Wild Bill Hickok came along.

Chapter Nineteen

A MARRIED MAN

Only a few years after being founded and acquiring its raunchy reputation, Cheyenne was undergoing that inevitable frontier progression toward becoming civilized. Law and order, not rowdiness, was what the majority of the more established residents wanted. The efforts of the local and county peace officers had proven effective, but the big difference was the outlook along the frontier shared by many new settlers.

"The new hero of the western towns would soon be the shrewd businessman, the booster and joiner, whose sons and grandsons today let their whiskers grow and strap on guns in celebration of 'Old Frontier Week,' or some such, and pay curious reverence to the 'badmen' their ancestors kicked out of town," writes Richard O'Connor. "Indubitably the Sons of Temperance won out over the Sons of Guns." He added that Hickok was now "a member of the old breed."

He was made to feel his years—though he had only just turned thirty-eight—on June 17, 1875, when he was arrested. Wild Bill was not arrested for rowdiness or shooting someone or brawling . . . but again for vagrancy. The loafing around had finally frustrated the local lawmen enough that Hickok was brought to the lockup, and he had to post a two-hundred-dollar bail to be let out. It was unlikely that he was the most visible or "active" loafer in Cheyenne—and with his sartorial splendor, he would hardly be mistaken for being a bum—so the thinking may have been that cuffing Wild Bill Hickok sent a loud message.

And that message was clear: Those uncomfortable with the direction toward a civilized society could move on. There was still plenty of frontier left to explore, some of it offering gold. By this time, the Grant administration had accepted that it simply did not have the political will and the military manpower to prevent the exploration and settlement of the Black Hills. The president authorized a treaty commission to travel west with an offer of six million dollars to buy the Black Hills from the Lakota Sioux.

Putting aside the belief among tribal leaders that the land was not to be bought or sold by anyone, this seemed a small amount for such precious and priceless territory. Red Cloud and Spotted Tail and other leaders said no. They told the commission to go back east and take all the white intruders with them. The response of the Grant administration was to declare victory and announce that it had purchased the Black Hills. The view was that before long the Sioux, who had fewer ways to feed their people and suffered through every winter, would come to their senses and accept the six-million-dollar payment. When that day came, the money would be waiting for them in a Treasury Department escrow account.*

---

*The escrow account continues to exist. With interest, today the initial six million dollars offered has grown to over one billion dollars. The Lakota Sioux have steadfastly refused to take it, demanding instead that the Black Hills be returned to them.

As a result of the "sale," the army ended all efforts to restrict access to the Black Hills. In the spring of 1876, the Sioux would prepare for war. Crazy Horse would again lead the attacks, this time under the command of Sitting Bull. Meanwhile, explorers, gold-seekers, freight companies, settlers, and the simply curious streamed into the newly acquired territory.

Hickok, however, was not yet in a hurry to journey into the Black Hills. By this point, he may have felt even less able physically to undertake long days of prospecting. In addition, during the rest of 1875 and into the winter, his eyesight had continued to fade, perhaps at an accelerated rate as he continued without any treatment other than the blue-lensed glasses to reduce the painful impact of the sunlight. By this time, he may have felt familiar enough with his surroundings in Cheyenne that he thought he was not as much at risk as he would be out in the open. Now, bravado and his reputation were better protection than his pistols.

Joseph Rosa comments that Hickok "displayed an air of confidence that he obviously did not feel. It is alleged that several times, at risk of losing face" by not responding to a challenge, "he laughed off would-be glory hunters by hinting that his eyes had 'gone back on me.'" Rosa speculates that this could also be "a gesture of contempt for the individual concerned—that even without his eyes Hickok believed he could still beat them—and would not deign to waste his time and energy. Regardless of the reaction, Wild Bill Hickok never wasted time in explanation. He continued to maintain that princely aloofness that had marked him through life when he meant to make it obvious he wished to be left alone."

With the exception of that one vagrancy charge, he was. But when the new year began with celebrations across the country for the centennial of the United States, Hickok determined to get moving in the spring. He had been hearing about Deadwood, where some people were getting rich overnight. And then life took an unexpected turn: Mrs. Agnes Lake came to Cheyenne.

This was not by chance. She and Hickok had continued to write each other. He addressed her as Mrs. Lake and then more often as Agnes, and she would address him only as James. He may have asked her to visit him, though midwinter in Wyoming was not a desirable time to travel, especially for a lady used to the warmer destinations of the circus season. And Hickok was probably reluctant to admit he needed her; his pride would not allow that hint of weakness. Most likely, Agnes, a successful businesswoman and far from being a delicate flower, decided to go west because she loved Wild Bill Hickok and they had danced around their feelings long enough.

Her stated reason for arriving in Cheyenne was to visit with S. L. Moyer, a businessman who was related to Agnes in some fashion, and his family. February was not the most appealing time of year to undertake such a journey, but Agnes still had a circus to operate and take on the road come spring. And from their correspondence, she knew Hickok was there and had not followed through on plans to go to the Black Hills. Just in case, if she truly wanted him, she had better get to Cheyenne before he did find sufficient motivation to prospect for gold—and while the tender feelings he had expressed in letters were still fresh in his heart.

Agnes stayed at Moyer's home, and it did not take long before Hickok learned of this. After letting Agnes get settled in with the Moyer family, on March 4, Hickok called on her there. He may have done this because of those tender feelings, or simply as a courtesy, or perhaps, given his uncertain circumstances, he was not as opposed to marriage and circus life as he had been years earlier.

Neither one of them had a lot of time to play with. Hickok would

WILD BILL · 251

be thirty-nine that May, with plenty of mileage on him. On her last birthday, Agnes had turned forty-nine. She now even had a married daughter. The previous November, Emma had married Gil Robinson, who represented yet another generation of Robinsons in the circus industry. Conceivably, Agnes could be a grandmother in the near future.

Accepting the march of time, Wild Bill and Agnes did not waste any of it. The result of their conversation behind closed doors in the parlor of the Moyer house that day was the two emerging to announce that they were to be married. If that was not surprising enough, they insisted that they would have the ceremony performed the very next day.

On March 5, 1876, James Butler Hickok and Mrs. Agnes Lake were married. The ceremony took place at the Moyer home, performed by the Reverend W. F. Warren, a Methodist minister. It was witnessed by the Moyer family and a handful of Hickok's Cheyenne acquaintances.

That evening, Mr. and Mrs. Hickok got on a train that took them to St. Louis, where they transferred to another train, this one to Cincinnati. They would honeymoon there for two weeks, with Agnes introducing her new husband to her hometown, friends, extended family, and no doubt a few strangers who were astonished to find the famed Wild Bill Hickok in such sedate surroundings.

During this time, the plan they formulated was that Agnes would remain in Cincinnati to attend to circus business, which could include exploring a way to turn all or most of the management over to others, possibly Emma and especially Gil Robinson, given his family's "wagon show" background. Hickok's exploring would be in the Black Hills area. When he did indeed find things going his way, he would either send for his wife or return in triumph.

"I expect to join him sometime in the Fall," Agnes wrote to Polly Hickok, her new mother-in-law. "He is going to take a party to the Black Hills and I expect to remain [in Cincinnati] until he sends for me. It is hard to part so soon after being married but it is unavoidable and I am content."

The evening came when Agnes saw her new husband off on the train that would take him to St. Louis and then back to the new frontier. After just the two weeks of marriage, they would never see each other again.

This would also be true of the Hickoks in what was now Troy Grove, Illinois. On his way west, James Butler stopped there to see his mother and siblings. This may have been for only a couple of days. He was now excited about getting to the Black Hills, making a solid strike at the gaming tables or in the field. When he saw his family again after that, it would be as a successful man, not as a fading frontier legend.

By the third week in March, Hickok was back in Cheyenne. He had no time for loafing; he was a newly married man on a mission. But nothing happened right away. As *The Cheyenne Daily Leader* reported, winter was lingering there, and Hickok did not make much headway in mounting an expedition. Possibly, everyone who intended on going to the Black Hills had already left, and a fresh pack of prospectors had not yet arrived by the chilly beginning of spring. Not long after unpacking his bag in Cheyenne, Hickok left, taking the train back to St. Louis.

He could have simply ridden off to the Black Hills himself, but it is possible he hoped to have others along because of his diminishing eyesight, and thus for added protection. Seething about the invasion of Paha Sapa, the Sioux and a few allied tribes were continuing to rally around Sitting Bull and Crazy Horse. No white man, especially

one on his own who might have difficulty seeing danger approach-
ing, was safe. It was believed that when full spring took hold on the
Plains, there would be a war similar to the two years of conflict with
Red Cloud a decade earlier.

St. Louis might prove more fertile ground to gather a company of
adventurers. There, Hickok had posters and flyers printed up and distributed "announcing that he is raising a company for the Black Hills
and Big Horn country, which will leave St. Louis, Jefferson City,
Sedalia and Kansas City, on Wednesday, May 17th," according to the
April 30 edition of *The Cheyenne Daily Sun*, which had received
one of the flyers. Hickok further explained: "We hope to secure a large
body of men for this expedition, not only for better self-protection on
the route, but also to enable us to get cheaper rates of transportation,
and lower figures on our supplies, and make a formidable settlement
in the famous gold region."

However, it does not seem that the expedition gained much
traction . . . or any volunteers at all. Soon, Hickok was back in Cheyenne, without an entourage, but at least he found that his fast friend
Charley Utter had returned from visiting his family in Colorado.

Utter's plan was to organize a Black Hills transportation service,
hauling both freight and passengers. A related business would be a
Pony Express that would deliver mail between Fort Laramie and
Deadwood. His partners would be John James Ingalls and Richard
Seymour, as well as his brother Steve Utter. The entrepreneurs were
putting together a wagon train of men and women who wanted to go
to Laramie, and many would continue on to Deadwood.

This was just the push and opportunity Hickok needed. He decided to throw in with Colorado Charley's venture. And now he would
finally have news to give Agnes. He would not have been surprised
though still a bit chagrined to learn that his wife had written to his

family in Illinois, "I have not heard from him and I feel so bad about it that I can not sleep at night, but the only consolation that I have is that he is where he cannot communicate. If I was sure it was that I would not feel so bad. But I am afraid that he is sick; and if so he will not write nor allow anyone else to do so."

Agnes's reference to Hickok being "sick" could have been about a flare-up of the rheumatism or to his vision difficulties, or an ailment only the couple knew. In any case, he now had something to write about. The caravan of wagons Hickok and Utter had pulled together left Cheyenne on June 27—with no knowledge of that week's disaster at Little Bighorn.

The only mishap along the way was the loss of Hickok's cane. On the night of June 29, he had stuck it in the ground near the top of his bedroll and then stretched out for the night. Somehow, in the caravan's haste to get a good start at dawn, Hickok had forgotten about it. When the travelers came to a ranch, Hickok asked the owner, John Hunton, if he would send someone back for it and at his earliest opportunity have it sent on to him in Deadwood.*

Actually, for Hickok, there was one more mishap on the journey: at Fort Laramie, the caravan was joined by thirty more wagons . . . and Calamity Jane, who, unhappily for Hickok, would be linked to him for the rest of his days, and well beyond.

---

*This Hunton did, but he was apparently in no hurry to deliver it to Deadwood. Hunton wound up keeping the cane until 1921, when he donated it to the Wyoming Historical Society.

Chapter Twenty

DEADWOOD DAYS

After inviting Calamity Jane and the travelers with wagons to join them, the expedition led by Wild Bill Hickok and Colorado Charley Utter that left Fort Laramie numbered around a hundred people. With their wagons and horses and mules and livestock and dogs, it had become quite a caravan. In a way, Hickok now had his own traveling wagon show, imitating his new wife's occupation.

Calamity Jane joined some of the other men in the wagon train in wearing buckskin . . . not necessarily by choice. After her partying excesses with the soldiers from Fort Laramie, she did not have clothes left to go traveling. Hickok and the others lent her enough items to make for a suitable outfit.

A last-minute addition to the party was a young man named Anderson. He had been a teenager when he and Hickok first met a few years earlier at Fort McPherson, and they had become reacquainted in Cheyenne. At the last minute, Hickok invited him to join the Deadwood excursion.

The twenty-two-year-old Joseph Foster Moore Anderson hailed from Holmes County in Ohio. As the youngest of eight children—his exhausted mother died within days of his birth—he was "petted, pampered and spoiled until I became a sickly youngster," according to the Anderson memoir *I Buried Hickok* published decades later. He was raised by an aunt and uncle until he struck out on his own. Not long after he did, he became known as White Eye Anderson. One day on the prairie, he and a friend known as Yankee Judd were searching along a stream for beaver and otter. Suddenly, they were almost completely surrounded by Indians, who, exhibiting a cruel streak, set fire to the tall grass. As the wind pushed the flames toward them, the horses of the two young men took off, so they had to try to outrun the crackling flames. Fortunately, with the blaze licking at their boots, they found a large buffalo wallow with water about a foot deep.

They jumped in and lay as flat as they could and still managed to have a pocket of air inside the coats they had pulled over their heads. When he thought the fire had passed, Anderson sat up. Burning buffalo chips were swirling in the wind, and one of them hit him in the face above one eye. The two young men managed to trudge to a camp with friendlier Indians, and the elderly medicine man treated the burn wound with a mixture of mushy blue clay, roots, and buffalo manure. The new hair that grew in was stark white. The medicine man declared that this was a mark signifying that the Great Spirit would protect him. A reason to believe the medicine man knew what he was talking about was that Anderson would live to 1946, dying three weeks before his ninety-third birthday.

During the caravan's journey, Wild Bill Hickok had one more opportunity to encounter his friend Buffalo Bill Cody, who had left the stage and been pressed back into scouting because of the war with the Plains tribes. The paths of Hickok and Cody intersected at Sage

Creek in eastern Wyoming. There was no beer-drinking frivolity for the old friends this time, though. Hickok was on a personal mission to Deadwood, and Cody and the cavalry troopers were in search of hostile Indians in the wake of the Little Bighorn massacre of Custer and his men. They may have indulged in a sip of whiskey while wishing each other safe and productive travels. It had to have been a solemn parting, with Wild Bill and Buffalo Bill wondering if each would see the other again.

Calamity Jane was not the only female on the trip. Most of the members were male—prospectors, bartenders, and gamblers, all looking for new opportunities—but there were also at least a dozen travelers described as "ladies of easy virtue" by John Gray, one of the wagon riders. Two of them were known as Dirty Em and Madame Moustache. According to her memoir, Calamity Jane was not on this trip at all, claiming that she went to Deadwood as a Pony Express rider delivering mail and had gotten as far as Custer. However, the Pony Express service had long ceased to exist, and Colorado Charley did not initiate an express mail service to and from Deadwood until later in July.*

In his account of the trip to Deadwood, White Eye Anderson wrote that Calamity Jane had some recovering to do, but once she "got cleaned up and sober she looked quite attractive." Anderson did most of the cooking for the group, and she pitched in to help him. He viewed Jane as being "a big-hearted woman," and, he wrote, they "became good friends." Not so for Wild Bill. Anderson recalled that he "surely did not have any use" for Calamity Jane.

---

*The cost of sending a letter was twenty-five cents, and the employees of the mail service, often traveling in groups for protection against hostiles, could carry up to two thousand letters per trip.

She was useful to the wagon train, however. No man on the excursion was better than she was at driving a team of mules, and all were impressed by her bull-whacking skills. She had very good skills with guns, too. One day, a coyote was spotted about a hundred yards from the wagon train. Several men fired at it with their rifles to no avail. Calamity Jane whipped out a pistol and killed it with a single, well-aimed shot.

Though Wild Bill and Calamity Jane were together day and night as the caravan rumbled toward the Black Hills, they did not become romantic partners. Obviously, that is what has been portrayed over the years in novels, television shows, and several movies. For the rest of her life, Calamity Jane claimed more than a passing relationship between her and Hickok, and she even intimated that their Deadwood sojourn produced a child (though she had the year and state wrong). Not only was there no love affair, but from the accounts of others who knew them both during the summer of '76, Hickok could barely tolerate her presence.

His attitude toward Calamity Jane could be chalked up to being completely faithful to his wife. Hickok was, after all, still a groom of only three months. As he worked his way west in June, Hickok had written that he had fallen ill "but am feeling very well and happy now. I god Bless and Protect my Agnes in my Prair. Would I not like to Put my big hands on your Shoulders and kiss you rite now. Love to emma [and] one Thousand kises to my wife Agnes."

But it also seems that Calamity Jane's rough manner rubbed him the wrong way. Perhaps if they had met a few years earlier it would have been a different story because Hickok was no stranger to rough frontier women, including prostitutes and "Indian Annies." But he had a rather refined wife now whom by all the evidence he truly loved and admired. Sharing intimacies with Calamity Jane would have been a blatant betrayal of Agnes . . . in addition to Calamity Jane being a lot more trouble than he needed in his life that summer.

However, Wild Bill and Calamity Jane did share a love of whiskey. He had made sure before leaving Cheyenne that the necessary supplies for the trip included a five-gallon keg of the potent liquor. Every morning, the group would prepare for the day's ride by gathering around Hickok's wagon for a pick-me-up, and there would be more imbibing in the evening. No wonder the keg did not last long, especially, as Anderson recounted, with Calamity Jane being the one who "hit it more often than anyone else." Luck was with the party because they encountered a man named Shingle who was driving a wagonload of whiskey to Deadwood. He sold Hickok another five-gallon keg and continued on his way.

As they wet their whistles after dinner, the group sat around the campfire and swapped stories. Oddly, Hickok had little to say. Perhaps it was a strange sensation those warm evenings on the Great Plains to be reenacting a scene from *Scouts of the Plains*, which was itself a reenactment of thousands of such scenes on the frontier. He may have been in a somber mood, thinking about his wife left behind and the uncertainty of his future and their future together. Any pauses in conversation, however, were filled by Calamity Jane: "I think she told some of the toughest stories I ever heard," Anderson reported, "and there would always be a big crowd come over to the campfire to hear her talk."

After the wagon train arrived in Custer City, the travelers rested up for a couple of days. Then Hickok, Calamity Jane, the Utter brothers, and a handful of others—including, as the local newspaper noted, its "crew of depraved women"—decided to ride ahead to Deadwood. For Wild Bill, it would be his first glimpse of the town that had very quickly acquired a notorious reputation.

However, it was the former Martha Canary who turned out to be the most famous figure to arrive that day. The July 15 edition of *The Black Hills Pioneer* proclaimed, "'Calamity Jane' has arrived." The presence of the others, including Wild Bill Hickok, was not reported. The article was accompanied by a photograph showing Calamity Jane hoisting a mug of beer as a salute to her rough-hewn fans.

Deadwood was the most recent boomtown that had exploded with the westward expansion of the American frontier. Right after the Custer expedition into the Black Hills in the summer of 1874, the first shanties and tents were quickly thrown up in a gulch lined with dead trees—the settlement soon to be called Deadwood Gulch, then simply Deadwood. The gold rush was on, and the new town became the beneficiary of it, if making fast money can be considered a benefit amid increasing violence, filth, and disease.

By March 1876, more than six hundred prospectors were as busy as beavers in the hills around Deadwood. There were plenty of jobs for other men, too, such as laborers and shopkeepers and hotel and restaurant workers. By that summer, the thriving outpost in what was still Dakota Territory had close to ten thousand inhabitants, including over a thousand now who were "looking for color," an expression that meant finding evidence of a gold deposit. Some did find what they were looking for, but most did not—it was estimated that the average income for miners was less than a dollar a day, and they were scraping by in a town with rampant inflation.

Booming the most were the saloons and dance halls and their gaming tables. But other, more "legitimate" establishments, such as restaurants and small shops, were thriving, too. As the historian Sherry Monahan points out, residents "benefited from local fish and game, as well as having food shipped in," indicating that not everyone who emigrated to Deadwood did so to be a prospector. "Local farmers supplied residents and merchants with chicken, pigs, potatoes, turnips, cabbages, eggs and butter." Morgan & Eggots was a shop that sold breads, pies, fancy cakes, candy, and ice cream. Hilary's Lee Street Bakery offered baked goods and cakes for special occasions.

The Black Hills Pioneer began publishing in 1876, and a second newspaper, *The Black Hills Times*, would appear the following year. Later in 1876, a telegraph line strung from Denver would be completed.

When Hickok and his party arrived that July, the main street of Deadwood was still lined with tents and wooden structures, though many of the latter were no longer shacks but one- and two-story buildings consisting of better-cut wood. The street was still dirt, and there were no sidewalks. When weather turned the street into boot-sucking mud, planks were dropped on top of it to cross the street.

"During the daytime the street was packed with jostling men, horses, mules, oxen, and every conceivable manner of conveyance," writes Joseph Rosa. "At night the sidewalks rang with the thud and scuff of thousands of boots, and the saloons did a roaring trade."

Wood and cigar smoke drifted out of those crowded saloons and dance halls, accompanied by the sounds of tinkling pianos, some laughter, some angry shouting, and the occasional gunshot. The air also carried the scents of burning kerosene and coal, horses and their manure, cheap perfume, and men who had gone too long without bathing.

Fortunately, except in the depth of summer when the burning hot air was still, the air remained clear from regular washing. As John Edwards Ames describes the area in *The Real Deadwood*, "The Black Hills are a high-altitude island of timber surrounded by [a] level, barren, treeless plain. They are far less arid than the surrounding region because some of the peaks rise more than a mile high. Thus, they arrest rain clouds that otherwise quickly blow over the dry plains."

As would plague several of the booming cow towns in Kansas in the late 1860s and through the '70s, Deadwood was rife with violence because of the combustible combination of guns and alcohol. As more men poured into the saloons and more whiskey was poured into their glasses, arguments and errant elbows and jealousies and accusations of cheating at cards very quickly escalated to gunplay. That few men were any good at shooting kept the death toll down.

But Deadwood was really just getting started. The Black Hills historian Watson Parker tabulated thirty-four murders between 1876 and 1879, and it can be assumed that in the Black Hills and other remote locations nearby, other deaths by violence went unrecorded. Every so often, there would be a report of a "bedroll killing"—men would sneak up on sleeping or drunken prospectors in the middle of the night and club or knife them to death, then make off with whatever gold they had harvested.

Still, for most men, the risk was worth it because of the potential, if you survived, to live out the rest of your life in ease and comfort. In the summer of 1876, gold was valued at twenty dollars an ounce, and just in June and July, a million dollars' worth of it was gouged out of the Black Hills. Newspapers in some of the major U.S. cities referred to the region as the "richest 100 square miles on Earth."

A ruthless man with ambition and gunmen to protect the services he provided could get rich yet never have to set foot on a claim. Such an entrepreneur was Ellis Albert Swearengen. Al, as he was called, and his twin brother, Lemuel, were born in Iowa, the eldest of eight children. When the thirty-year-old Al Swearengen showed up in Deadwood in May 1876, he brought with him a wife, Nettie, and a desire to get rich quick, whatever way that had to be done. He

WILD BILL · 263

immediately managed to construct the Cricket, a saloon made of canvas and lumber. There was a bar, of course, and an expanding gambling operation and a small dance hall; he also hosted prizefights, and as prostitutes became available, he created small shanties out back that served dozens of men a night. The going rate was $1.50 per assignation.*

Into such surroundings came Wild Bill Hickok and his party, in full plainsman regalia. Passersby stopped in their tracks to witness the arrival of the most famous gunfighter of his time. Hickok and Colorado Charley were immediately recognizable with their long, flowing locks. Calamity Jane was outfitted as though she, too, had spent considerable time as a U.S. Army scout. (According to her tales, she had.) It was something like a royal procession down the sunbaked, dust-swirling street.

The journalist Richard Hughes observed the entrance of Hickok and his entourage and later reported, "They rode the entire length of Main Street, mounted on good horses and clad in complete suits of buckskin, every suit of which carried sufficient fringe to make a considerable buckskin rope." Hickok made for an impressive figure at the head of the column, and the others "basked chiefly in the reflected glory of their leader."

Harry Young, the young man Hickok had befriended and helped in Abilene several years earlier, was now a bartender at Nuttall and Mann's No. 10 saloon. He noted in his memoir, "A more picturesque sight than Hickok on horseback could not be imagined." Hickok rode up to the saloon, and the owner "greeted him with much enthusiasm

---

*It was not until the following year that Swearengen opened the Gem Theater, a much larger business portrayed in the HBO series *Deadwood*. Until it burned down in September 1879, it is believed to have earned at least five thousand dollars a night from alcohol, gambling, and prostitution, a huge take for the time.

and asked him to make the saloon his headquarters. This meant money for Mann, as Hickok was a great drawing card."

One of those in the ad hoc parade was Richard Seymour, who had been with the expedition from the beginning. Bloody Dick, as he was called, was believed to be—probably because he claimed it—the son of an aristocratic English family, who had come to America seeking adventure. He appeared on the frontier in 1874, serving as a packer for the U.S. Army, and he made the acquaintance of Buffalo Bill Cody. Both were on the Big Horn expedition and the Powder River campaign, and while he was stationed at Fort Robinson, Seymour's employment was listed as "assistant in charge of public train." Somewhere along the way, he and Colorado Charley had become friends, and Seymour was on the Deadwood expedition because he would partner with Utter and John James Ingalls* to create the express mail service between Deadwood and Custer City and beyond to Fort Laramie. Ingalls, a Massachusetts native, was a former Kansas newspaper editor now representing the state in the U.S. Senate.

The new arrivals set up camp on Whitewood Creek . . . all except Calamity Jane. Swearengen's dance hall was down to only two singers and dancers, which didn't make the mass of men who crowded in every night very happy. Calamity Jane was immediately hired. However, she could not be kicking up her heels in a buckskin outfit that still had trail dust wafting off it. Hickok and the other men passed the hat and gave Calamity Jane twenty dollars. Hickok's contribution was accompanied by a request that she wash behind her ears. Accordingly, she jumped in the creek to take a bath, then dressed again and went off to town.

---

*He was a second cousin of Charles Ingalls, whose daughter Laura Ingalls Wilder would write the frontier classic *Little House on the Prairie*.

After a few days, the lenders wondered if she had simply drunk up the loan, but then Calamity Jane returned, "all togged out in a good outfit of female clothes," Anderson recalled, and took care of the debt from a roll of bills she pulled out of her stocking.

Everyone but Hickok was repaid. He refused the return of the twenty dollars, saying, "At least she looks like a woman now."

Well, she was a woman, but she sure did not act like a proper lady of the time when her dander was up. Another female member of the Hickok party was a slight redhead everyone called Tit Bit. (Other colorfully named female companions of Calamity Jane's on the trip were known as Big Dollie, Smooth Bore, and Sizzling Kate.) Calamity Jane took her under her wing to show her how she could survive and even make a living in Deadwood. These activities included teasing men for drinks and meals, and sometimes providing favors. The relatively inexperienced Tit Bit was not discriminating enough to avoid taking on a man known as Laughing Sam as a client. He was a gambler with a shaky reputation, and he added to it by paying Tit Bit with a small pouch that he said contained gold dust but was instead a mixture of metal filings and sand.

Tit Bit, when the ruse was discovered, was not about to take on Laughing Sam . . . but she had a friend who, like Wild Bill, feared no one. Borrowing two pistols from Colorado Charley, Calamity Jane went back into Deadwood, found the saloon Laughing Sam was in, and entered to confront him. There was a hush as onlookers took in the scene of the well-known and usually fun-loving Calamity Jane training the two pistols on the seated gambler, whose reaction was far from laughter.

She filled the silence by declaring she would fill Laughing Sam with lead, but first she had to reveal to all what he had done. She did, using particularly pungent language. When Sam saw she was ready to squeeze the triggers, he reached not for his own gun but for two twenty-dollar gold coins, which he begged be given to Tit Bit. Calamity Jane left with them, and no one tried to cheat Tit Bit again.

It was the kind of action Wild Bill Hickok would have taken on behalf of a swindled friend. But he may not have had it in him anymore. Colorado Charley and others noted that Hickok seemed moody and often melancholy. One time when Utter pressed him a bit, Hickok responded with what was like one of the soliloquys he'd had to recite while onstage with Buffalo Bill, Texas Jack, and the rest of the cast. This time, though, what he was saying seemed heartfelt.

"I feel that my days are numbered," Hickok told his friend. "My sun is sinking fast. I know I shall be killed here, something tells me I shall never leave these hills alive, somebody is going to kill me. But I don't know who he is or why he is going to do it. I have killed many men in my day, but I never killed any man yet but what it was kill or get killed."

Utter figured Hickok was just tired from the journey. But it spooked him nonetheless.

Chapter Twenty-one

THE PREMONITION

Having heard about the event from Buffalo Bill Cody, Wild Bill Hickok and the advance guard of his caravan that set up camp just outside Deadwood were able to confirm the persistent rumors of a great loss at the hands of Indian warriors. Indeed, George Armstrong Custer was dead.

On the morning of June 25, Lieutenant Colonel Custer, accompanied by his brothers Tom and Boston and a nephew and brother-in-law, had led units of the Seventh Cavalry in an attack on an Indian village near the Little Bighorn River in Montana. Custer was unaware that the Lakota Sioux medicine man Sitting Bull had gathered 2,500 Sioux, Arapaho, and Northern Cheyenne warriors. Led by the war chiefs Crazy Horse and Gall, the mass of Indians surrounded and killed Custer and 261 of his men.

While this was a stunning victory for the Lakota Sioux and their allies, offering them stronger hope that the white invaders would melt away like spring snow, the actual result was an intensification of the military pressure on Indians throughout the Plains. What would be called the Great Sioux War of 1876 became an effort to force onto reservations the remaining native peoples who wanted to live independently, and while the army was at it, avenge the Little Bighorn massacre.

In a gruesome way, it was Buffalo Bill who was first to enact some revenge. About a week after having met Hickok and the caravan, Cody and the Fifth Cavalry were on patrol when they intercepted a band of Cheyenne warriors. A running battle began. The warrior Cody went after was named Yellow Hair—ironically, one of the nicknames Indians had for Custer. After shooting the warrior off his horse, Cody jumped off his own horse and scalped the dead Yellow Hair. Raising his fist, Cody cried out, "First scalp for Custer!" For years, in his stage productions, Cody would reenact this scene, to the delight of eastern audiences and the consternation of the Indian members of the cast.*

Reports of the Little Bighorn battle and skirmishes with Indian bands made people aware of the increased risk of travel across the frontier, especially the Plains. If Wild Bill Hickok had second thoughts about a new career as a gold prospector or just wanted to return to his bride, this was not the best time to take to the road. Or maybe it didn't matter, because the lanky gunfighter was in something of a limbo state.

When Hickok finally ambled into Deadwood to explore the infamous town and, presumably, how to go about forming an expedition into the Black Hills, he saw that there were indeed men who had found gold and perhaps were in the process of becoming rich . . . if

---

*The actual scalp and Yellow Hair's quirt and weapons were sent by Cody to his friend Moses Kerngood in Rochester, New York, who displayed them in his cigar store. The scalp can now be found at the Buffalo Bill Museum in Cody, Wyoming.

they didn't toss it all away on the whiskey and women the Deadwood saloons offered. At a creaky thirty-nine, though, with failing eyesight,* Hickok was more convinced than ever before that he was not about to be kneeling by the side of a creek sifting through dirt and sand all day.

He may have tried, however. In a letter to his wife dated July 17, Hickok wrote, "I have but a few moments left before this letter starts. I never was as well in my life; but you would laugh to see me now—just got in from prospecting. Will go away again tomorrow. Will write again in the morning, but God knows when the letter will start. My friend will take this to Cheyenne, if he lives."

If it was true that he had made an attempt at prospecting, more likely the exercise further persuaded Hickok that any riches he might glean would come at the gaming tables. The rest of the letter, signed J. B. Hickok, sounds completely sincere: "I don't expect to hear from you, but it is all the same. I know my Agnes and only live to love her. Never mind, Pet, we will have a home yet, then we will be so happy. I am almost sure I will do well here. The man is hurrying me. Good-bye, dear wife. Love to Emma."

When he was not in Deadwood, he relaxed at the Whitewood Springs camp and practiced drawing and shooting, just in case. In Deadwood, as the historian James D. McLaird put it, "Hickok spent only a few weeks in the Black Hills . . . and he wasted most of his time in Deadwood drinking, gambling, and shooting at targets."

No doubt, his prospecting ambitions, such as they were, were

---

* According to a document housed in the National Archives, on the way to Deadwood, Hickok visited the doctor at Fort Laramie, who noted that the gunfighter was "going blind from glaucoma." If Hickok was indeed given this blunt assessment, and the fact didn't put a stop to his plans, it probably made him all the more desperate to push on with the gold-seeking expedition.

hampered by his having agreed to Carl Mann's proposition. Saloon No. 10 became his home in Deadwood, and he was given a generous bar tab, with drinks often served by Harry Young. The bartender was one of many who could not get enough of Hickok's stories. By then, the famed gunfighter was forgetful or jaded enough that it did not matter which stories were true.

In his memoir *Hard Knocks*, Young would recall that since he had last seen Hickok, the frontiersman had "changed greatly and tried very hard to avoid notoriety, but unfortunately his past reputation was still a matter of public comment. Bill had attained much the same reputation as a prizefighter who has successfully sent all of his opponents down to defeat and become the acknowledged champion."

Hickok developed a set routine to get each day going: "The first thing Wild Bill would do in the morning was empty his pistols in target practice at an old cottonwood tree that grew on the bank of the creek," White Eye Anderson remembered. "Then he would take a stiff drink of whiskey and he would be ready for breakfast."

A cheerful event was the arrival in Deadwood of his old friend California Joe, who "had hardly changed since Wild Bill saw him last," writes Joseph Rosa. "His hair and beard were still matted, and he still had his great sense of humor." It was not uncommon for passersby in town to see Wild Bill, Colorado Charley, and California Joe heading for the No. 10 saloon, where they would swap tales of life on the prairie.

That month, with the summer broiling the dust-covered streets of Deadwood, Hickok's camp was visited by a reporter from *The Springfield Republican*, a newspaper in Massachusetts. Leander Richardson had been dispatched to inform readers back home about the Black Hills gold rush.

He met Colorado Charley first, who in turn suggested that Richardson meet his friend Wild Bill. In the "middle of a bright sunny afternoon" the two men found Hickok sitting on a board lying on the ground in front of a saloon. "His knees were drawn up in front of him as high as his chin, and he was whittling at a piece of wood with a large pocketknife."

Richardson wrote that after Utter asked Hickok to stand up for an introduction, "Wild Bill slowly arose. He came up like an elevator, and he came up so high that I thought he was never going to stop. He was unusually tall, and quite spare as to flesh, but very brawny and muscular."

The reporter became enamored right away with the legendary gunfighter, even more so when Hickok, much the veteran performer, tossed a tomato can in the air and shot it twice before it landed on the ground. And Richardson was mightily impressed one afternoon when they strolled through Deadwood and a gun battle broke out between two men on the main drag. As citizens sought cover, Hickok paused to observe the shoot-out and offered the trembling reporter sarcastic comments about their poor marksmanship.

Another time, there was an altercation in a bar, and when the proprietor produced a shotgun, the patrons hurried for the exit. But Hickok stopped Richardson, saying, "Young man, never run away from a gun. Bullets can travel faster than you can. Besides, if you're going to be hit, you had better get it in the front than in the back. It looks better."

Richardson marveled at his cool and asked Hickok how he could control his nerves during an armed confrontation. The gunfighter replied, "When a man believes the bullet isn't moulded that is going to kill him, what in hell has he got to be afraid of?"

Richardson was surprised by the desire for order and cleanliness in the midst of chaotic living for most residents. However, in this case, it was Colorado Charley representing that even more so than Wild Bill. Both men still bathed every day, either in the creek or in a Deadwood bathhouse, but Utter's fastidiousness went well beyond that of his friend. Richardson reported that one night Hickok returned drunk to the camp, and seeing Utter's tent empty, and the rather expensive blankets in it proving too tempting, he ignored Utter's "do not enter" prohibition and fell asleep within.

When Utter came back from town and saw Hickok sprawled across his blankets, he dragged him out by his feet. Muttering oaths, Utter took the blankets, shook them out thoroughly, and hung them on tree branches for a good airing. A bemused Hickok gazed at his friend's activities for a few minutes, then "with a parting grunt, climbed into his wagon and went peacefully to sleep again."

Colorado Charley may also have had a bone to pick with Hickok over gambling. It and his daily quota of liquor went hand in hand. The problem was, Hickok was losing at poker more than he was winning, and when funds were low, Utter, who had done very well in real estate and other ventures back home, provided Hickok with more money. Deadwood had become a mecca for professional cardsharps, and they were simply better players than the shootist. It was also possible that Hickok was being cheated regularly and his eyes could not discern the tricks.

A rumor began to spread that put Hickok's life in danger, the kind of danger he had faced in Hays City and Abilene when he was younger and had clear eyesight. A story circulated that the legendary gunfighter had been recruited to come to Deadwood. "He had never been north of Cheyenne before this, although many in Deadwood knew him, some only by reputation," commented Harry Young. "A good many gunmen of note were in town and his arrival caused quite a commotion."

The rumor claimed that an attempt to impose law and order in Deadwood was about to get under way, and the one who would do the imposing was Wild Bill Hickok. The new marshal would bring to the Sodom and Gomorrah of the Dakotas the same kind of six-shooter discipline he had brought to Abilene. Hickok knew nothing about such an effort, but hearing about it, he immediately understood that gunmen and even businessmen like Swearengen who felt threatened might arrange for his death even before he could contemplate pinning on a badge.

There were actual feelers put out for men who would do the hit, by Tim Brady and Johnny Varnes (and probably Swearengen), who controlled some of the gambling operations in town. One of the fellows in Deadwood with an unsavory reputation was the gunman Jim Levy, who turned the job down, intimidated by Hickok's reputation. Another man-killer who was approached was Charlie Storms.

Storms was just the kind of gunman Hickok had to be wary of—envious of the reputations a few other men had earned, and waiting for an opportunity to do something about it. In 1876, Storms was a gray-whiskered fifty-three with a long résumé, not much of it good. He hailed from upstate New York, lived for a time in Mexico—possibly as a mercenary in the routine uprisings and suppressions there—then went cross-country in 1849 to seek his fortune (unsuccessfully) in the California gold rush. It is not known what he did during the Civil War years, but afterward, he roamed the frontier as a hired gun and a gambler. Storms's travels took him to Virginia City, Leadville, Dodge City, and Deadwood, where he had survived several gunfights.

However, he refused to take a shot at Wild Bill that summer of '76. Storms moved on, revisiting old haunts that would still have him, and in 1881, he was in Tombstone, Arizona. There, on February 25, he had the misfortune of encountering men he could not intimidate and, worse, outdraw. Storms was drinking a lot of whiskey in the Oriental Saloon. This new watering hole was co-owned by Wyatt Earp, and helping to manage it and provide security was Bat Masterson. The two best friends had reunited a few years after being lawmen together in Dodge City. Masterson certainly knew Storms, even considered him somewhat of a friend, yet the large consumption of whiskey and the man's penchant for gunplay had the saloon's manager on alert.

Another misfortune for Storms was he was losing at faro, the most popular card game at the time on the frontier, and the dealer was Luke Short. The diminutive dealer was a good friend to both Bat and Wyatt, and his temper sometimes caused him some trouble. On this particular whiskey-soaked evening, Storms criticized the quality of the dealing and connected it to his ongoing streak of bad luck. When Short was considerably less than sympathetic, Storms slapped him.

Short went for his gun, but an instant later, "I jumped between them and grabbed Storms, at the same time requesting Luke not to shoot," Bat wrote about the incident.

The former sheriff of Ford County, Kansas, took Storms outside and told him to go to his hotel room and get some sleep. It appeared that Storms complied. Luke Short then stepped outside the saloon, and as Bat was explaining what had transpired, Storms reappeared "without saying a word, at the same time pulling his pistol." Short pulled his faster and Storms "was dead when he hit the ground." Short turned to Bat and said, "You sure pick some of the damnedest friends, Bat."*

---

*Storms may have been mostly a good-for-nothing gunman, but he contributed to the creation of the bulletproof vest. Dr. George Goodfellow noted that though a

Colorado Charley heard the rumor about Wild Bill becoming the Deadwood marshal, and he feared that his friend would not survive a confrontation with a determined assassin, or especially several of them. One evening during supper at their campfire, Utter suggested that the camp be moved. When Hickok asked where, Utter replied, "It might be a good scheme to organize a little party and go over to Standing Rock and cut out some ponies."

Hickok appeared to consider this. It was fun to find a remuda of Indian ponies, chase off a couple of sentries, and steal the horses. They could be brought to the nearest fort and sold. But he shook his head. Hickok suspected his friend's motives, and he was not leaving Deadwood because there might be danger. Plus, this was not a good time to go stirring up some Indians.

"Those fellows over across the creek have laid it out to kill me," he told Utter, "and they're going to do it or they ain't. Anyway, I don't stir out of here unless I'm carried out."

According to several accounts, one day in Deadwood, Hickok was approached by six men who said they had business with the man expected to be marshal. Even in his best days, Wild Bill would have had a tough go of it in a shoot-out with six men, but now, with the shape his eyes were in . . .

He did not hesitate. In an instant, his Colt pistols were out of their holsters and aimed at the figures before him. "I understand that you cheap, would-be gunfighters from Montana have been making remarks about me," Hickok said with a firm voice, his hands steady, fingers on the triggers. "I want you to understand unless they are

bullet struck Storms in the heart, not a drop of blood had exited the wound. The Tombstone physician extracted the intact bullet and found it wrapped in silk from the victim's handkerchief. Dr. Goodfellow began experimenting with bullet-resistant clothing, beginning with layers of silk, then moving on to other materials.

stopped there will shortly be a number of cheap funerals in Dead-wood. I have come to this town not to court notoriety but to live in peace and do not propose to stand for insults."

The strategy worked—it dawned on the six men that not only did someone have the drop on them, but that someone was the legend-ary gunfighter Wild Bill Hickok. The way he could shoot with both hands, he could kill all six of them and still have six bullets left. The Montana men moved on. After word of the confrontation spread through Deadwood, there were no more plots to kill Hickok.

But there was by now in Deadwood a man named Jack McCall.

Sometimes known as Crooked Nose Jack, McCall had been born in Jefferson County, Kentucky, twenty-four years earlier. As a teen-ager, he worked various jobs as he wended his way west, and in 1869, he was with a buffalo-hunting outfit on the Kansas-Nebraska border. McCall spent some time in Wyoming, and in Deadwood in 1876, he was going by the name of Bill Sutherland. Some people glanced twice at him on the street—not because of his short sandy-brown hair and spare mustache but for his crossed eyes.

In what is believed to be the last letter Hickok wrote—and cer-tainly the last one to his wife—he expressed a very dim view of his immediate future: "Agnes Darling, if such should be we never meet again, while firing my last shot, I will gently breathe the name of my wife—Agnes—and with wishes even for my enemies I will make the plunge and try to swim to the other shore."

Did Hickok indeed have a premonition? J. W. Buel, who as a young reporter had known Hickok, wrote years later, "The very few intimate friends Bill had were well acquainted with his peculiar belief in spir-itualism. He claimed to be clairvoyant, especially when danger threat-ened, and the narrow escapes he had gave some evidence of the reality of his spiritual sight."

So his actual sight was fading, but his "spiritual sight" was intact and may have become sharper. At the end of July, once again Hickok said to his friend, "Charley, I feel this is going to be my last camp, and I won't leave it alive."

Chapter Twenty-two

DEAD MAN'S HAND

W hen August began, Wild Bill Hickok had not only forgotten prospecting in the Black Hills but had to recognize his path to riches did not lie in gambling, either. In the three weeks since he arrived in the Deadwood area, he had lost more money than he'd won. However, he kept returning to the familiar confines of Nuttall and Mann's No. 10 saloon. There he was often surrounded by friends, and he felt less exposed to dangers he might not be able to see until it was too late. It was not just being prudent—for the first time in his life, Hickok felt fear, or something close to it.

The somber pronouncements he offered about his life ending soon indicated that fear. But by remaining stuck in a saloon, and especially losing money, he was breaking his promise to his wife. Agnes was no longer on the road with the circus; she was waiting faithfully, and with increasing trepidation, in Cincinnati to hear from her husband. Hickok was in a difficult position of being unable to move forward but too ashamed to go backward. Thus, he dithered in Deadwood, perhaps waiting for fate to intervene.

Joseph Rosa in *The West of Wild Bill Hickok* offers an interesting view, contending that the events in Deadwood were like the final moves in a chess match, and he echoes what Hickok had just written to Agnes: "That Hickok knew his enemies were determined to get him is no longer disputed, yet his coolness while awaiting their move was remarkable. His friends tried to persuade him to leave town for a while and join California Joe on a buffalo hunt. But he refused. To Wild Bill that would have been tantamount to admitting fear, or worse, cowardice."

On the night of August 1, Hickok was in his usual spot, a chair against the wall, playing cards at the No. 10 saloon. One of the participants in the poker game was Jack McCall, who had been drinking steadily that evening. Hickok may have thought his luck was turning because there were enough winning hands to pretty much clean McCall out. Feeling bad for McCall, who seemed stupid but harmless, Hickok gave him money to buy breakfast and advised him not to play cards again until he could cover his losses. At first, McCall refused the handout, but Hickok insisted.

The following day, Wednesday, August 2, Hickok entered Nuttall and Mann's No. 10 saloon at 3 P.M. dressed in his longtime favorite outfit, which included the Prince Albert frock coat, calfskin boots, and black sombrero. As usual, he had bathed, then had a noonish breakfast with Colorado Charley, and when he entered the saloon, he was easily the best-dressed and most presentable man in the place. He wore his gun belt the usual way, with the pistols up near his hips, handles out.

Hickok chatted with Harry Young at the bar and downed a shot of whiskey. He saw a poker game already in progress that included Carl Mann, Charles Rich (only seventeen years old), and Captain William Massie. The latter was a forty-five-year-old former captain of steamboats that plied the Missouri River who had contracted gold fever, then discovered he preferred poker to prospecting. Rich was in the seat against the wall. Usually, Hickok did not even have to ask, the man in the wall chair would immediately give it up, but in this instance, Rich did not. Reluctantly, Hickok sat in a chair on one side of the poker table. At least it gave him an unobstructed view of the saloon's front door, and he was aware that a few steps behind him there was a rear exit.

The game continued for close to an hour. None of the men apparently had any other pressing business, and playing poker in the cool and dark confines of the saloon was as good a way as any to pass the sultry summer afternoon. The only sour note was that several times Hickok asked the teenager Rich to exchange seats with him, and the latter refused—he was either being unnecessarily obstinate or was having a run of good luck and did not want to change a thing. Mann and Massie, who was opposite Hickok at the table, noticed the plainsman's unease, but they did not have the coveted chair against the wall to offer. It didn't help Hickok's mood that the cards were going against him.

Lady Luck continued to defy him. Hickok called to Young for a loan of fifty dollars, as he was almost cleaned out. The bartender brought that amount in chips over to the table. Referring to Massie, Hickok remarked, "The old duffer broke me on the last hand." Those would turn out to be Wild Bill Hickok's last words.

Jack McCall entered the No. 10 saloon. For his purpose, it paid to be a somewhat small and nondescript man, and little notice was taken of him. He stood at the bar and over time worked his way along it, toward the poker table with Hickok and his companions. If Hickok had spotted him entering the front door, he dismissed McCall . . . or that is one explanation. Surely, he would have recognized McCall from only the night before and regarded him for a few moments, still viewing him as stupid and harmless. However, it is possible that Hickok did not see him well enough to recognize him.

In any case, McCall loitered at the bar. There were no sudden movements, as the man did nothing to attract attention. For once, it seems, the sixth sense Hickok had always had about danger was not working that afternoon.

Quietly and unobtrusively, McCall eased himself behind Hickok. Rich dealt cards to the three other men. Hickok held in his hands a pair of aces, a pair of eights, and a queen. At about 4:10, McCall stepped forward and placed the muzzle of a .45-caliber revolver against the back of Hickok's head and pulled the trigger. There was the sudden loud sound of a shot, and McCall cried out, "Damn you, take that!" Hickok jerked forward. He was motionless for a few moments, then fell sideways out of the chair.

Massie was startled by the sudden commotion and confused by a numbness he felt in his left arm. Such was Hickok's reputation that at first Massie thought that the gunfighter, angry at losing money to him, had shot him. But as soon as Hickok fell to the floor, Massie saw McCall and his smoking gun standing there. He would soon learn that the bullet fired into Hickok's skull had exited below his right cheekbone and then became lodged in Massie's wrist.*

McCall waved his pistol at others in the saloon and shouted,

---

*Massie never had one of the most infamous bullets of the American West removed. Over the years during his travels, when he arrived somewhere he announced that "the bullet that had killed Wild Bill Hickok had come to town." It was buried with William Massie after he died in St. Louis in 1910.

"Come on, you sons of bitches!" There was an abrupt rush for the front door. McCall, after attempting to fire the gun at Harry Young, tossed it aside and ran out the exit door. A saddled horse was there, but McCall fell off it because the saddle had been loosened. He resumed running. He paused to try to hide in a butcher shop. McCall could hear out on the street one, two, then many voices yelling, "Wild Bill has been shot!" and "Wild Bill is dead!"

There was, alas, no doubt about that. Hearing the shouts, Colorado Charley rushed to the No. 10 saloon, where he met Ellis Peirce, a Deadwood barber, who determined that Hickok had "bled out quickly." Doc Peirce was the closest the town had to a coroner.* Hickok had died immediately . . . and he never saw it coming. In one hand were the cards he had been dealt, to be forever known as a Dead Man's Hand. It was also found that of the six bullets in McCall's pistol, five were defective, meaning the only "good" bullet in the gun was the one shot into Hickok's head.

Obviously, McCall had not planned an escape because he left his hiding spot and simply ran down the main street, kicking up dust as he went like a frightened rabbit. Harry Young, after recovering from the initial shock of seeing Hickok shot, was giving chase, and by ones and twos, others on the street joined in. Most people, however, fled, seeking shelter. It was being shouted along the street that it was Wild Bill Hickok who was doing the shooting, taking revenge on Deadwood for his bad luck at cards.

McCall was apprehended before he got too much farther. The August 5 edition of *The Deadwood Pioneer-Times* would report

---

*In his coroner's report, Peirce included that Hickok's corpse, when laid out, looked like a wax figure and that "Wild Bill was the prettiest corpse I have ever seen."

matter-of-factly, "The murderer Jack McCall was captured after a chase by many citizens and a guard placed over him."

Never one to miss an opportunity, and especially now that her "lover" was dead, Calamity Jane offered that when she heard about the killing, "I at once started to look for the assassin and found him at Shurdy's butcher shop and grabbed a meat cleaver and made him throw up his hands."

The actual whereabouts of Calamity Jane that afternoon are unknown, but she definitely was not in Nuttall and Mann's No. 10 saloon, before or after Hickok's murder. Thus, also untrue is her tale of sorrowfully cradling his body.

Now that the mob had McCall, the question was what to do with him. This was debated at a public meeting held the next day, Thursday, August 3, at the Bella Union Theater. A few voices suggested that they lynch the killer and be done with it. Deadwood did not have a jail nor a court, certainly no sitting judge, so lynching was at least an expedient solution. But the one settled upon was to convene a miner's court, which had become a standard practice on the far reaches of the frontier when there was no practical legal alternative.

At first blush, the murder of Wild Bill Hickok looked like an easy prosecution. There were several witnesses who testified to McCall's shooting the victim.* And since McCall had crept up from behind and shot Hickok in the back of the head, any claim of self-defense would be ludicrous. McCall may have been disgruntled about Hickok wiping him out during a poker game and then lecturing him about it, but that did not justify cold-blooded murder.

When the trial began, McCall's defense was that he had shot

---

*One of the witnesses was Captain Massie, who displayed the bullet wound in his wrist.

Hickok as revenge for killing his brother back in Abilene and that if he could, he'd shoot him again. This explanation was completely untrue—Hickok had killed no one related to McCall in Abilene, plus McCall had three sisters and no brother. However, the ad hoc jury had no way of knowing this. Avenging a family member was an acceptable motive for shooting someone, but it was still a surprise when two hours after the trial concluded, the jury returned a not guilty verdict. *The Black Hills Pioneer* commented, "Should it ever be our misfortune to kill a man, we would simply ask that our trial take place in some of the mining camps in these hills."

The New North-West publication in Montana intoned about the murder and acquittal, "Numerous other crimes of a like nature have been committed. All go unpunished, leaving us in a state of chaos."

Whatever the actual reason for McCall's act, the result was the same. Colorado Charley, with some assistance from Doc Peirce, took charge of the funeral arrangements. In a notice in *The Black Hills Pioneer,* he announced the funeral would also be that Thursday, at the Whitewater Springs camp. Those who wished to could visit Wild Bill lying in repose before the burial.

For several hours, miners and shopkeepers and saloon girls and others filed past the coffin to pay their respects. Peirce clipped a lock of Hickok's hair and gave it to Colorado Charley, who in turn gave it to the reporter Leander Richardson. He would keep it for thirty-one years; then it was presented to Agnes.*

Even in death, Wild Bill's appearance impressed others. A reporter for *The Chicago Inter Ocean* wrote, "His long chestnut hair, evenly

---

*Its journey not yet completed, sometime after Agnes's death, the lock of Hickok's hair was on the move again, eventually becoming part of the Wilstach Collection at the New York Public Library.

WILD BILL · 285

parted over his marble brow, hung in waving ringlets over the broad shoulders; his face was cleanly shaved excepting the drooping mustache, which shaded a mouth which in death almost seemed to smile." He couldn't help but add that Hickok's heart, now stilled, "had beat with regular pulsation amid the most startling scenes of blood and violence."

Wisely wasting no time, Jack McCall left Deadwood. But the law was not finished with him. McCall lit out for Wyoming and probably thought he was safe there. As word spread that he was the man who had killed Wild Bill Hickok, many who encountered him must have been shocked. *This* was the man who had gunned down a legend? And gotten away with it?

He did not wind up getting away with it. Thanks to the badgering of Colorado Charley, Wyoming authorities determined that McCall's trial was not legal because Deadwood was in Indian Territory, not in a state or territory officially part of the United States. An arrest warrant was issued, and on August 29, McCall was apprehended by a deputy U.S. marshal in Laramie. His second, and legal, trial would take place in Yankton, South Dakota.

The jury at that trial, which began on December 4 of that same year, was not as gullible. Looking on during the proceedings was Lorenzo Hickok, who had traveled from Troy Grove in Illinois to represent the grieving Polly and the rest of the family. There was some satisfaction this time when McCall was found guilty and sentenced to hang.

The sentence was carried out on March 1, 1877. That morning, McCall was marched up the stairs of the hanging platform, where a priest awaited. The two kneeled and prayed. Then McCall's arms and legs were tied. A black hood was pulled down over his head. McCall, now standing, was granted one more prayer. After the noose was placed around his neck, McCall's last words were, "Draw it tighter, Marshal." The trap was sprung, and McCall became the first man to be legally executed in Dakota Territory.

The killer was interred in a Catholic cemetery in Yankton. Fourteen years later, when the cemetery was being moved to make room for an insane asylum, McCall's body was exhumed. The noose was still around his neck. He was reburied, but the location remains unknown.

Wild Bill Hickok was buried in the Deadwood cemetery on Friday. Colorado Charley had a marker created that read: "Wild Bill, J.B. Hickok killed by the assassin Jack McCall in Deadwood, Black Hills, August 2d, 1876. Pard, we will meet again in the happy hunting ground to part no more. Good bye, Colorado Charlie, C.H. Utter."

The two did meet again, in a way, and not in a happy hunting ground. In 1879, Utter traveled from Colorado to Deadwood to supervise the relocation of Hickok's body to its present location, in the Mount Moriah Cemetery. Because of previous problems with vandals and souvenir hunters, the grave is surrounded by a cast-iron fence, with a U.S. flag flying nearby.

Agnes Lake Hickok may not have known about her husband's death until an article on the killing in Deadwood appeared in a Cincinnati newspaper. Perhaps it struck her that both of her husbands had been murdered by guns fired at point-blank range and in the month of August.

She could not leave home to go to Deadwood because her daughter Emma was about to give birth. On August 15, she became a grandmother when Agnes Emma Robinson was born. Both her grief and her desire to visit Hickok's grave were strong; however, Emma had a slow recovery, the baby was especially fussy, and Gil Robinson was traveling with his circus. In November, Agnes wrote a letter to the

WILD BILL · 287

Hickok family that informed, "I can see him day and night before me. The longer he is dead, the worse I feel."

It would not be until September 1877 that Agnes made the journey to Deadwood. She was accompanied by two western acquaintances, Buckskin Charley Dalton and Texas George Carson. She sat at her husband's grave for several hours, then made arrangements for a headstone before departing Deadwood. She went to Cheyenne, where on the twenty-seventh, the fifty-one-year-old Agnes married the twenty-eight-year-old Carson.

It may seem no more than an odd coincidence that within six weeks of each other in 1876, and with the nation's centennial in between, the American West had lost its two most famous and legendary figures in George Armstrong Custer and Wild Bill Hickok, and both still only in their thirties. With the former, a rousing victory at Little Bighorn could have catapulted him to the White House that fall, or possibly no later than 1880, when James Garfield, another young Civil War general, was elected. At the least, if Custer had escaped death, chances are his popularity would only have increased.

Hickok, though, seems to have sensed that the American West was passing him by. The two-gun lawing he had employed in Hays City and Abilene was being replaced by peace officers, with the emphasis on "peace." The Old West that the Wild Bill Hickok legend had popularized was already receding into history. As Joseph Rosa put it, "It might be said that Wild Bill's death was a destiny fulfilled, that McCall's pistol was an instrument of fate. It might also be said, with truth, that Wild Bill had outlived his time and had to die."

Hickok had died with his era. And he had seen it coming.

EPILOGUE

Poor Bill was afterwards killed at Deadwood, in the Black Hills, in a cowardly manner," wrote Buffalo Bill Cody toward the end of his first memoir. "Thus ended the career of a life-long friend of mine who, in spite of his many faults, was a noble man, ever brave and generous hearted."

Though he traveled far and wide on the American frontier, meeting many people along the way, and many of those he met knew who he was, Wild Bill Hickok had very few good friends. Cody qualifies as one of them. From pre–Civil War days when Cody was still an adolescent to their last meeting in July 1876, Hickok and Cody genuinely liked and respected each other. With the exception of Hickok's strong distaste for acting, when the paths of the two friends crossed, they enjoyed each other's company and the adventures they shared on the frontier.

In a way, they were connected after Hickok's death, too. With him and Custer gone and lawmen like Wyatt Earp and Bat Masterson yet to become legends, Buffalo Bill became the most famous American

West figure. Over time, he paid less attention to the frontier and more to cultivating a larger-than-life image—and making lots of money— on his touring Wild West shows. They became hugely popular, in both the United States and Europe. The first edition was the circus-like production titled *Buffalo Bill's Wild West*, founded in North Platte, Nebraska, in 1883. A later incarnation featured Sitting Bull with a band of twenty (former) warriors. The plentiful profits allowed Bill and Louisa Cody to construct the Scout's Rest Ranch, an eighteen-room mansion on a four-thousand-acre ranch outside North Platte.

Restless again, Buffalo Bill founded Cody, Wyoming, in 1895 and opened the Hotel Irma there, named after his daughter. Between his productions and three autobiographies, for a time Cody was considered the most recognizable celebrity in the world. This did not stop him from some bad decisions or spare him some bad luck that almost broke him financially, but he survived to a ripe old age for the time. Buffalo Bill Cody was a month shy of his seventy-first birthday when he passed away in January 1917.

For over a century, there has been an angry dispute about where his grave belongs. Louisa had him buried on top of Lookout Mountain, west of Denver, though Cody, Wyoming, lays claim to him and for decades threatened to steal the corpse and take it north. Such renewed threats in 1948 were taken so seriously that the Colorado National Guard was called out to surround the burial site. At present, Buffalo Bill and Louisa remain atop Lookout Mountain.

Another very good friend was Colorado Charley Utter. He was in Deadwood in September 1879 when a fire destroyed much of the town, his possessions included. Some of the town was rebuilt; the rest, left where it was. By then, many miners had moved on, new bouts of gold fever taking them to Colorado, Idaho, and New Mexico. The following year, Utter left his wife and lived in Durango, Colorado, then Socorro, New Mexico, where he operated a saloon and fell in love with Minnie Fowler, a faro dealer.

His wanderings were not over, however. By 1888, Utter was living in Panama in Central America. He was a doctor and pharmacist, practicing medicine among the local Indian population, which included delivering babies. The last reported sighting of him was at age seventy-two, blind and sitting in a rocking chair outside his pharmacy in Panama City.

And there was California Joe Milner. Hickok was once reported to have said when reunited with him in Deadwood, "I have but two trusty friends: one is my six-shooter and the other is California Joe." On the day of Hickok's murder, California Joe was out hunting. When he returned to town, he immediately prepared to set off again, this time to hunt the killer. He was assured that Jack McCall was in custody, so like many others, he repaired to a saloon to toast the memory of Wild Bill.

After the funeral, California Joe returned to his main occupation: guiding military and civilian outfits in and around the Black Hills and across the Plains. One day in late October, at Fort Robinson, he got into a scuffle with Tom Newcomb, who worked in the post's butcher shop. Guns were drawn, but California Joe suggested they have a drink instead of fighting. Newcomb thought that was a good idea. However, later that afternoon, as California Joe stood talking to friends in the sutler's store, Newcomb entered with a rifle and shot him in the back. California Joe died at age forty-seven. The killer was not charged with a crime, and after being released from custody at Fort Robinson, he disappeared.

After her visit to Deadwood, Wild Bill's only true wife, Agnes Lake Hickok, returned to the Midwest—shedding Texas George Carson along the way—and doted on her family. Sadly, the daughter

Emma gave birth to in June 1878 lived only eleven days. Emma returned to performing, and Agnes cared for her surviving granddaughter, who was called Daisy. The following year, Emma was one of the featured equestrians in P. T. Barnum's New and Greatest Show on Earth and was often billed as "America's Side Saddle Queen."

𝄞 Emma and Gil Robinson divorced in 1883, and she and her mother and daughter relocated to New Jersey. Four years later, Emma was performing with Annie Oakley in the traveling Buffalo Bill Cody production. When it traveled to London, she was accompanied by Agnes and Daisy. Billed as Emma Hickok, she was a big hit, and her performances included one for Queen Victoria. Back home, in 1893, Emma remarried Gil Robinson.

Agnes's remaining years were quiet ones. She lived with Emma, Gil, and Daisy. The latter married, and then Agnes became a great-grandmother when another Emma was born. The family was living in Somers Point, New Jersey, in 1907 when Agnes's health began to fail. Like her first two husbands, she died in August, three days before she would have turned eighty-one.

Obituaries of the once-famous circus impresario appeared in newspapers around the country. They referred to Agnes as either "Circus Queen" or "Wild Bill's Widow." After her body remained in a public vault for two months, it was transported to Cincinnati, where Agnes was buried next to her first husband, Bill Lake.

It would be Calamity Jane who would spend eternity with Wild Bill Hickok. She remained in Deadwood after Hickok's death. Calamity Jane was credited with nursing victims of a smallpox epidemic in the area in 1878. This was now home for her, even as the town's prospects declined. She did eventually move on, though, living on a ranch in Montana, then heading south. In Texas, she met and married Clinton Burk (or Burke), and in 1887, she gave birth to a daughter named Jane, who was raised by foster parents after Calamity Jane returned to her wandering ways. These included a stay in Boulder, Colorado, and starring in Buffalo Bill's productions and making other appearances to give sharpshooting exhibitions and tell tall tales, including the Pan-American Exposition in Buffalo in 1901.

While she was with the traveling Kohl & Middleton's Dime Museum as a performer and storyteller, a booklet was created to sell to audiences. It purported to be Calamity Jane's autobiography, though the author is given as Marthy Cannary. Much of the narrative is fiction, but the booklet served its purpose of connecting the audience with an authentic "legendary" figure of the Old West . . . and providing supporting "evidence" for the tales she told while wearing buckskin and brandishing a rifle.

Calamity Jane's love of whiskey became a severe addiction, to the point where she could not earn a living as a performer—or as anything else—anymore. In the spring of 1903, she was back in the Black Hills, making some money doing cooking and laundry in a brothel. That summer, while on a train to Terry, South Dakota, and drinking heavily, she collapsed. When the train arrived, she was carried to the Calloway Hotel. There she died, on August 1, of pneumonia and inflammation of the bowels.

She was buried next to Wild Bill Hickok in Mount Moriah Cemetery in Deadwood. One account contends that this was Calamity Jane's dying wish, carried out by the Society of Black Hills Pioneers. Another explanation is that several men who had planned the funeral thought that burying Calamity Jane there would be an amusing posthumous joke on Wild Bill. In any case, that day, as the hearse carried her body up to the cemetery, it was followed by those who had packed into the First Methodist Church for the funeral service, giving Calamity Jane a send-off she would have appreciated.

A postscript to the Wild Bill Hickok and Calamity Jane "romance" involves Jean Hickok McCormick, the daughter of Wild Bill and Calamity Jane—or so she claimed.

She was born on September 25, 1873, in Montana, the result of an affair Calamity Jane had with Hickok while she was employed as an army scout. Calamity Jane gave the child up for adoption, and Jean was raised by a couple named O'Neil. At the age of sixty-eight, in 1941, the U.S. Department of Public Welfare granted old-age assistance to Jean Hickok McCormick after being presented evidence that not only had Hickok and Calamity Jane had a liaison, but they'd been married at Benson's Landing in Montana Territory (now Livingston, Montana) in September 1873. Several years later, Jean published a book that included letters written to her by her mother, Calamity Jane—somehow overlooking that Calamity Jane was illiterate. Jean died in February 1951 in Billings, Montana, still claiming to be the couple's daughter.

One more postscript: The tale of the romance claimed by Calamity Jane would have died a natural death as her memoir faded from memory. However, in 1936, sixty years after Wild Bill Hickok's death, the film *The Plainsman* was released. The plot has President Abraham Lincoln, before leaving for Ford's Theatre on April 14, 1865, personally assigning Hickok on a mission to track down who was illegally selling guns to hostile Indians on the frontier. Arriving in Hays City, Hickok encounters the newly married and dandified Buffalo Bill Cody. He also finds Calamity Jane, who has been pining away for Wild Bill's return to the frontier. All three become involved in the mission, and it is later, when he and Calamity Jane are facing a gruesome death at the hands of Painted Horse and his gun-toting savages, that Hickok reveals his true love for her.

In the screenplay, facts are mixed in with embellishments and fabrications (even Jack McCall makes an appearance, eleven years before shooting Hickok), but audiences cared most about the combined talents of Gary Cooper and Jean Arthur and the director, Cecil B. DeMille. *The Plainsman* was boffo at the box office and is still considered a classic western epic, and over the decades, it has continued to impress on the public mind that the saga of Wild Bill Hickok and Calamity Jane was one of great love stories in American history . . . as has the fact, not the legend, that the two lie next to each other for eternity.

Acknowledgments

As usual, I owe a large thank-you to the curators, librarians, archivists, and others whose diligent work, too often unsung, allows writers like me to have a career. Their passion for accuracy and thoroughness keeps us all honest. With *Wild Bill*, I am especially grateful to staffers at the Kansas State Historical Society (where the Hickok Family Collection can be found), and Nancy Sherbert in particular; the Buffalo Bill Center of the West in Wyoming; the Kansas Heritage Center; the Abilene Preservation League; the Dickinson County Heritage Center; the South Dakota State Historical Society; the Nebraska State Historical Society; the Denver Public Library; the Library of Congress; the National Archives and Records Administration; and the Wilstach Collection, housed in the New York Public Library. Thanks also to the libraries and other repositories where the archives of newspapers can be found. Most are no longer publishing, but while they may be gone, they certainly are not forgotten. Other researchers and curators who should be acknowledged are Patricia Andersen, Dell Darling, Laurie Langland, Martha Miller, Matthew Reitzel, Michael Runge, and Janice Scott. And I must recognize the expertise and courtesy of Virgil Dean of Lawrence, Kansas, who was kind enough to give the manuscript a good read and alert me to errors. Whatever mistakes still managed to slip through are totally my responsibility.

Wild Bill would not exist without the initial suggestion and subsequent enthusiasm and support of Marc Resnick, my editor at St. Martin's Press. Others there who have been wonderful to know and work with include Steve Cohen, Sally Richardson, Rebecca Lang, Tracey Guest, Danielle Prielipp, Hannah O'Grady, Sara

Ensey, and Jaime Coyne. Another big reason why this book exists is the long-standing guidance and friendship of Scott Gould at RLR Associates.

My dear friends continue to . . . well, tolerate me, and for that, I am very grateful. And my children, Kathryn Clavin Vun Kannon and Brendan Clavin, continue to be even more important to me than . . . well, anything else.

Selected Bibliography

BOOKS

Ames, John. *The Real Deadwood: True Life Histories of Wild Bill Hickok, Calamity Jane, Outlaw Towns, and Other Characters of the Lawless West.* New York: Chamberlain Bros., 2004.

Athearn, Robert G. *William Tecumseh Sherman and the Settlement of the West.* Norman: University of Oklahoma Press, 1956.

Barnitz, Albert. *The Diary of Major Albert Barnitz* (unpublished manuscript). Beinecke Library, Yale University.

Bell, Bob Boze. *Classic Gunfights.* Phoenix, AZ: Tri-Star Boze Publications, 2013.

Brown, Dee. *Trail Driving Days.* New York: Charles Scribner's Sons, 1952.

Buel, J. R. *Heroes of the Plains.* London: Forgotten Books, 2018.

Burkey, Blaine. *Wild Bill Hickok: The Law in Hays City.* Hays, KS: Ellis County Historical Society, 1973.

Carter, Robert A. *Buffalo Bill Cody: The Man Behind the Legend.* New York: John Wiley & Sons, 2000.

Clavin, Tom. *Dodge City: Wyatt Earp, Bat Masterson, and the Wickedest Town in the American West.* New York: St. Martin's Press, 2017.

Cody, Louisa Frederici. *Memories of Buffalo Bill.* New York: D. Appleton, 1919.

Cody, William F. *Buffalo Bill's Life Story: An Autobiography.* New York: Skyhorse Publishing, 2010.

Collins, Robert. *Kansas Train Tales.* N.p.: CreateSpace, 2009.

Connelley, William E. *Wild Bill and His Era: The Life and Adventures of James Butler Hickok.* New York: Press of the Pioneers, 1933.

Custer, Elizabeth Bacon. *Following the Guidon.* Norman: University of Oklahoma Press, 1976.

Custer, George Armstrong. *My Life on the Plains.* Norman: University of Oklahoma Press, 1962.

Dary, David. *True Tales of Old-Time Kansas.* Lawrence: University Press of Kansas, 1984.

Dawson, Charles. *Tales of the Oregon Trail.* Bellevue, WA: Big Byte Books, 2017.

Dexter, Pete. *Deadwood.* New York: Random House, 1986.

Drury, Bob, and Tom Clavin. *The Heart of Everything That Is.* New York: Simon & Schuster, 2013.

Dykstra, Robert R. *The Cattle Towns.* New York: Knopf, 1968.

Ebbutt, Percy G. *Emigrant Life in Kansas.* London: British Library, 2010.

Eisele, Wilbert E. *The Real Wild Bill Hickok.* Denver, CO: William H. Andre, 1931.

Etulain, Richard W. *The Life and Legends of Calamity Jane.* Norman: University of Oklahoma Press, 2014.

Fisher, Linda A., and Carrie Bowers. *Agnes Lake Hickok: Queen of the Circus, Wife of a Legend.* Norman: University of Oklahoma Press, 2009.

Hardin, John Wesley. *Gunfighter.* n.p.: Creation Books, 2000.

Herring, Hal. *Famous Firearms of the Old West.* Guilford, CT: Globe Pequot Press, 2011.

Jackson, Donald. *Custer's Gold: The United States Cavalry Expedition of 1874.* Lincoln: University of Nebraska Press, 1966.

Jameson, Henry B. *Early Days in Abilene, Kansas.* Abilene, KS: Reflector-Chronicle Publishing Corp., 1940.

Jucovy, Linda. *Searching for Calamity: The Life and Times of Calamity Jane.* Philadelphia: Stampede Books, 2012.

McCoy, Joseph G. *Historic Sketches of the Cattle Trade of the West and Southwest.* Middletown, DE: Pantianos Classics, 2017.

McLaird, James D. *Calamity Jane: The Woman and the Legend.* Norman: University of Oklahoma Press, 2005.

———. *Wild Bill Hickok and Calamity Jane: Deadwood Legends.* Pierre: South Dakota State Historical Society Press, 2008.

Mersman, Joseph J. *The Whiskey Merchant's Diary: An Urban Life in the Emerging Midwest.* Athens: Ohio University Press, 2007.

Miller, Nyle H., and Joseph W. Snell. *Great Gunfighters of the Kansas Cowtowns, 1867–1886.* Lincoln: University of Nebraska Press, 1963.

———. *Why the West Was Wild: A Contemporary Look at the Antics of Some Highly Publicized Kansas Cowtown Personalities.* Norman: University of Oklahoma Press, 2003.

Monaghan, Jay. *The Great Rascal: The Life and Adventures of Ned Buntline*. New York: Bonanza Books, 1951.

Nash, Jay Robert. *Encyclopedia of Western Lawmen & Outlaws*. New York: Da Capo, 1992.

North, Luther and Donald F. Danker. *Man of the Plains*. Lincoln: University of Nebraska Press, 1961.

O'Connor, Richard. *Wild Bill Hickok*. New York: Doubleday, 1959.

Otero, Miguel Antonio. *My Life on the Frontier 1864–1882*. London: Kessinger Publishing, 2010.

Pierce, Dale. *Wild West Characters*. Phoenix, AZ: Golden West, 1991.

Robinson, Gil. *Old Wagon Show Days*. Cincinnati: Brockwell Company, 1925.

Root, Frank A., and William Connelley. *The Overland Stage to California*. London: Forgotten Books, 2016.

Rosa, Joseph G. *Age of the Gunfighter: Men and Weapons on the Frontier 1840–1900*. Norman: University of Oklahoma Press, 1995.

———. *They Called Him Wild Bill: The Life and Adventures of James Butler Hickok*. Norman: University of Oklahoma Press, 1964.

———. *The West of Wild Bill Hickok*. Norman: University of Oklahoma Press, 1994.

Russell, Don. *The Lives and Legends of Buffalo Bill*. Norman: University of Oklahoma Press, 1960.

Spring, Agnes Wright. *Good Little Bad Man: The Life of Colorado Charley Utter*. Boulder, CO: Pruett Publishing, 1987.

Steckmesser, Kent Ladd. *The Western Hero in History and Legend*. Norman: University of Oklahoma Press, 1997.

Stiles, T. J. *Custer's Trials: A Life on the Frontier of a New America*. New York: Knopf 2015.

Stillman, Deanne. *Blood Brothers: The Story of the Strange Friendship Between Sitting Bull and Buffalo Bill*. New York: Simon & Schuster, 2017.

Stratton, Joanna L. *Pioneer Women: Voices from the Kansas Frontier*. New York: Touchstone, 1982.

Tallent, Annie. *The Black Hills*. London: Forgotten Books, 2017.

True West, eds. *True Tales and Amazing Legends of the Old West*. New York: Clarkson Potter, 2005.

Verckler, Stewart P. *Cowtown Abilene: The Story of Abilene, Kansas, 1867–1875*. Whitefish, MT: Literary Licensing, 2011.

Webb, Dave. *Adventures with the Santa Fe Trail*. Dodge City: Kansas Heritage Center, 1989.

Wilstach, Frank J. *The Plainsman, Wild Bill Hickok*. Garden City, NY: Sun Dial Press, 1937.

ARTICLES

"A Trip To the Black Hills." *Scribner's*, February 1877.

Banks, Leo W. "Gambling, Gold and Women." *True West*, September 2017.

Boardman, Mark. "Buffalo Bill Lies Here—or Here." *True West*, December 2016.

Bommersbach, Jana. "The Ball that Killed Wild Bill." *True West*, January 2015.

———. "Hot Air & Kind Words." *True West*, January 2018.

Brown, Norman Wayne. "The Birth of a Wicked Son Reimagined." *True West*, March 2017.

"Buffalo Hunt at Niagara Falls." Nebraska State Historical Society, 2005.

Cerney, Jan. "Agnes Lake Hickok: Queen of the Circus, Wife of a Legend." *Western American Literature*, Spring 2010.

Cushman, George L. "Abilene, First of the Kansas Cow Towns." *Kansas Historical Quarterly*, August 1940.

Dippie, Brian W. "Its Equal I Have Never Seen: Custer Explores the Black Hills in 1874." *Columbia: The Magazine of Northwest History*, Summer 2005.

Eastman, Charles A. "Roman Nose—Cheyenne War Chief." Legends of America, 2017 (reprinted from 1918).

Flippin, W. B. "The Tutt and Everett War in Marion County." *Arkansas Historical Quarterly*, Summer 1958.

Garfield, Marvin H. "Defense of the Kansas Frontier 1866–1867." *Kansas Historical Quarterly*, August 1932.

Hough, Emerson. "Joseph Slade—Hanged by Vigilantes." Legends of America, 2003 (reprinted from 1903).

Koster, John. "Legendary California Joe." *Wild West*, April 2018.

Landry, Alysa. "Native History: Custer Attacks Peaceful Cheyenne in Oklahoma." Indian Country Media Network, November 2013.

"Last Days of a Plainsman." *True West*, November/December 1965.

Lewis, Alfred Henry. "How Mr. Hickok Came to Cheyenne." *Oamaru Mail*, April 1904.

Lyons, Chuck. "Deadwood's Black Friday Fire." *Wild West*, April 2018.

"Memories of Buffalo Bill." *Ladies' Home Journal*, July 1919.

Nichols, George Ward. "Wild Bill." *Harper's New Monthly Magazine*, February 1867.

Rosa, Joseph G. "California Joe: Great Scout and Plainsman." *True West*, April 2002.

Spangenberger, Phil. "Colt's Paterson—the Foaling of a Legend." *True West*, May 2017.

"True Story of Wild Bill–McCanles Affray in Jefferson County, Nebraska, July 12, 1861." *Nebraska History Magazine*, 1927.

Turner, Thadd. "'Texas Jack' Omohundro." Buffalo Bill Center of the West.

Weiser, Kathy. "James H. Lane—Grim Leader in the Free-State Fight." Legends of America, 2016.

———. "Jesse Chisholm—Blazing a Trail." Legends of America, 2014.

———. "Missouri Bushwhackers—Attacks Upon Kansas." Legends of America, 2017.

———. "Rock Creek Station, Nebraska and the McCanles Massacre." Legends of America, 2017.

———. "Wild Bill Hickok & the Deadman's Hand." Legends of America, 2016.

NEWSPAPER ARCHIVES

Abilene Chronicle

Anaconda Standard

Atchison Daily Champion

Atchison Weekly Free Press

Black Hills Pioneer

Black Hills Times

Brownsville Advertiser

Cheyenne Daily Leader

Cheyenne Daily News

Cheyenne Daily Sun

Chicago Inter Ocean

Daily Miners' Register

Deadwood Black Hills Pioneer

Deadwood Pioneer-Times

Denver Post

Denver Republican

Denver Tribune

Ellis County Star

Hays City Sentinel

Hays Daily News

Jefferson City News Tribune

Junction City Weekly Union

Kansas City Daily Journal of Commerce

Kansas City Star

Lawrence Daily Tribune

Leavenworth Daily Commercial

Leavenworth Daily Conservative

Leavenworth Times and Conservative

Lincoln Daily State Journal

Manhattan Independent

Mendota Bulletin

Missouri Weekly Patriot

New York Herald

Niagara Falls Gazette

North Topeka Times

Omaha Daily Bee

Omaha Weekly Herald

Rochester Democrat and Chronicle

Springfield Weekly Missouri Patriot

Topeka Capital

Topeka Daily Commonwealth

Topeka State Record

Topeka Weekly Leader

Weekly Missouri Democrat

Yankton Press and Dakotan

Index

Abilene, Kansas, 86, 88, 110
  circus shows in, 179, 185–86
  growth of, 152–65, 191
  Hickok as sheriff of, 151, 164–65,
    166–78, 186–91, 195–96, 231,
    233, 272–73, 287
  Smith as sheriff of, 159–64, 170,
    195, 232
The Abilene Chronicle, 186
abolitionists. *See also* Civil War
  in Kansas, 18–25, 27–30, 52–55
  Underground Railroad by, 12–13
Adam Forepaugh's Circus and
    Menagerie, 184
African Americans
  slavery of, 12–13, 18–25, 27–30,
    52–55, 198
  in Union Army, 116–18, 118*n*, 120,
    123–24, 135
the Alamo saloon, Abilene, 169–70
Alexis, Grand Duke of Russia,
    213
Allen, Ethan, 9

American Fur Company, 24
American Geographical Society,
    208
Ames, John Edwards, 261
The Anaconda Standard, 244
Anderson, Joseph Foster Moore
    "White Eye," 255–56, 259, 265,
    270
Anderson, Josephine, 54
Anderson, William "Bloody Bill,"
    54
Apache tribe, 104, 134
Arapaho tribe, 34, 227
Armes, George, 117–18
Armstrong, Eli, 70
Armstrong, John B., 173
Arthur, Jean, 294
Atchison, David, 24
Atchison, Kansas, 19, 39, 118, 133
  Pomeroys (baseball team), 103
Atchison, Topeka, and Santa Fe
    Railway, 85
Athearn, Robert G., 77

Badger (Oglala Sioux man), 207–8
Bailey, Frederic H., 184–85
Bailey, James Anthony, 181
Barnes (Confederate soldier), 59
Barnett, Sidney, 201–4, 213
Barnitz, Albert, 68, 71
Barnum, P. T., 181, 184–85, 291
Bascom, C. J., 145
baseball teams, 102–3
Bass Outlaw, 173
Bassett, Charlie, 134
Battle of Adobe Walls (Civil War), 35
Battle of Bad Axe (Black Hawk's War),
    11
Battle of Beecher Island (Indian wars),
    121–24, 136
Battle of Brandy Station (Civil War), 64
Battle of Galveston (Civil War), 176
Battle of Glasgow (Civil War), 64
Battle of the Hundred-in-the-Hands
    (Red Cloud's War), 227–28, 227n
Battle of Little Bighorn (Great Sioux
    War of 1876), 144, 228, 245, 254,
    257, 267–68, 287
Battle of Little Blue River (Civil War),
    64
Battle of Magdala (Ethiopia), 99
Battle of Mine Creek (Civil War), 65
Battle of Pea Ridge (Civil War), 49,
    51–52, 59
Battle of the Rosebud (Great Sioux
    War of 1876), 245
Battle of the Saline River (Indian
    wars), 117–18
Battle of Shiloh (Civil War), 97–98
Battle of Slim Buttes (Great Sioux War
    of 1876), 208
Battle of Stillman's Run (Black Hawk's
    War), 10
Battle of Tupelo (Civil War), 117

Battle of Washita River (Indian wars),
    124–25, 226
Battle of Westport (Civil War), 64–65
Battle of Wilson's Creek (Civil War),
    49, 51, 53
Battle of Wisconsin Heights (Black
    Hawk's War), 11
Bear Flag Revolt (California), 34
Bellevue Hospital Medical College,
    New York, 207
Beni, Jules, 40, 42n
Bennett, James Gordon, 98
Benoit, Kansas, 90
Benteen, Frederick, 65, 65n
Big Creek Land Company, Kansas, 110
Big Hank (cowboy), 161, 162
Billings, Montana, 293
Binghamton, New York, 224–25
Bitter, John, 147
Black Hawk (Sauk chief), 10–11
Black Hills
    gold speculation in, 228–31, 243–44,
        249–52, 260, 262, 268–70, 278,
        289
    Indian territory mandates in, 227–30,
        243–46, 248–49, 248n, 252–53,
        254, 257, 267–68
The Black Hills Pioneer, 260, 261, 284
The Black Hills Times, 261
The Black Hills (Tallent), 236–37
Black Kettle (Cheyenne chief), 125
Black Nell (horse), 62
Blancett, Truman, 36
Boone, Daniel, 14, 99
Border Ruffians (guerrilla group),
    21–25, 27–30, 53–55, 198
Bowers, Carrie, 185
Bowlby (saloon proprietor), 235–36
Bozeman Trail, 227–28
Brady, Tim, 273

Bridger, Jim, 39, 93

Brink, J. W. "Doc," 46

British Band (of Indians), 10–11

Brooks, Preston, 21

Bross, William, 197

brothels. *See* prostitutes

Brown, John, 19, 21–22, 30, 53, 53*n*

Buel, J. W., 59, 211–12, 276

"Buffalo Bill." *See* Cody, William
   Frederick "Buffalo Bill"

Buffalo Bill's Life Story (Cody), 26

Buffalo Bill's Wild West show, 200, 289,
   291, 292

Buffalo Land (Webb), 148

"Buffalo Soldiers" (Tenth U.S. Cavalry
   Regiment), 116–18, 118*n*, 120,
   123–24, 135

Bull's Head Tavern, Abilene, 175–78,
   187

Buntline, Ned, 211–14, 217, 218, 222,
   223

Burk, Clinton, 291

Burk, Jane, 291–92

Burke, John, 215–16, 216*n*, 219–21,
   222*n*

Burr, Aaron, 3

Burroughs, S. A., 169

Bushwhackers (guerrilla group), 29, 52,
   198

Butler, Ben, 9

Calamity Jane (Martha Jane Canary),
   242*n*
   birth/background of, 240–43, 240*n*
   Burk's marriage to, 291
   children born to, 258, 291–92, 293
   Deadwood residency by, 263–66,
      283, 291
   death/burial of, 292–93, 294
   embedded with troops, 243–46

Hickok's relationship with, 179, 246,
   254, 255–60, 264–65, 283, 291–94
movie representations of, 293–94
nickname's origins, 242–43

California, Bear Flag Revolt in, 34

"California Joe." *See* Milner, Moses
   Embree "California Joe"

California Trail, 43

Canary, Charlotte, 240–41

Canary, Martha Jane. *See* Calamity Jane

Canary, Robert, 240–41

Carpenter, Louis, 123–24

Carr, Eugene, 124, 126–27

Carr, Thomas Jeff, 232–33, 239

Carson, Christopher "Kit," 14, 63, 93,
   96, 99, 159, 169
   background of, 33–35
   Hickok's friendship with, 33, 35

Carson, Maria Josefa Jaramillo, 34–35

Carson, "Texas" George, 287, 290

Carson, Tom, 169, 170

Carson City, Nevada, 139

Cassidy, Butch, and the Sundance Kid,
   233

The Cattle Towns (Dykstra), 154

cattle trade, 84–90
   in Abilene, 152–65, 166–70, 174–78,
      187, 191
   "Spanish Fever" in, 156, 156*n*

Chandler (Red Leg commander), 61

Cherokee Nation, Oklahoma, 85

Cheyenne, Wyoming, 242–43, 245
   cultural evolution of, 247–48
   gold rush's impact on, 231–39

The Cheyenne Daily Leader, 252

The Cheyenne Daily News, 238

The Cheyenne Daily Sun, 253

Cheyenne tribe, 34
   Dog Soldiers of, 107, 122
   massacres of, 120, 124–25, 226

Cheyenne tribe (*continued*)
  war parties of, 105–7, 117–25,
    129–31, 227, 267–68
Chicago Inter Ocean, 244, 284
Chisholm, Jesse, 85–86
Chisholm Trail, 86, 153–54
Chivington, John, 124
cholera, 32, 128–29, 155
Cincinnati, 179–80, 251
  Red Stockings (baseball team), 102
circuses/traveling shows
  Adam Forepaugh's Circus and
    Menagerie, 194
  Buffalo Bill's Wild West, 200, 289,
    291, 292
  during Civil War, 181–82
  The Daring Buffalo Chase of the Plains,
    200–204
  Frederic H. Bailey's Circus and
    Menagerie, 184–85
  Hickok's performances in, 200–204,
    211–22, 259
  Hippo-Olympiad and Mammoth
    Circus, 179, 182–87, 198–99, 200,
    223–24, 236, 250
  John Robinson's Circus, Menagerie,
    and Museum, 184
  Kohl & Middleton's Dime Museum,
    292
  Mammoth Circus & Gymnastic
    Arena Company, 180–81
  Mazeppa, 182
  Native Americans in, 200–204, 224,
    289
  Scouts of the Plains, 214–25, 259
  Scouts of the Prairie, 211–14
Civil War, 9, 31, 86, 89, 92, 104, 149.
    See also Union Army
  Battle of Adobe Walls in, 35
  Battle of Brandy Station in, 64

Battle of Galveston in, 176
Battle of Glasgow in, 64
Battle of Little Blue River in, 64
Battle of Mine Creek in, 65
Battle of Pea Ridge in, 49, 51–52, 59
Battle of Shiloh in, 97–98
Battle of Tupelo in, 117
Battle of Westport in, 64–65
Battle of Wilson's Creek in, 49, 51, 53
Carson's service in, 35
Cody's service in, 61–62, 114
end of, 65
Grierson's Raid in, 117
guerrilla factions in, 22, 52–57
Hickok's service in, 2, 35, 47, 48–52,
    57–65, 73–74
Price Raid of 1864 in, 49
Reconstruction post-, 76, 105
Shenandoah Valley campaign in, 119
traveling shows during, 181–82
Clay, Henry, 2
Cody, Arta Lucille, 115, 211, 211*n*
Cody, Elijah, 26
Cody, Eliza, 115
Cody, Irma Louise, 211*n*, 289
Cody, Isaac, 26–27
Cody, Kit Carson, 211, 211*n*
Cody, Louisa Frederici, 114–16, 211,
    211*n*, 218, 222, 289
Cody, Orra Maude, 211, 211*n*
Cody, Samuel, 26
Cody, William Frederick "Buffalo Bill,"
    230, 264
  Buffalo Bill's Wild West show by, 200,
    289, 291, 292
  childhood of, 25–28, 33
  death/burial place of, 289
  Hickok's friendship with, 25–28,
    36–37, 61–62, 114–16, 126–27,
    130, 131, 197, 212–22, 256–57, 288

marriage of, 114–15
military service/scouting by, 61–62, 109, 114, 116, 119, 124, 126–27, 130, 144, 256–57, 268, 268*n*
movie representations of, 293
nickname's origins, 115
as Pony Express rider, 39–41
pulp/dime store novels on, 93, 196, 211
Scouts of the Plains show by, 214–25, 259
Scouts of the Prairie show by, 211–14
Cody, Wyoming, 289
Coe, Philip Haddox, 175–78, 187–88, 190, 210
Coleman, Frank, 20
Colorado, 198
    Cody's burial in, 289
    Fort Evans, 127
    Fort Lyon, 120–21, 130–31
    Sand Creek Massacre in, 120, 124
Colorado Charley. *See* Utter, Charles H. "Colorado Charley"
Colorado National Guard, 289
Comanche tribe, 35, 86, 119
    in Wild West shows, 202–4, 224
Conkie, John, 167
Connelley, William, 7, 15, 35, 36–37, 58–59, 62–63
Cooke, Philip St. George, 24
Cooper, Gary, 294
cow towns, 84–90, 109–10, 262
    Abilene as, 152–65, 166–70, 174–78, 187, 191
Cowtown Abilene (Verckler), 157, 175
Crawford, Jack, 244
Crawford, S. J., 105
Crazy Horse (Oglala Lakota leader), 227–28, 249, 252
    at Battle of Little Bighorn, 228, 267
    at Battle of the Rosebud, 245

Creek Nation, Oklahoma, 85
the Cricket, Deadwood, 263
Crockett, Davy, 99
Crook, George, 244–46
Cummins, Jim, 174
Curry, Jim, 111, 145–46
Curtis, Samuel, 51, 58, 60, 64
Custer, Boston, 267
Custer, George Armstrong, 78–79, 81, 105–6, 143, 213, 229–30, 243
    Battle of Little Bighorn by, 144, 228, 245, 254, 257, 267–68, 287
    death of, 257, 267–68, 287, 288
    desertion from army by, 125, 226–27
    Washita Massacre by, 124–25, 226
Custer, Libbie, 78–79, 90, 125
Custer, Tom, 267

The Daily Miners' Register, 198
Dale, William, 181
Dalton, "Buckskin" Charley, 287
The Daring Buffalo Chase of the Plains show, 200–204
Darnell, William, 65
Davis, Jefferson, 11
Dead Man's Hand, 282
Deadwood, South Dakota, 142, 246, 290, 293
    Calamity Jane's residence in, 263–66, 283, 291
    fire in, 289
    gold speculation in/near, 250–52, 260, 262, 268–70, 278
    Hickok's death/burial in, 288, 292, 294
    Hickok's residence in, 255–66, 267–77, 278–87
    origins/growth of, 260–63
Deadwood (Dexter), 193
The Deadwood Pioneer-Times, 282–83

Delano, Columbus, 228

DeMille, Cecil B., 94, 294

The Denver Post, 36

The Denver Tribune, 198

Department of the Missouri, 118

Dexter, Pete, 193

DiCaprio, Leonardo, 37

Dippie, Brian, 230

"Dirty Em" (prostitute), 257

Dodge, Grenville, 232

Dodge, Henry, 11

Dodge, Richard Irving, 243

Dodge City, Kansas, 11, 32, 90, 110, 118, 134, 167, 232, 243, 274

Dow, Charles, 20

Doyle, James, 22

Drovers Cottage, Abilene, 152, 154–55

Drum, Tommy, 145–46

Dykstra, Robert, 154

Earp, Wyatt, 42, 91, 93, 118, 134, 189, 274, 288
  Clanton's gunfight with, 42

Eastman, Charles A., 121

Eckles, R. A., 136

Edwards, J. B., 161, 166

Edwards, John Newman, 206

Eighth Missouri State Militia, 58

Ellsworth, Allen, 128

Ellsworth, Kansas, 90, 109, 189
  Fort Ellsworth at, 115, 128–29

Emancipation Proclamation, 12

Eothen (schooner), 208

Etulain, Richard W., 240, 242

Evans, A. W., 124

Evans, Richard, 137

Ewert, Theodore, 229

Ewing, Thomas, Jr., 52

Farmers' Protective Association, Abilene, 191

Ferrin, Andrew, 40

Fetterman, William, 227

Fifth Cavalry Corps (Confederate), 143

Fifth U.S. Cavalry, 144, 268

First Transcontinental Railroad, 39

Fisher, Linda A., 185

Flynn, Errol, 144

Following the Guidon (Custer), 78–79

Forepaugh, Adam, 184

Forrest, Nathan Bedford, 117

Forsyth, George, 122–23

Fort Abraham Lincoln, North Dakota, 229

Fort Bridger, Wyoming, 39, 242

Fort Cobb, Oklahoma, 125

Fort Dodge, Kansas, 209, 210

Fort Ellsworth, Kansas, 115, 128–29

Fort Evans, Colorado, 127

Fort Fetterman, Wyoming, 245–46

Fort Harker, Kansas, 125, 128

Fort Hays, 106, 110, 118, 135–36, 142, 149

Fort Kearny, Nebraska, 77

Fort Laramie, Wyoming, 244–46, 253–54, 255

Fort Leavenworth, Kansas, 64, 86, 116–17

Fort Lyon, Colorado, 120–21, 130–31

Fort McPherson, Nebraska, 144, 201, 255

Fort Phil Kearny, Wyoming, 227

Fort Riley, Kansas, 74–77, 78, 98, 106, 109, 117

Fort Robinson, Nebraska, 264, 290

The Fort Scott Monitor, 37

Fort Wallace, Kansas, 123, 130, 133

Fowler, Minnie, 290

Fox tribe, 201

Frederic H. Bailey's Circus and
   Menagerie, 184–85
Free Soil movement, 27
Free State Army, Kansas (guerrilla
   group), 20–25, 27–30
Frémont, Jessie, 34
Frémont, John C., 34, 72
French and Indian War, 124
Frontier Guard (Union militia), 55–56
Frontier Store, Abilene, 89
Frontier Times, 238

Gainsford, James, 170
Gall (Lakota leader), 267
gambling, 87–88, 138, 274
   in Abilene, 167, 170, 176
   in Cheyenne, 232–38
   in Deadwood, 257, 260–64, 269, 272
   in Hays City, 138, 142, 145–46
   by Hickok, 67–69, 91, 100, 109, 138,
      145–46, 196–97, 199, 205, 212,
      221, 222, 224, 226, 231, 233,
      234–38, 263–64, 269, 272,
      278–81, 282
Garfield, James, 287
"Garry Owen" (song), 125, 229
Geary, John, 24
Geronimo (Apache leader), 104
Gibbon, John, 244, 244n
Gibbs House, Fort Hays, 110
glaucoma, 200
Glenn, S. C., 43
Gold Room, Cheyenne, 234–36, 234n,
   237
gold speculation, 14, 43, 143, 241
   by Hickok, 249–52, 268–70, 278
   at Pikes Peak, 198
   in South Dakota, 228–31, 243–44,
      249–52, 260, 262, 268–70, 278, 289
   in Wyoming, 228–39, 243–44

Golden Rule House, Leavenworth, 115
Gomerville, Colorado, 120–21
Gordon, James, 45–46, 94
Grant, Frederick Dent, 230
Grant, Ulysses S., 63, 65, 105, 118,
      125, 228, 244, 248
Grapewin, Charley, 144
Gray, John, 257
Great American Desert, 2, 32, 76, 83,
      95, 101, 159
Great Sioux War of 1876, 268n
   Battle of Little Bighorn in, 144, 228,
      245, 254, 257, 267–68, 287
   Battle of the Rosebud in, 245
   Battle of Slim Buttes in, 208
The Great Train Robbery (movie), 94
Greeley, Horace, 66
Green Mountain Boys (Revolutionary
   War), 9
Grierson, Benjamin, 117
Grierson's Raid, 117
Gross, C. F., 174
Grouard, Frank, 246
gunfight(s)
   accidental killings in, 187–89, 191
   Earp-Clanton, 42
   Hickok-cattle herders (Jefferson
      County), 112–13
   Hickok-Coe, 187–88
   Hickok-McCanles, 42–47, 67, 94
   Hickok-Mulvey, 138–39
   Hickok-Strawhun, 146–48
   Hickok-Sullivan, 141
   Hickok-Tutt, 1–4, 68–72, 91, 94
   Storms-Short, 274
   thwarted, 145–46, 190, 275–76

Hamilton, Alexander, 3
Hance, George, 75
Hancock, Winfield Scott, 104–6, 119

Handsmeller (Oglala Sioux man), 207–8

Hannah (freed slave), 13

Hard Knocks (Young), 270

Hardin, John Wesley, 171–73, 177–78

Harper's New Monthly Magazine, 1, 72–73, 78, 90–91, 93–100

Harris, Charles, 150

Harte, Bret, 39

Harvey, James, 136–37, 146

Hasel, Jessie, 178

Hatfield and McCoy feud, 2

Hays City, Kansas, 81, 90, 109–11, 133–34
  Hickok as sheriff of, 135–39, 140–51, 164, 195, 231, 233, 272, 287
  judicial system of, 137–38

Henry, T. C., 157–61

Heroes of the Plains (Buel), 59, 211–12

Hersey, Elizabeth, 88

Hersey, Timothy, 88–90, 152, 154

Hiccocks, John, 8

Hiccocs, William, 8

Hickok, Aaron (great-grandfather), 8–9

Hickok, Agnes Mersman Lake (wife)
  birth/childhood of, 179–80
  children adopted by, 181–82
  as circus owner, 179, 182, 184–87, 198–99, 200, 223–24, 236, 250
  as circus performer, 182, 236
  death of, 291
  Hickok's courtship of, 186–87, 223–24, 236, 250
  Hickok's marriage to, 251–54, 258–59, 269, 276, 278–79, 284, 286–87, 290–91
  Lake's marriage to, 180–82

Hickok, Celinda (sister), 12, 132–33, 236, 252

Hickok, Horace (brother), 5, 11–16, 23, 48, 132–33, 236, 252

Hickok, Howard, 13, 18

Hickok, Ichabod, 8

Hickok, James Butler "Wild Bill." *See also* gunfight(s)
  ancestors of, 7–11
  arrow injury of, 130–32
  bear encounter by, 37–38
  birth/childhood of, 11–16
  burial place of, 132*n*, 286, 292, 294
  Calamity Jane's relationship with, 179, 246, 254, 255–60, 264–65, 283, 291–94
  Carson's friendship with, 33, 35
  Cheyenne residency by, 231–39, 247–54
  children allegedly fathered by, 258, 293
  Cody's friendship with, 25–28, 36–37, 61–62, 114–16, 126–27, 130, 131, 197, 212–22, 256–57, 288
  as constable of Monticello, 28–30, 74
  in *The Daring Buffalo Chase of the Plains,* 200–204
  Deadwood residency by, 255–66, 267–77, 278–87
  death/burial of, 209, 278–87, 282*n*, 284*n*
  deputy's accidental killing by, 187–89, 191
  in Free-Stater forces, 20–25, 27–30
  gambling by, 67–69, 91, 100, 109, 138, 145–46, 196–97, 199, 205, 212, 221, 222, 224, 226, 231, 233, 234–38, 263–64, 269, 272, 278–81, 282

gold speculation by, 249–52, 268–70, 278

guns of, 70, 91, 106, 166, 290

Harper's New Monthly Magazine's profile on, 1, 72–73, 78, 90–91, 93–100

"Indian Annie's" relationship with, 110, 178, 258

Jefferson County gunfight by, 112–13

Lake's courtship by, 186–87, 223–24, 236, 250

Lake's marriage to, 251–54, 258–59, 269, 276, 278–79, 290–91

McCanles's gunfight with, 42–47, 67, 94

military service/scouting by, 2, 35, 47, 48–52, 57–65, 73–74, 100–107, 116–21, 125–27, 130–31, 133

Moore's relationship with, 58–59, 68–69, 74, 217

movie representations of, 293–94

myths/exaggerations about, 7, 35, 42, 50, 57–58, 62–63, 67, 93–99, 209–11, 270, 293–94

New York Herald's profile on, 97–99

nicknames' origins, 18, 50–51

Owen's relationship with, 24–25, 29–30, 31, 36

portraits of, *5,* 31–32, *81, 193*

premonitions by, 266, 276–77, 278

pulp stories on, 130, 196, 211

rheumatism of, 230–31, 254

Schull's relationship with, 44, 46–47

as sheriff of Abilene, 151, 164–65, 166–78, 186–91, 195–96, 231, 233, 272–73, 287

as sheriff of Hays City, 135–39, 140–51, 164, 195, 231, 233, 272, 287

shooting exhibitions by, 91–92, 144–45, 200, 226

spiritualism of, 276–77

Springfield residency by, 67–74, 95, 207

Tutt's gunfight with, 1–4, 68–72, 91, 94

as U.S. marshal, 74–75, 108–13, 114–16, 118, 133–35

vision difficulties of, 199–200, 212, 218, 221–22, 231, 254, 272

as wagon train teamster/driver, 28, 32, 36–38, 50

in Wild West productions, 200–204, 211–22, 259

Hickok, Lorenzo (first brother), 9

Hickok, Lorenzo (second brother), 10–16, 17, 22, 23, 29–30, 31, 48, 50, 66–67, 75, 77, 132, 236, 252, 285

Hickok, Lydia (sister), 12, 131–33, 236, 252

Hickok, Martha Edwards, 132

Hickok, Oliver (brother), 9–13, 15, 48, 132

Hickok, Oliver (grandfather), 8–9

Hickok, Pamelia Butler "Polly" (mother), 9–16, 17, 23, 24, 29, 74, 131–33, 236, 252, 285

Hickok, William Alonzo (father), 9–14, 19

The Hickok Legend (Hickok), 18

Hippo-Olympiad and Mammoth Circus, 179, 182–87, 198–99, 200, 223–24, 236, 250

Historic Sketches of the Cattle Trade of the West and Southwest (McCoy), 156, 164

Hitchcock/Hickock, Elizabeth, 8

Hitchcock/Hickock, Joseph, 8

Hitchcock/Hickock, Samuel, 8
Hitchcock/Hickock, William, 8
Homer, Illinois. *See* Troy Grove,
    Illinois
Hood, John Bell, 182
Hotel Irma, Cody, 289
Houston, Dana, 133, 135, 137
Hoyt, George, 53
Hudson, Charles, 15
Hughes, Richard, 263
Hunton, John, 254
Hutt, Joe, 145

I Buried Hickok (Anderson), 256
Illingworth, William, 230
Illinois, Troy Grove, 11–12, 14–16, 67,
    132–33, 132*n*, 252, 285
Illinois and Michigan Canal company,
    15
Independence, Missouri, 50–51, 66–67,
    75, 209, 210, 226
"Indian Annie," 110, 178, 258
Indian Territory, Oklahoma, 19, 64,
    84–85, 125
Ingalls, John James, 253, 264, 264*n*

Jackson, Stonewall, 77
James, Frank, 54, 173–74, 204–6
James, Jesse, 54, 93, 173–74, 204–6
Jameson, Henry, 158, 162, 166, 169,
    178
Jayhawkers (guerrilla group), 21–25,
    27–30, 36, 52, 61, 198
    extortion by, 153
Jefferson County, Nebraska, gunfight
    at, 112–13
Jenney, Walter, 243
Jennison's Jayhawkers, 61
John Robinson's Circus, Menagerie,
    and Museum, 184

Johnson, Andrew, 9, 228
Jones, Sam, 20
Judd, Yankee, 256
Judiciary Act of 1789, 108
Junction City, Kansas, 114–16, 139
The Junction City Weekly Union, 149

Kansas
    Abilene, 86, 88, 110, 151, 152–65,
        166–78, 179, 185–91, 195–96, 231,
        232, 233, 272–73, 287
    abolitionists in, 18–25, 27–30, 52–55
    Brigade, 56–57
    cattle trade/cow towns of, 84–90,
        109–10, 152–70, 174–78, 187, 191,
        262
    Dodge City, 11, 32, 90, 110, 118,
        134, 167, 232, 243, 274
    Ellsworth, 90, 109, 115, 128–29,
        189
    Free State Army in, 20–25, 27–30
    geography of, 83–84
    Hays City, 81, 90, 109–11, 133–34,
        135–39, 140–51, 164, 195, 231,
        233, 272, 287
    land giveaway in, 18–19, 26
    Leavenworth, 19, 22–24, 30, 31, 37,
        47, 48, 64, 86, 115–17, 133
    Marais des Cygnes Massacre in,
        29–30
    Monticello, 28–30, 74
    population statistics in, 83
    Pottawatomie Massacre in, 22
    pro-slave *v.* anti-slave skirmishes in,
        18–25, 27–30, 52–55
    railroad expansion in, 85, 87, 90,
        152–58, 191
    Topeka, 19, 83, 116, 133, 151, 190,
        226
    Wakarusa War in, 20–21, 21*n*

Kansas City, Missouri, 199–201, 224,
226
Antelopes (baseball team), 102–3
Kansas City Industrial Exhibition,
205–7
The Kansas City Journal, 212
The Kansas City Star, 103, 145
The Kansas City Times, 206
Kansas-Nebraska Act of 1854, 18–19,
26
Kansas Pacific Railway, 85, 110, 115,
128, 152–54
Kansas State Historical Society, 5, 81,
193, 199
Kearny, Stephen, 34, 143
Killian, Jacob, 182–83
Kingsbury, E. W., 129
Kiowa tribe, 85
Kohl & Middleton's Dime Museum
show, 292
Kress, William, 208
Ku Klux Klan, 12

Lake, Agnes. *See* Hickok, Agnes
Mersman Lake
Lake, Alice, 181–82
Lake, Bill (aka Bill Lake Thatcher),
180–83, 291
Lake, Emma. *See* Robinson, Emma
Lake
Lakota Sioux. *See also* Sioux Nation
Black Hills as territory of, 227–30,
243–46, 248–49, 248n, 252–53,
254, 257
Oglala band of, 227–28, 267–68
Lanahan, "Rattlesnake" Pete, 149–50
Lane, James, 20–25, 27, 29, 54–55
nicknames of, 56
Osceola Massacre by, 56–57
Larkin, Arthur, 129

laudanum, 208
"Laughing Sam" (gambler), 265–66
Lawrence, Kansas, 19–22
Confederate guerrilla raid on, 54–55
Leavenworth, Kansas, 19, 22–24, 30,
31, 37, 47, 48, 115, 133
Fort Leavenworth at, 64, 86, 116–17
The Leavenworth Daily Commercial,
147–48
The Leavenworth Daily Conservative,
96–97, 147
*The Leavenworth Times and
Conservative,* 137, 147
Lecompton, Kansas, 23–24
Lee, Robert E., 65, 77, 119
Levy, Jim, 273
The Life and Legends of Calamity Jane
(Etulain), 240
Lincoln, Abraham, 11, 55–56, 77, 105,
293
Little, Theophilus, 176
Longstreet, James, 77
Lookout Mountain, Colorado, 289
Lorentz, Upton, 238
Ludlow, William, 243–44
Lyon, Nathaniel, 48–49, 53
Lyon House Hotel, Springfield, 3

MacArthur, Arthur, Jr., 104
MacArthur, Douglas, 104
"Madame Moustache" (prostitute), 257
M'Afee, C. B., 71
Magic City of the Plains. *See*
Cheyenne, Wyoming
Making-Out-Road (Cheyenne woman),
34
Mammoth Circus & Gymnastic Arena
Company, 180–81
Manhattan, Kansas, 19
Manifest Destiny, 76–77, 99

Mann, Carl, 263–64, 270, 280

Mann, James, 173

Marais des Cygnes Massacre (Kansas), 29–30

Marion County War (aka Tutt-Everett War), 2

Marmaduke, General, 62, 64

massacres

Marais des Cygnes, 29–30

Osceola, 56–57

Pottawatomie, 22

Sand Creek, 120, 124

Washita, 124–25, 226

Massie, William, 280–81, 281n

Masterson, Bat, 93, 118, 134, 176, 189, 274, 288

Maximilian, Emperor of Mexico, 176–77

Mazeppa (traveling show), 182

McCall, Jack (aka Bill Sutherland), 294

background of, 276

Hickok's murder by, 279–86, 290

McCandless, A. D., 199

McCanles, Charles, 43

McCanles, David, 42–47, 67, 94

McCanles, James, 43

McCanles, Mary, 43

McCanles, William, 45–46

McConnell, Andrew, 162–63

McCormick, Jean Hickok, 293

McCoy, James, 154

McCoy, Joseph, 90, 152–57, 160, 164–65

McCoy, William, 154

McCulloch, Ben, 51–52

McDonald, James, 162–63

McLaird, James D., 269

McPherson, James, 53

Medal of Honor, 124, 211, 213

media representations/storytelling, 75, 78–79, 106

in Harper's New Monthly Hickok feature, 1, 72–73, 78, 90–91, 93–100

hype/exaggeration in, 7, 35, 42, 50, 57–58, 62–63, 67, 93–99, 206, 209–11, 243, 270, 293–94

via movies on Wild West, 42n, 93–94, 293–94

in New York Herald's Hickok feature, 97–99

via pulp novels, 130, 196, 211

Meline, James, 67

Memoirs (Carson), 34–35

Mersman, Catharina, 179–80

Mersman, Frederick, 179–80

Mexico, 127, 273

in Mexican-American War, 20, 34, 39, 49, 104, 143

Revolution in, 176–77

Miles, Moses, 162–63

Miller, Clell, 174

Milner, Moses Embree "California Joe," 143–44, 197, 270, 279

death of, 290

Milner, Nancy, 143

Minutemen, 8, 53

Missouri, 58, 118

Bushwhackers, 29, 52, 198

Compromise of 1820, 19

Independence, 50–51, 66–67, 75, 209, 210, 226

Osceola Massacre in, 56–57

St. Louis, Missouri, 114, 186, 252–53

Sedalia, 50, 153

Springfield, 1–4, 62, 67, 68–74, 91, 94, 95, 152, 207

The Missouri Weekly Patriot, 71

Monahan, Sherry, 260

Montana, 241, 293

Battle of Little Bighorn in, 144, 228, 245, 254, 257, 267–68, 287

The Montana Post, 241

Monticello, Kansas, 28–30, 31, 74

Moon, W. S., 89

Moore, Susannah, 58–59, 68–69, 74, 217

Morlacchi, Giuseppina, 214–15, 217–19, 222n–23n

Morrow, David "Prairie Dog," 134–35

Moses & Bloomfield, Fort Hays, 110

Motz, Simon, 138

Mount Moriah Cemetery, Deadwood, 286–87, 292–93, 294

Moyer, S. L., 250–51

Mrs. Agnes Lake's Hippo-Olympiad and Mammoth Circus, 179, 182–87, 198–99, 200, 223–24, 236, 250. *See also* Hickok, Agnes Mersman Lake

Mulvey, Bill, 138–39, 140

My Life on the Plains (Custer), 106, 143

Nash, Matilda, 198

Native Americans, 25, 34–35, 76–77, 85, 87, 115–16, 133–34, 198, 207, 213, 256. *See also specific tribes*

Battle of Little Bighorn by, 144, 228, 245, 254, 257, 267–68, 287

Black Hawk's War by, 10–11

diseases spread to, 83

massacres of, 120, 124–25, 226

relocation of, 83–84, 268

Sand Creek Massacre of, 120, 124

treaty negotiations with, 10, 100–107, 227–30, 244, 248, 248n

war parties of, 105–7, 117–27, 129–31, 227, 245, 249, 267–68, 268n

Washita Massacre of, 124–25, 226

in Wild West shows, 200–204, 224, 289

Navajo tribe, 134

Nebraska

Fort Kearny, 77

Fort McPherson, 144, 201, 255

Fort Robinson, 264, 290

Jefferson County gunfight in, 112–13

Kansas-Nebraska Act and, 18–19, 26

Rock Creek Station in, 38, 42–47

Wild West shows in, 289

The New North-West, 284

New York City, New York, 224

Wild West shows in, 214–19

The New York Evening Post, 72

The New York Herald, 97–99, 214

New-York Tribune, 66

The New York World, 214

Newcomb, Tom, 290

Newton, Henry, 243

Newton, Kansas, 90

Niagara Falls, 200–204

Niblo's Garden, New York City, 214–19

Nichols, George Ward, 72–74, 78, 90–91, 93–100

North Platte, Nebraska, 289

Norton, A. S., 183

Norton, Brocky Jack, 170

Nuttall and Mann's No. 10 saloon, Deadwood, 263–64, 270, 279–83

Oakley, Annie, 200, 291

O'Connor, Richard, 233, 247

Oglala Lakota tribe, 227–28, 267–68

Oglala Sioux, 41, 122, 207–8

Oklahoma

Fort Cobb, 125

Indian Territory of, 19, 64, 84–85, 125

Washita Massacre in, 124–25, 226

Old Man Jones, Abilene, 89

Old Wagon Show Days (Robinson), 184

Omohundro, John "Texas Jack,"
143–44, 201
death of, 223*n*
in Wild West shows, 213, 215,
217–20, 222, 222*n*–23*n*, 266

Oregon Trail, 39, 43, 121

Osceola Massacre (Missouri), 56–57

Otero, Miguel, 139

Overland Stage Company, 31, 38–47,
88–89

Overland Trail, 39

Owen, John, 24–25, 28, 36

Owen, Mary Jane, 24–25, 29–30, 31,
36

Owen, Richard Bentley, 73–74, 95

P. T. Barnum's Circus, Menagerie, and
Museum, 184–85

P. T. Barnum's New and Greatest Show
on Earth, 291

Paha Sapa, 227–28, 243, 252. *See also*
Black Hills

Pan-American Exposition of 1901,
Buffalo, 292

Panic of 1837, 11–12

Panic of 1873, 90, 229, 236

Parker, Quanah, 10

Patinuxa (Shawnee woman), 25

Patterson, Colonel (Revolutionary
War), 8

Patterson (boxer), 150–51

Pawnee Killer (Sioux warrior), 107

Pawnee tribe, 107, 133, 201, 207, 213

Peirce, Ellis, 282, 284

Penrose, William, 125–27

Phelps, John, 71

Philips, John Finis, 65

Pierce, Franklin, 18–19

Pikes Peak, Colorado, 198

Pine Ridge Reservation, South Dakota,
107

Plaine Joan (ship), 8

The Plainsman (movie), 293–94

Pleasonton, Alfred, 62–64

Pohlschneider, Maria Agnes. *See*
Hickok, Agnes Mersman Lake

Polk, James, 2

Pomeroy, S. C., 55

Pony Express, 38–41, 253, 257, 257*n*,
264

Pope, John, 77–78, 102

Porter, Edwin, 94

Portland, Maine, 221

Pottawatomie Massacre (Kansas), 22

prairie dogs, as pets, 134–35

Price, Sterling "Old Pap," 49, 51–53,
59–65, 73

Price Raid of 1864 (Civil War), 49

prizefighting, 150–51, 263

prostitutes, 67–68, 87, 129
in Abilene, 157, 167
in Cheyenne, 232–33
in Deadwood, 257, 258, 259, 263,
265–66, 269
disease spread by, 199–200
in Hays City, 110

pulp stories/dime novels
on Cody, 93, 196, 211
on Hickok, 130, 196, 211

Quantrill, William, 49, 53–57

Quantrill's Raiders, 54–57

railroad, 39, 85, 87, 90, 229
cattle industry's use of, 152–58, 191

The Railway Advance, 110

Ralston, Jack, 208

The Real Deadwood (Ames), 261

Rebs, Johnny, 50

Reconstruction era, 76, 105

Red Cloud (Indian leader), 10, 41, 122, 227–28, 253

Red Cloud's War, 122, 227–28, 253

Red Legs (guerrilla group), 52–53, 61, 198

Red River Station, Texas, 86

The Revenant (movie), 37

Revolutionary War, U.S., 8–9

rheumatism, 230–31, 254

Rice, Dan, 184

Rich, Charles, 280

Richardson, Leander, 270–72, 284

Riley, Bennett, 75

Rio Grande, Texas, 86

Robinson, Agnes Emma "Daisy," 286, 291

Robinson, Charles, 22

Robinson, Emma Lake, 251, 286
    as circus performer, 181, 223, 236, 291

Robinson, Gil, 184, 251, 286, 291

Robinson, John, 184

Rock Creek Station, Nebraska, 38, 42–47

Rockwell & Company's New York Circus, 181

Rocky Mountain Detective Association, 232

Roman Nose (Cheyenne leader), 119, 121–23, 136

Roosevelt, Franklin Delano, 78

Root, Frank, 133

Rosa, Joseph G., 38, 42, 57–58, 110, 132, 148, 174, 191, 199, 232, 249, 261, 270, 279, 287

Roughing It (Twain), 40

Rowlands, John. *See* Stanley, Sir Henry Morton

Russell, Majors, and Waddell company, 31, 38

Sac tribe, 201

The St. Louis Republican, 140–41

The St. Louis Weekly Missouri Democrat, 210

St. Louis, Missouri, 114, 186, 252–53

saloons, 87, 109–11, 129, 185, 226
    in Abilene, 89, 156–58, 160–62, 167–70, 175–78, 187–89
    characteristics of, 32–33
    in Deadwood, 260–66, 269–70, 272, 278

Salt Lake City, Utah, 241–42

San Antonio, Texas, 86

Sanborn, John, 63

Sand Creek Massacre, Colorado, 120, 124

Santa Fe, New Mexico, 35, 37–38, 39

Santa Fe Trail, 34, 35, 128

Sauk tribe, 10–11

Scarborough, George, 173

Schull, Sandra, 44, 46–47

Schwatka, Frederick, 207–8

Scott, Winfield, 11

Scouts of the Plains show, 214–25, 259

Scouts of the Prairie show, 211–14

Scout's Rest Ranch, North Platte, 289

Second Battle of Bull Run (Civil War), 77

Second Battle of Sacket's Harbor, New York (War of 1812), 9

Second Ohio Volunteer Cavalry, 68

Secret Service, precursor to, 55

Sedalia, Missouri, 50, 153

Selman, John, 173

Seventh Iowa Cavalry, 128

Seventh Kansas State Militia, 61–62

Seventh U.S. Cavalry, 124–25, 144, 227–28
  at Battle of Little Bighorn, 144, 228, 245, 254, 257, 267–68, 287
Seymour, Richard, 253, 264
Shakespeare, William, 7, 196
Shawnee tribe, 25
Shenandoah Valley campaign (Civil War), 119
Sheridan, Philip, 118–20, 122, 124–25
Sherman, William, 22
Sherman, William Tecumseh, 49, 72, 77, 94, 102, 104, 118
The Shootist (Swarthout), 100
Short, Luke, 274
Simpson, Lewis, 28, 37
Singing Grass (Arapaho woman), 34
Sioux Nation, 105–7, 119
  Battle of Little Bighorn by, 144, 228, 245, 254, 257, 267–68, 287
  Lakota Sioux in, 227–30, 243–46, 248–49, 248n, 252–54, 257, 267–68
  Oglala Sioux in, 41, 122, 207–8
  Treaty of Fort Laramie by, 227–30, 244
Sitting Bull (Lakota leader), 10, 252
  Battle of Little Bighorn and, 228, 249, 267
  in Wild West shows, 200, 289
Slade, Joseph Alfred "Jack," 39–42, 42n
slavery. *See also* Civil War
  Kansas skirmishes over, 18–25, 27–30, 52–55, 198
  Underground Railroad and, 12–13
smallpox, 32, 291
Smith, Edmund Kirby, 64
Smith, Thomas "Bear River," 158–63, 170, 195, 232
Smoky Hill Trail, 111

Society of Black Hills Pioneers, 292
Soule, John Babsone Lane, 66
South Dakota
  Black Hills of, 227–31, 243–46, 248–54, 248n, 257, 260, 262, 267–70, 278, 289
  Deadwood in, 142, 246, 250–52, 255–66, 267–77, 278–87, 288–94
  gold speculation in, 228–31, 243–44, 249–52, 260, 262, 268–70, 278, 289
  Indian treaties regarding, 227–30, 244
  Pine Ridge Reservation in, 107
  Yankton, 285–86
Spain
  civil war of, 99
  in Spanish-American War, 104
"Spanish Fever" (aka "Texas Fever"), 156, 156n
Springfield, Missouri, 62, 67, 73–74, 95, 152, 207
  Tutt-Hickok duel in, 1–4, 68–72, 91, 94
The Springfield Patriot, 97
The Springfield Republican, 270
The Squaw Man (movie), 94
Stanley, Henry Hope, 97
Stanley, Sir Henry Morton, 97–99
Stevens, Lucile, 174
Stilwell, Jack, 123
Storms, Charlie, 273–74, 274n–75n
The Story of the Great March (Nichols), 72
Strawhun, Samuel, 137, 146–48
Stuart, J. E. B., 64, 119, 143
Sullivan (gunman), 141
Sumner, Charles, 21
Sutherland, Bill. *See* McCall, Jack
Swarthout, Glendon, 99–100
Swearengen, Ellis Albert, 262–63, 273
Swearengen, Lemuel, 262

Swearengen, Nettie, 262
syphilis, 199–200

Tallent, Annie, 236–37
Taylor, Zachary, 11
Tenth U.S. Cavalry Regiment "Buffalo
	Soldiers," 116–18, 118n, 120,
	123–24, 135
The Terre Haute Express, 66
Terry, Alfred, 244–45
Tewodros II of Ethiopia, 99
Texas
	cattle industry in, 85–87, 129, 143,
		152, 154–65, 156n, 166–70,
		174–75, 187, 191
	Rangers, 173
"Texas Jack." *See* Omohundro, John
	"Texas Jack"
Thayer, Isaac, 136
They Called Him Wild Bill (Rosa), 42
They Died with Their Boots On (movie),
	144
Third U.S. Cavalry, 207, 215
Thirty-Sixth Texas Cavalry
	(Confederate), 177
Thomas, George, 181
Thompson, Ben, 175–78, 187, 189
Thompson, Billy, 189
Thompson, C. H., 89
Tilghman, William, 118
"Tit Bit" (prostitute), 265–66
Titusville, Pennsylvania, 219–21
Tombstone, Arizona, 273–74
Topeka, Kansas, 19, 83, 116, 133, 151,
	190, 226
The Topeka Daily Commonwealth, 140,
	206, 209, 231
The Topeka Leader, 109, 116
Treaty of Fort Laramie (1868), 227–30,
	244

Treaty of St. Louis (1804), 10
Troy Grove, Illinois (formerly Homer),
	11–12, 14–16, 67, 132–33, 132n,
	252, 285
Trudeau, Pierre, 123
"The Truth About Wild Bill" (Hance),
	75
Tutt, Davis, 1–4, 68–72, 91, 94
Tutt, Hansford "Hamp," 2
Tutt, Lewis, 72
Tutt-Everett War (aka Marion County
	War), 2
Twain, Mark, 39–40
Twenty-Seventh Arkansas Infantry
	Regiment, 2
Tyler, John, 78

Underground Railroad, 12–13
Union Army. *See also* Civil War
	Carson's service in, 35
	Cody's service in, 61–62, 114
	Frontier Guard and, 55–56
	Hickok as military police in, 63,
		73–74
	Hickok as scout in, 48–52, 63
	Hickok as spy for, 57–63, 64–65
Union Pacific Railroad, 158, 232
United States Hotel, Portland, 221
United States Hotel, Santa Fe, 35
U.S. Department of Public Welfare,
	293
USS *Minnesota* (battleship), 98
Ute tribe, 198
Utter, Charles H. "Colorado Charley,"
	197–99, 234, 289–90
	Deadwood residency by, 237–38,
		253–61, 263–66, 270–72, 275,
		277, 279, 282, 284–86
	Hickok's death and, 282, 284–86
Utter, Steve, 253, 259

Van Dorn, Earl, 51
Varnes, Johnny, 273
Verckler, Stewart P., 89, 157, 167, 175
Victoria, Queen of United Kingdom, 291
Vigilance Committee, Hays City, 136–37, 146

Wakarusa War (Kansas), 20–21, 21*n*
War of 1812, 8–9, 10
Warren, W. F., 251
Washington, George, 108, 183
Washita Massacre, Oklahoma, 124–25, 226
Webb, Charles, 172
Webb, William, 110, 148
Webster, Alonzo, 136–37, 136*n*, 146
Weiss, Joe, 137, 146
Wellman, Horace, 44–46
The West of Wild Bill Hickok (Rosa), 279
Wheeler, O. W., 155
"Whirling Rope." *See* Omohundro, John "Texas Jack"
Whistler (Oglala Sioux man), 207–8
Whiting, Charles C., 108, 111, 116, 133
Wichita, Kansas, 86, 90
Wild Bill, the Indian-Slayer (pulp story), 130

"Wild Bill." *See* Hickok, James Butler "Wild Bill"
Wild Bunch gang, 233
Wilkinson, Allen, 22
William Tecumseh Sherman and the Settlement of the West (Athearn), 77
Williams, Mike, 170, 187–89, 191
Wilson, Ben, 110
Wilson, Birdie, 110
Wilson, John, 182
Wilstach, Frank, 223
Woods, James, 45–46, 94
Wyoming
   Cheyenne, 231–39, 242–43, 245, 247–48
   Cody, 289
   Fort Bridger, 39, 242
   Fort Fetterman, 245–46
   Fort Laramie, 244–46, 253–54, 255
   Fort Phil Kearny, 227
   gold speculation in, 228–39, 243–44
"Wyoming Frank" (cowboy), 162

Yankton, South Dakota, 285–86
Young, Harry "Sam," 142, 243, 263, 270, 272, 279–80, 282
Younger, Cole, 54, 173–74

Turn the page for a sneak peek at
Tom Clavin's next book

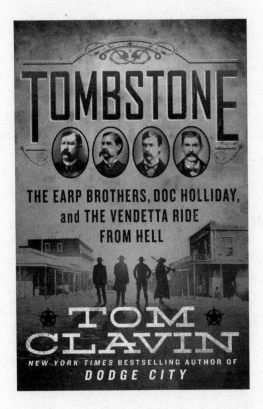

Available April 2020

"THE FIGHT'S COMMENCED"

Frank McLaury and Billy Clanton rode into Tombstone a few minutes after noon on that almost wintry Wednesday, October 26, 1881. They were accompanied by a rancher and cattle-dealer neighbor John Randolph Frink, who intended to buy six hundred head from the McLaury brothers. When the trio stopped at the Grand Hotel, the first man they encountered was Doc Holliday.

Being that he had no quarrel that day with Frank or Billy, Doc shook hands with the latter and asked, "How are you?" Then, for Doc it was the time of day for breakfast, and he walked away to find some.

It was at the hotel bar, as he drank what was presumably his first drink of the day, that Frank learned of the attack on his brother. A friend of the Clantons, William Allen, found the older McLaury there and reported what Wyatt had done. Frank and Billy left the bar, took hold of their horses, and according to what Allen later reported, Frank said, "I will get the boys out of town."

Until around 3 P.M., the day would have many moving parts. And there would be many versions offered by a mixture of participants, witnesses, and gossips of what transpired, some of them at odds and other accounts being outright contradictions. With all the moving parts, if an "actor" on this day had said or done something differently, there may not have been the Gunfight at the O.K. Corral. One gets the sense, though, that it or something like it was bound to happen. Those involved appear to have had a let's-get-it-done attitude.

Certainly one contributing factor was that the older McLaury brother did not do what he said he would—"get the boys out of town." Instead, he and Billy Clanton ran into Billy Claiborne. Just turned twenty-one, he fancied himself another Billy the Kid. The other cowboys tolerated the pretension, and some even referred to him as "the Kid." Born in Mississippi, as a teenager William Floyd Claiborne was a cowhand for John Slaughter in Texas. In 1879, at the end of a cattle drive west, Claiborne decided to remain in Arizona, doing mining and cowboy work around Charleston. There, to get October 1881 going, he had shot and killed a man.

The name of the departed was James Hickey. Alcohol had been his best friend for three days, with his last stop being the Queen's Saloon. As he staggered out of it, he encountered Claiborne. Apparently, they had had a run-in before, and new insults were traded. When Hickey advanced on him, Billy whipped out his pistol and shot him just below his left eye, killing him. Claiborne's first trial ended in a mistrial, and in the second trial, which took place only after the third attempt to collect enough jurors, Billy was found not guilty. It was believed that given the young gunman's quick-trigger temper, no juror wanted to vote otherwise.

Claiborne was in Tombstone that day for one of the hearings

on the Charleston killing, and when he had seen Ike Clanton and his battered condition, he had taken Ike to a doctor. At the Grand Hotel, Billy Clanton asked to be taken to Dr. Charles Gillingham's office so he could collect his brother and bring him to their ranch.

Ike, with his head bandaged, agreed to go. He told Billy and Frank McLaury that he had already asked the stableman at the West Coast Corral to hitch horses to his wagon. However, a decision was made not to leave and instead they walked over to Spangenberg's While there may have been an innocuous reason for going there, such as needing fresh ammunition for their respective ranches, being seen at that particular store and with the events of that morning being talked about on the streets of Tombstone, assumptions were made that the men were buying guns in preparation to take on the Earps.

This assumption found Virgil. He also overheard a couple of cowboys talking about an impending fight. Things were getting more ominous. Virgil headed over to the Wells Fargo office and borrowed a 10-gauge shotgun. When he emerged, he may have looked for one or both of his brothers. As it happened, Wyatt was still working on the cigar outside of Hafford's Saloon. He had observed McLaury and the Clantons walk into the gun shop. After one last puff, Wyatt walked to Spangenberg's to see for himself what was going on within.

McLaury's horse must have been curious, too, because it got up onto the sidewalk and poked its head into the shop. Wyatt reached for the horse and pulled it back by its bridle. Suddenly, Billy Claiborne was in the doorway with his hand on the butt of his pistol. McLaury brushed past him and stepped outside. Wyatt informed him that a horse in a shop violated a city ordinance. If the tension in Tombstone had not been so high, McLaury might have laughed

326 ★ TOM CLAVIN

at the trivial transgression. Instead, he took his horse from Wyatt, backed it into the street, and tied it up more securely.

Meanwhile, Wyatt was looking through the now empty doorway. He saw Ike and Billy Clanton pushing cartridges into their belts, further evidence that there would be a confrontation. Wyatt had to conclude that this would be the day when the faction of ranchers and cowboys settled affairs with their nemeses, the Earps and the law-and-order system they reluctantly represented. As Casey Tefertiller observes, "When men hear the sound of death pounding in their ears, they assume every action or innuendo by their foes to have some hidden meaning."

Virgil was just leaving the Wells Fargo office when Bob Hatch, a friend of the Earps who owned a saloon and poolroom, hurried up to him. "For God's sake, get down there to the gun shop," he implored. "They are all there and Wyatt is all alone." Then he burst out, "They are liable to kill him before you get there!"

Virgil did not have to be told twice. He found Wyatt in the street outside Spangenberg's and the other four men back in the shop. He also saw cartridges being put into belts and had to assume the Clantons and Frank McLaury would emerge armed.* People in the street assumed the same thing. Word was being passed around that Tom McLaury, after a doctor had treated his head, had been seen on the street and it looked as if a pistol were stuck in his pants.

Wyatt returned to standing outside Hafford's, with Virgil beside him. To them, the scenario was that for once Ike Clanton had as much bite as bark and truly was fixing for a fight. In the brothers'

---

* Virgil and Wyatt could not have known that the elder Clanton had tried to purchase a gun but George Spangenberg, seeing Ike's boozy and battered condition, refused to sell one to him.

view, sometime that morning Ike had sent a message to the Clanton and McLaury ranches requesting help, and Billy and Frank had responded. They could not figure Billy Claiborne other than he was a young hothead aligned with the cowboys, and only a few weeks ago he had gunned a man down. The odds were not pretty if Tom, now armed, met up with the four men inside the shop. If the five men were about to leave Tombstone, they could keep their guns and go. But if they planned to stay, Virgil and Wyatt would have to attempt to arrest them.

Finally, the sheriff made an appearance. Behan had indeed slept late and had not begun the day until after 1 P.M. He was enjoying a shave at Barron's Barber Shop when a couple of men found him to tell him that a gunfight was about to happen. The half-shaved sheriff got up and hurried out of the shop. He ran into a visiting Charlie Shibell, who probably was relieved to no longer be wearing a badge with such a storm brewing. Together, they went in search of Virgil. On the way, a man named Coleman stopped them to say the Clantons and McLaurys were looking for a fight, and he advised Behan, "You should go and disarm that bunch."

They arrived outside Hafford's and asked Virgil what was happening. Virgil replied, "There are a lot of sons-of-bitches in town looking for a fight, and now they can have it."

For once, Virgil did not appear open to reason. Still, Behan suggested that he stick to his duty as police chief and ask the other men to give up their weapons. "I will not," Virgil stated. "I will give them their chance to make a fight."

This alarmed Behan. A situation out of control that could end with gunshots would not reflect well on any peace officer. It may have occurred to him that because of his decision, his deputies Billy Breakenridge and Dave Neagle were still away chasing outlaws, so he would have to single-handedly stop a shoot-out. If he did not, with so many onlookers observing that afternoon's street theater, stray bullets could kill innocent people. Even Shibell, who still carried the stain of colluding with cowboys to steal the previous year's election for sheriff, did not want to see a worst-case scenario played out. To give Virgil a chance to cool off, he and Behan persuaded him to step into Hafford's Saloon. Virgil refused a whiskey, but Behan knocked one back.

By this time, Tom McLaury had joined his brother and Ike and Billy Clanton and Billy Claiborne. The five men stopped by the Dexter Livery and Feed Stable—ironically, co-owned by the enterprising Johnny Behan—where the younger Clanton had left his horse. However, they did not appear to be in any hurry to leave town or to do anything at all. They ambled to the O.K. Corral, which was across the way, on Allen Street between Third and Fourth Streets. There they dawdled, heatedly discussing what to do next. This was reported to the chief of police. "They mean trouble," one man told Virgil. "They are all armed, and I think you had better go disarm them."

Getting an impression of Tombstone on this Wednesday that most citizens did not want to provide was H. F. Sills, a railroad engineer who had just arrived in town. He saw several men standing around "talking some trouble they had had with Virgil Earp, and they made threats at that time, that on meeting him they would kill him on sight." One of them said that "they would kill the whole party of the Earps when they met them."

Stills walked up the street and asked who Virgil Earp and the Earps were. Virgil was pointed out to him, and he identified himself as the city marshal when Stills asked. The engineer reported what he had overheard, then like many others on the street, he stood aside and watched for what would happen next.

Since its informal activation in September, the Citizens Safety Committee had continued to exist. The head of it, William Murray, stepped into Hafford's. He took Virgil aside and confided, "I know you are going to have trouble and we have plenty of men and arms to assist you."

By this time, Virgil might have calmed down from his agitated state of a few minutes earlier, at least enough to realize that if men went for their guns, it could mean all-out war in the streets of the city. Right now the issue was limited to the long-simmering acrimony between the Clantons and McLaurys and the Earp brothers. But if there were dozens of armed citizens, the day could be a very bloody one indeed. Worse, if Ike Clanton's call for help had reverberated, a contingent of cowboys led by Curly Bill Brocius or Johnny Ringo could be on its way right now. As marshal and being Virgil, the last thing he wanted was chaotic violence and bodies bleeding into the dust.

"As long as they stay in the corral," Virgil told Murray, "I will not go down to disarm them. If they come out on the street, I will take their arms and arrest them."

This was still bold talk, considering that to avoid a more widespread confrontation it would be just Virgil and Wyatt against five armed men. But help was on the way, and it was not a vigilance committee.

As was his custom, after his early afternoon breakfast Doc Holliday had strolled to the Alhambra Saloon. There might already be a card game under way to join, or he would just amuse himself with solitaire. He would certainly be immediately recognizable to anyone who entered the saloon after him. As described by Gary L. Roberts, "Doc was dressed like a dandy in a gray suit and a pastel shirt with a stiff collar and tie. He wore a slouch hat and a long, gray overcoat and carried a silver-headed cane."

The Alhambra was where Morgan found Holliday. After being informed of that morning's events and perhaps regretting that in an unusual fit of bonhomie he had shaken Billy Clanton's hand, Doc accompanied Morgan to find Virgil and Wyatt. Citizens immediately directed them to Hafford's Saloon.

Wyatt was still standing outside, and Doc asked him what was going on. "We're going to make a fight," Wyatt replied.

The only other question Doc Holliday had was, "You're not going to leave me out, are you?"

"This is none of your affair."

"That is a hell of a thing for you to say to me."

"It's going to be a tough one."

Doc grinned. "Tough ones are the kind I like."

Inside Hafford's Saloon, Behan, the whiskey burning in his belly, told Virgil that he would ask the Clantons and McLaurys and Claiborne to give up their guns. "They won't hurt me," Behan declared, either boasting or with false courage. "I will go down along and see if I can disarm them."

To be fair to the sheriff, because a potential confrontation was within city limits, this was more the problem of the local police than his. And it was to Johnny Behan's credit that he offered to try to persuade armed men to stand down. On the other hand, he was a political animal. If he had stayed in bed that day or been called to business elsewhere in Cochise County, Behan would have been off the hook. But he was on the scene for all to see. If he abandoned the city marshal to his fate, the voters in Tombstone would remember that. And there was a big upside: if he did actually disarm the five men and violence was avoided, voters would remember that, too.

Virgil responded that the immediate issue was the men were wearing weapons within the city limits. If they surrendered their guns or got on horses and rode away, there would be no further trouble. And if they stayed in the O.K. Corral, they would be left to themselves, though Virgil was not about to wait all day to do his job or be able to concentrate on other matters.

He was approached by John Fonck, who had served as a police captain in Los Angeles. He offered to round up several men to stand with Virgil if he took on the ranchers and cowboys. The marshal responded that if those men were at the corral getting horses to leave, he would let them do so. But Fonck had just come from the O.K. Corral, and he told Virgil that the five men had left and were now on Fremont Street.

That tore it. Virgil could not allow them to roam all over downtown displaying weapons. But Behan interceded, saying he would meet up with those men and disarm them. Virgil nodded.

As he walked down the street toward where the Clanton and McLaury brothers and Billy Claiborne were reported to be, Behan was either quaking in his boots or picturing himself as a hero. When he reached them, he said, "Boys, you must give up your arms. You have got to give up your arms."

He was met with silent stares, so the sheriff pressed ahead: "Boys, you must go up to the sheriff's office and lay off your arms, and stay there until I get back. I'll go disarm the Earps."

Behan either did not say the last sentence or did say it—as he later testified—but he knew it was highly unlikely that his fellow lawman Virgil and his deputies would hand him their guns. If he said it, it was to further persuade the five men that there would be no fight and they could safely disarm.

But then he glanced up Fremont Street and saw the Earp brothers and Doc walking toward him. Now, whether Behan had meant what he said or not, getting the marshal's party to give up their guns or to at least stop in their tracks was the only way to avoid bloodshed. "Wait here," he told the others. "I will go up and stop them."

Virgil was a patient man . . . but Behan had taken too long. Standing outside Hafford's, he may have deputized Doc. Because of being so frequently called upon, Wyatt and Morgan were already designated as "special officers" and had law-enforcement powers. All four men had six-shooters stuck in their belts. Virgil took the walking stick and handed the borrowed shotgun to Doc, either because the latter's long overcoat might make his pistol hard to get to or because brandishing a shotgun at the cowboys might be like shaking a red cape at a bull. Plus, Virgil knew that Doc was no marksman with a handgun.

The four men waited another minute or two, then began marching down Fourth Street. Wyatt was on the left, and to his right were Virgil, Morgan, and Doc, with Virgil a couple of steps ahead. When they reached Fremont Street, they turned west, seeing Fly's boardinghouse and photo studio up ahead. Also up ahead, in a vacant lot next to Fly's property, were five men who, as far as the lawmen knew, were armed and demanding a fight.

When Behan saw the four lawmen steadfastly approaching, he hurried from the vacant lot to intercept them. They met in front of Bauer's Meat Market. "Gentlemen," Behan began, "I am sheriff of this county and I am not going to allow any trouble if I can help it."

The Earp brothers and Doc Holliday brushed past him. It was abundantly clear that by this point the sheriff had lost all credibility with Virgil. Behan's passive approach to the cowboys was now coming back to haunt him; he was nothing more than someone to be ignored so the real work could be done. Behan followed behind the four men, practically begging them to halt, but he could no longer delay the inevitable. "For God's sake," the sheriff implored, "don't go down there or you will get murdered."

As they marched on, Virgil and Wyatt heard the sheriff add, "I have disarmed them all."

Behan would later deny he made that statement, but that is what Virgil and Wyatt heard and they relaxed a bit. Wyatt, Morgan, and Doc were still prepared to back Virgil's play, but if the sheriff had indeed taken the weapons from the five men, there would be no shooting. Virgil pushed his pistol into the left side of his pants and now in his gun hand he held the walking stick, as though he would wave it and the men in the lot would disappear. Wyatt and Morgan had their six-shooters in their right hands, but now they put them away on their right sides. Doc's pistol and the shotgun were hidden under the long gray coat, except when the wind pushed it open. Behan stopped trying to keep up with them as they strode down Fremont Street and dropped back.

Someone called out, "There they come!" Dozens of eyes turned to see four men marching toward destiny.

David Wells

Tom Clavin is a #1 *New York Times* bestselling author and has worked as a newspaper and website editor, magazine writer, TV and radio commentator, and a reporter for *The New York Times*. He has received awards from the Society of Professional Journalists, Marine Corps Heritage Foundation, and National Newspaper Association. His books include *The Heart of Everything That Is, Halsey's Typhoon,* and *Reckless.* He lives in Sag Harbor, New York.